Contents

The Walk-through

Data Appendices

The World

Once, long ago, the world of Yukes, Clavats, Selkies and Lilties was pure and good. But the coming of a meteor foretold grave times, as the world was quickly swallowed by a poisonous cloud of Miasma. The people learned that they could keep the Miasma at bay by constructing large crystals that received their power from Myrrh—a rare substance that is found only in a Myrrh Tree.

The Tale Begins . . .

You are a member of a caravan—a position of great importance and responsibility. Each year, caravans set out from villages all over the world in a quest to find the Myrrh that will power their crystals and hold off the Miasma for another season. The dangers are legion—monsters of all shapes and sizes have sprung up since the Miasma took hold, including massive creatures that guard each and every tree. Only the strongest and most capable are able to join caravans, for if they fall, their friends, families and homes will all fall with them.

The Tribes

You can choose from four tribes when you begin a new game. Each has both a male and a female aspect.

Clavats

Clavats are a fairly well-balanced tribe. Although they don't lead the pack in any single area, their ability to use both magic and weapons with decent results is a huge plus. Clavats have good Defense ratings, so stick them in the front of any multiplayer party.

INITIAL STATS	
HP	8
STRENGTH	6
DEFENSE	7
MAGIC	13

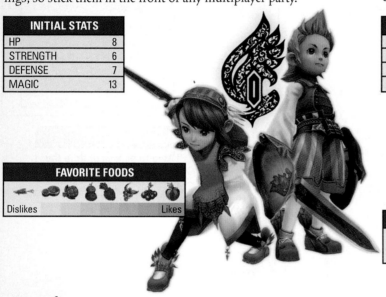

FAVORITE FOODS	
Dislikes	Likes

Lilties

Don't be fooled by the Lilties' small stature and baby faces—they are the most fearsome warriors in the land. Their offensive prowess is without equal, which makes them excellent frontline fighters. They don't like magic much, however, so stick to melee combat.

INITIAL STATS	
HP	8
STRENGTH	8
DEFENSE	8
MAGIC	10

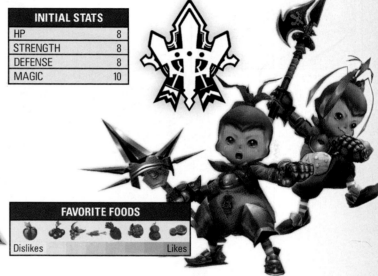

FAVORITE FOODS	
Dislikes	Likes

Yukes

The Yukes are a mysterious tribe that have dedicated themselves to the study of magic. As a Yuke, you will be able to cast spells faster (and with greater effect) than any other tribe, but low Strength and Defense will be a burden. Try to stay in the back of the fight.

INITIAL STATS	
HP	8
STRENGTH	5
DEFENSE	5
MAGIC	15

FAVORITE FOODS	
Dislikes	Likes

Selkies

A tribe composed of thieves and brigands, Selkies have a bad reputation. Their forte in combat is the Focus Attack—it charges up faster than any other race's—so give them a strong weapon and let them leap into the fray.

INITIAL STATS	
HP	8
STRENGTH	7
DEFENSE	6
MAGIC	12

FAVORITE FOODS	
Dislikes	Likes

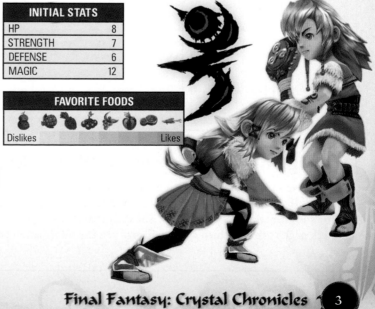

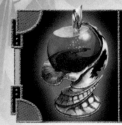

Controls

It's time to learn how to move, Kupo! Master the basics so you can control your character effortlessly in the world of Final Fantasy.

Single-Player Controls

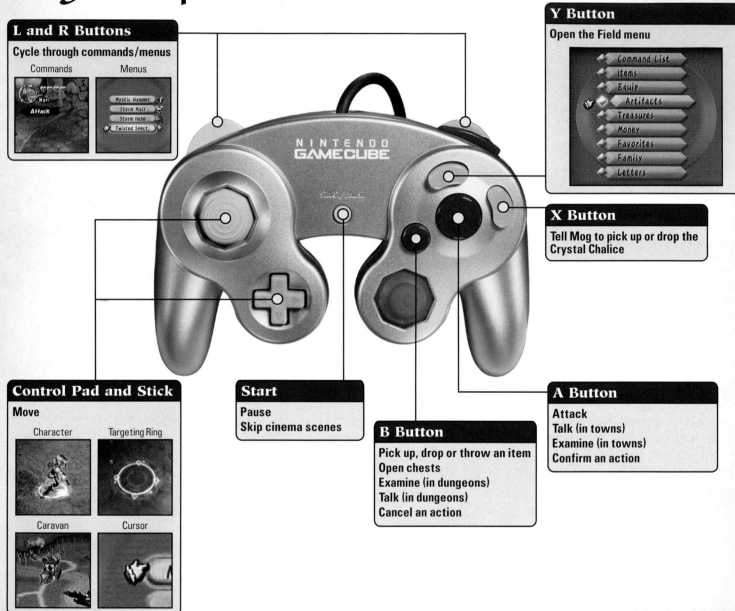

L and R Buttons

Cycle through commands/menus

Commands — Menus

Mystic Hammer
Storm Mail
Storm Helm
Twisted Spect.

War!
Attack

Y Button

Open the Field menu

Command List
Items
Equip
Artifacts
Treasures
Money
Favorites
Family
Letters

X Button

Tell Mog to pick up or drop the Crystal Chalice

A Button

Attack
Talk (in towns)
Examine (in towns)
Confirm an action

B Button

Pick up, drop or throw an item
Open chests
Examine (in dungeons)
Talk (in dungeons)
Cancel an action

Start

Pause
Skip cinema scenes

Control Pad and Stick

Move

Character — Targeting Ring

Caravan — Cursor

Using the GBA in Single-Player Mode

If you have a Game Boy Advance but are playing alone, you can still connect it and receive helpful information. If you plug the GBA into the second Controller slot, it will function as a map or a screen that shows information about enemies. The data that is displayed depends on the color of your Moogle. Check page 15 to see which colors will give you the information you want.

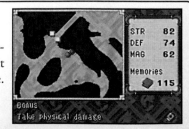

STR 82
DEF 74
MAG 62

Memories
◆ 115

Bonus
Take physical damage

Multiplayer Controls

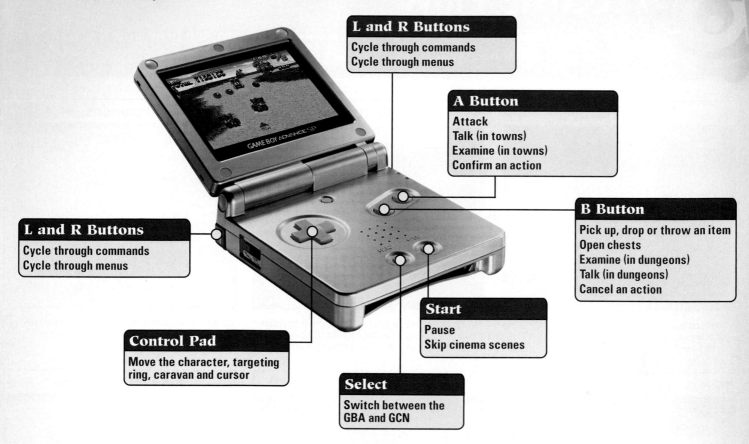

L and R Buttons
Cycle through commands
Cycle through menus

A Button
Attack
Talk (in towns)
Examine (in towns)
Confirm an action

B Button
Pick up, drop or throw an item
Open chests
Examine (in dungeons)
Talk (in dungeons)
Cancel an action

L and R Buttons
Cycle through commands
Cycle through menus

Control Pad
Move the character, targeting
ring, caravan and cursor

Start
Pause
Skip cinema scenes

Select
Switch between the
GBA and GCN

Using the GBA

When you play in multiplayer mode, each player must use a GBA. The handheld device functions as both a controller and a mini information display. You will look at the GBA to access your items, inventory, letters and other options. It will also function as a map, an enemy or treasure chest locator or a screen that displays monster information.

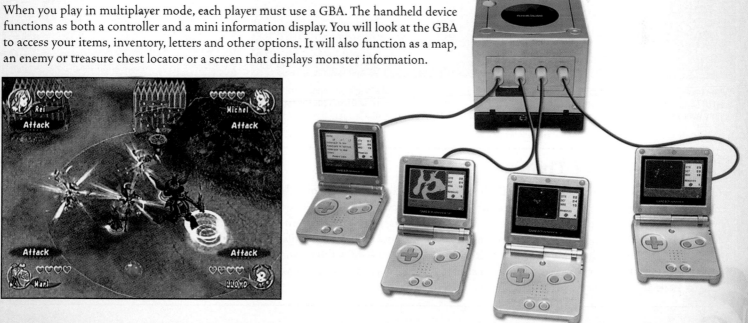

Game Flow

So how does the game work? Take a look below to see how you'll move and operate while you're playing Crystal Chronicles.

Party Formation

When you begin, you must choose a character. If you select an empty slot, you can create a new character. Up to eight can be stored on one card.

The World Map

When you leave a town or dungeon, you'll take control of the caravan. Use the caravan to move from place to place, then press A to enter the area you want.

Dungeons

Dungeons contain monsters and Myrrh. You will also find artifacts, materials, scrolls and more inside dungeons.

The Myrrh Tree

When you beat the dungeon boss, you will receive a drop of Myrrh. The tree will replenish its Myrrh supply every two years.

Letters

If you get Myrrh, a Mail Moogle will appear with a letter. You can then read it and send the writer an item, money or nothing at all.

Artifact Selection

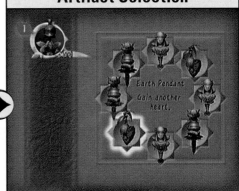

Finally, you will get to keep one of the artifacts you found in the dungeon. If you are playing a multiplayer game, each character will choose an artifact.

The Passage of Time

Crystal Chronicles is divided into years. Each time you get a drop of Myrrh, one-third of a year will pass. When you get three drops, you will return to your hometown and have a party, then set out on a new year. If you have visited a dungeon within the past two years, you can't get Myrrh from that area—but you can still enter the dungeon, fight monsters, beat the boss and take an artifact. If you choose to fight in dungeons without Myrrh, you can do so as much as you want without causing time to pass. There is no time limit in the game—and you'll see more of the storyline if you take your time—so feel free to move at a leisurely pace.

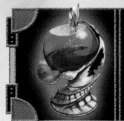

World Map Menu

The World Map menu is where you'll do most of the busy work before you start playing the game.

 ## Set Out

The Set Out option allows you to create new characters (if you have room) or choose which existing character you want to take on your adventure. In single-player mode, character creation happens on-screen. In a multiplayer game, it takes place on the GBA.

When you create a new character, you must give him or her a name and choose the sex, then select the race and appearance. Finally you will choose the occupation of your character's parents.

 ## Diary

Each time you encounter a road event (which will appear in the form of a cut scene), you will write about it in your diary. You'll also write in the diary each time you visit a new town or defeat a dungeon boss. Your diary entries for the year will be read at the annual party in your hometown, but you can go to the main menu and read your diary at any time.

Bring a Friend

If you want to import a friend's character to your game, place your Memory Card in slot A, and the Memory Card with the visiting character in slot B. Visiting characters take only their equipped weapon, armor, helmet and accessory—no items or gil will transfer. When you send the character back, he or she will take only the artifacts gained—any items or money will be lost.

 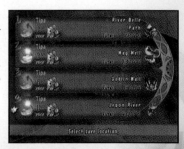

 ## Options

The Options screen lets you change a few key features. You can alter the volume of sound effects and music, toggle your position markers on or off, and change the color balance of any linked GBAs. Use the Enhanced color option if you're not using a GBA SP.

Save Game

While you're on the world map, you can save your game at any time. There are four save slots available. It's a good idea to use all four in case you want to return to an older saved game.

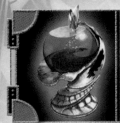

Main Menu & Radar

You'll be able to access the main menu and radar screens in towns and dungeons. Radar screens appear only on a GBA.

Main Menu

Command List

The Command List is where you set actions that you can use during battle. Attack and Defend are default options and can't be removed, but you can fill the empty slots with Magic, food or certain items (such as Phoenix Down). You begin the game with four slots, and you can acquire up to four more.

Items

All of your possessions are stored in the Items section of the main menu. From there you can use an item, drop it or destroy it. You can also get information about an item by highlighting it with the cursor.

Equip

You can arm your character with four different pieces of equipment—a weapon, a suit of armor, and two miscellaneous items: helmets, shields, pendants and the like. The possibilities vary depending on the character's race.

Artifacts

After you beat a dungeon and choose an artifact to keep, it will appear in the Artifacts section of the main menu. There you can see how many artifacts you have, what they do and how many you have yet to collect.

Treasures

When you pick up an artifact in a dungeon, it will be stored in the Treasures section of the main menu. You can hold only four artifacts at a time, but you'll never receive more than four unless you're exploring the Abyss.

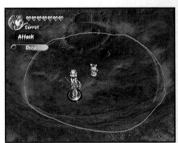

Once you pick up an artifact, you cannot drop or destroy it. You will immediately receive the bonus stats from any artifact that is in your inventory, but the bonus will last only as long as you are in the dungeon. If you leave a dungeon early, you will lose all the artifacts. If you beat the boss, you can choose one artifact to add to your permanent collection.

Money

You gots to get paid! All of your gil is stored in the Money section of the menu. If you are in a multiplayer game and want to drop gil so another player can take it, you can do so from the Money screen.

Favorites

Your food likes and dislikes are displayed in the Favorites section. If you eat food that you like, you'll gain a lot of HP and a bonus to your stats. If you eat food you dislike, you'll get a tiny amount of HP and suffer a statistical penalty.

DEFENSE +2	MAGIC +2	STRENGTH +2

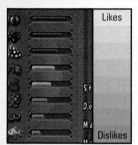

Even if you don't like a particular foodstuff, send it down the hatch. The more you eat something, the more you will grow to enjoy it. If you eat all the food you come in contact with, you'll eventually love everything.

Family

To gain your family's favor, say nice things in letters and always include a gift. If you send a gift that matches a person's job (such as seeds to a farmer) the person will like you more. If your father likes you, you'll get money and a discount on any items he sells.

FAMILY RELATIONSHIPS

Bad   Good

Letters

All of your letters are stored in the Letters section of the main menu. You can reread old letters whenever you want. Sometimes you'll get a gift inside your letter. If you don't take it out right away, you can come back and take it any time you have space in your inventory.

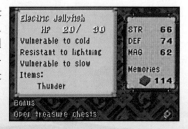

Radar Screens

Area Map

You can see a map of a dungeon on a GBA. The GBA also shows your stats, memory count and objective for the current dungeon. If you're playing in multiplayer mode, only one person will have the map.

Scouter

The Scouter is perhaps the most useful readout in the game. When you strike a monster, you'll learn its HP, strengths and weaknesses plus what item (if any) it is carrying.

Monster Locator

Monsters appear as yellow Xs on the screen. The boss will appear as a red X. Your radar content in single-player mode is determined by your Moogle's color—plug the GBA into the second Controller slot to use the radar.

Treasure Chest Locator

The Treasure Chest Locator works just like the Monster Locator—except it lets you see where the loot is stashed. The chests appear as blue, purple and red dots.

The Crystal Chalice

Your life and the lives of your family all rest upon a small container known as the Crystal Chalice. Treat it with care!

Once you leave a town, the Crystal Chalice is the only thing that holds Miasma at bay. It creates a circular force field around your character, allowing him or her to breathe comfortably. It also holds the Myrrh that you collect from dungeons. The chalice has the ability to assume different elemental types, which serves two purposes. First, the large Miasma Streams that cut through the land are tied to the elements, so your chalice must be of the correct type to pass through. Second, many of the elemental attributes will give your character a bonus when applied to the chalice.

The Chalice's Elemental Attributes

Fire	Water	Wind	Earth	???

If the chalice has a Fire attribute, you won't burn when attacked by a Fire-based spell.	If the chalice has a Water attribute, you won't be frozen when attacked by an Ice-based spell.	If the chalice has a Wind attribute, you will receive protection from a thunder spell's Paralysis effect.	The Earth element protects you from the staus effects of Poison and Petrification. It's very handy in certain areas.	The mystery element can pass through Miasma of any elemental type but provides no magical protection.

Merchants

Sellers traverse the land hawking their wares. If you have gil and the proper items, you can barter with the shopkeepers.

Shops

Shops sell many things depending on where they are located. The standard items are food and basic materials (such as iron), but you can sometimes find exotic goods for sale. If you have excess items, you can sell them at a shop.

Blacksmiths

If you have a scroll, the matching materials and some gil, a blacksmith will craft a new item for you. Each smith has limited skills, so you may have to travel a great distance to find someone who can help you. The blacksmith in Shella can make many rare items.

Ports

After the third year, ships will appear at various ports around the world. You can use the ships to reach distant lands, but you'll have to cough up gil. In a multiplayer game, each player must pay the toll. If you find certain items, the boatman will give you a discount.

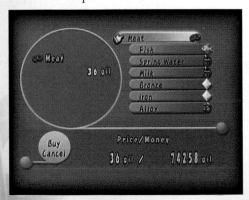

Family Occupations

While awaiting your caravan's return, your parents will continue living and working. Pick a job for them that can help you on your journey.

As soon as you create a character on your Memory Card, his or her parents will move into your town and set up shop. You can make use of any shops in your town, so you might want to make eight characters, even if you're going to play with only one.

① Fisherman

As a fisherman, your father will give you fish once a year. The amount you receive changes according to how well you get along with the family and how advanced their Production Level is. (See the next page for info on a family's Production Level.)

② Miller

The miller enjoys getting seeds, especially wheat. If you send a Wheat Seed, you'll get a loaf of Bannock Bread. After two years, your parents will give you a bag of flour.

③ Farmer

Farmers love to receive seeds of all types, so send them as gifts whenever you can. If you send a Wheat Seed, your parents will give you a loaf of Bannock Bread. Two years later, you'll start to get bundles of wheat.

④ Rancher

The rancher will give you a slice of meat at the beginning of each new year. After three years, he will also start to give you bottles of milk. Send him a cow from the Fields of Fum when you get the chance.

A Quick Guide to Production Levels

Your family's production level depends on your relationship with your father. If you reply to his letters in a friendly way and send him gifts, he will like you and increase his production level. As the level goes up, he will be able to make more and better items (in the case of a blacksmith or tailor) or give you access to better equipment (as a merchant or alchemist). There is no way to monitor your production level in the game—you must judge it based on how much your family likes you.

Cash on the Barrelhead

Your family loves you, but they still have to make a living. If your family has one of the four jobs listed below, you'll have to pay to get something as opposed to receiving a freebie. You can get better prices, however, by being on good terms with your father. Check the chart to the right to see what kinds of deals you can get by buttering up the old man.

DISCOUNTS & FAMILY RELATIONSHIPS		
65% Discount		30% Discount
55% Discount		Full Price

⑤ Merchant

The merchant has a small selection of items for sale at first, and he will get more as his production level rises. In addition to purchasing items from the merchant, you can sell your unwanted goods—the prices vary depending on your relationship. If another player has a merchant father, you can use him also.

ITEM AVAILABILITY (BASED ON PRODUCTION LEVEL)	
EARLY	Meat, Bronze, Alloy, Fish, Milk, Iron, Spring Water
LEVEL 1	Mythril, Gold, Silver, Bronze Shard, Iron Shard
LEVEL 2	Magma Rock, Chilly Gel, Thunderball
LEVEL 3	Ultimite, Dark Sphere

⑥ Blacksmith

The blacksmith is a handy parent to have. If you bring him the proper materials and scrolls, he will craft armor and weapons for you. He can make only simple items at first; he'll gain the ability to make more as his production level rises. If another player has a blacksmith father, you can use him also.

CRAFTABLE ITEMS (BASED ON PRODUCTION LEVEL)	
EARLY	Novice's Weapon, Warrior's Weapon, Bronze Armor, Iron Armor, Iron Shield, Bronze Gloves, Iron Gloves, Bronze Belt, Iron Belt
LEVEL 1	Master's Weapon, Mythril Shield, Mythril Gloves, Mythril Sallet, Mythril Belt
LEVEL 2	Legendary Weapon, Diamond Armor, Diamond Gloves, Diamond Sallet, Diamond Belt
LEVEL 3	Greatest Weapon

⑦ Tailor

The tailor doesn't work with needle and thread—he makes all kinds of useful accessories instead. You must bring the tailor the proper materials and scrolls to receive an accessory, and like the other occupations, he can make better items when he has a high production level. If another player has a tailor father, you can use him also.

CRAFTABLE ACCESSORIES (BASED ON PRODUCTION LEVEL)	
EARLY	Flame Craft, Frost Craft, Lightning Craft, Clockwork
LEVEL 1	New Clockwork, Blue Yarn, Tome of Wisdom, Tome of Speed, Fiend Kit, Faerie Kit, Eyewear Techniques, Goggle Techniques
LEVEL 2	White Yarn, Gold Craft, Secrets of Wisdom, Secrets of Speed, Daemon Kit, Angel Kit, Designer Glasses, Designer Goggles
LEVEL 3	Ring of Invincibility

⑧ Alchemist

The alchemist studies the mysteries of the world and its inner workings—and as such, he knows how to create new items. Starting at year two, he will give you one new scroll each year. As his production level rises, you'll get better scrolls. Good gifts for alchemists include scrolls, materials and seeds.

SCROLL AVAILABILITY (BASED ON PRODUCTION LEVEL)			
LEVEL 1	Iron Armor	LEVEL 7	Lightning Craft
LEVEL 2	Warrior's Weapon	LEVEL 8	Master's Weapon
LEVEL 3	Flame Armor	LEVEL 9	Ring of Light
LEVEL 4	Clockwork	LEVEL 10	Diamond Armor
LEVEL 5	Mythril Armor	LEVEL 11	Ring of Invincibility
LEVEL 6	Frost Craft	LEVEL 12	Greatest Weapon

Secret Items

It pays to explore every nook and cranny of the world—there are lots of hidden treasures just waiting to be found.

Certain areas in the game contain hidden items. Go to the locations listed on the chart below and search until the Examine icon appears. When it does, press the A Button to pick up the secret goodie. The items will appear in the order shown on the list to the right—regardless of where you search. When you find the 25th item (an Ancient Potion), the list will start over at the beginning (a Wheat Seed). Once you find a hidden item, you won't be able to find another one until you defeat a dungeon and get a drop of Myrrh.

SECRET ITEMS BY TURN			
1	WHEAT SEED	14	VEGETABLE SEED
2	BRONZE SHARD	15	JADE
3	BRONZE	16	VEGETABLE SEED
4	IRON SHARD	17	SILVER
5	FRUIT SEED	18	GOLD
6	ALLOY	19	MYTHRIL
7	FRUIT SEED	20	PRESSED FLOWER
8	IRON	21	REMEDY
9	FRUIT SEED	22	BANNOCK
10	MARK OF SHELLA	23	SPRING WATER
11	SPRING WATER	24	SPRING WATER
12	VEGETABLE SEED	25	ANCIENT POTION
13	RUBY		

SECRET ITEM LOCATIONS		
TIPA PENINSULA	TIPA	PG. 29
IRON MINE DOWNS	MARR'S PASS	PG. 40
VALE OF ALFITARIA	ALFITARIA	PG. 52
VEO LU	SHELLA	PG. 64
PLAINS OF FUM	FIELDS OF FUM	PG. 71
LYNARI ISLE	LEUDA	PG. 103

Adventures on the Road

As your caravan moves through the land, you'll learn the story of Crystal Chronicles through two kinds of events.

Fixed Events

Fixed events are cinema scenes that occur at the same time in every game. Examples are the story of the Black Knight and the events of the curly-haired wanderer named Gurdy. Fixed events play heavily into the story and should be studied carefully.

Random Events

Random events will occur at different times, depending on the progress of your game, where you are and a host of other intangibles. Among other random events, you'll meet a group of Yukes who think that a loaf of bread represents the world, and fight a long-running battle against a group of incompetent bandits. See pages 118-121 for a list of all fixed and random events.

Moogle Nests

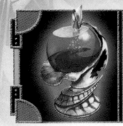

Each area of the world contains a Moogle Nest—a cozy nook where the furry creatures have carved out a nice life for themselves.

Moogle Nests exist in towns and dungeons. When you approach a nest entrance, the Examine icon will appear—press B to enter the nest. Once inside, you can collect stamps, paint your Mog (in single-player mode) or play Blazin' Caravans (in multiplayer mode).

Stamps and Nest Locations

When you speak to a Moogle for the first time, he or she will offer you a Moogle Stamp (23 in all). When you collect all the stamps in a set, you will unlock a minigame called Blazin' Caravans—a Mario Kart-like game that can be played only on the GBA in multiplayer mode. The stamp card to the right shows the location of each stamp, while the lettered screenshots show where the corresponding Moogle Nest is located. If you can't find a nest, use the page number in the corner of the screenshot to find a map of the area.

Stamp card grid:
A B C D E F
G H I J K
L M N O P Q
R S T U V W

A Moschet Manor

PG. 59

B The Mine of Cathuriges

PG. 46

C Tida

PG. 53

D Goblin Wall

PG. 34

E Port Tipa

PG. 29

F Mushroom Forest

PG. 41

G Mount Vellenge

PG. 112

H Mag Mell

PG. 111

I Lynari Desert

PG. 104

J Conall Curach

PG. 91

K Daemon's Court	**L** The Fields of Fum	**M** Rebena Te Ra	**N** Alfitaria	**O** Shella
 PG. 72	 PG. 71	 PG. 97	 PG. 52	 PG. 64

P Marr's Pass	**Q** Selepation Cave	**R** Tipa	**S** West Jegon River	**T** River Belle Path
 PG. 40	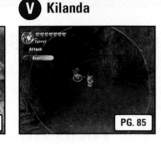 PG. 77	 PG. 29	 PG. 71	 PG. 30

U Leuda	**V** Kilanda	**W** Veo Lu Sluice
 PG. 103	 PG. 85	PG. 65

Your Moogle Friend

In single-player mode, you will be accompanied by a helpful Moogle named Mog. His most important duty is to carry the chalice so you can fight, but he will also cast an occasional spell. If you cast a spell along with your Moogle, you can fuse the two to create more powerful spells.

A Moogle Masterpiece

You can paint your Moogle and cut his hair inside any Moogle Nest. The color of your Moogle affects what spell he will cast (he won't stick to a certain spell all the time—he's just more likely to cast it), and what information you'll see if you connect a GBA to the second Controller port. The length of the Moogle's hair affects how quickly he becomes tired in certain dungeons.

COLOR	MAGIC	RADAR DISPLAY
COLORLESS	RANDOM	AREA MAP
RED	FIRE	MONSTER LOCATOR
BLUE	BLIZZARD	CHEST LOCATOR
GREEN	THUNDER	SCOUTER

Moogle Mumblings

Your Moogle isn't shy when it comes to speaking up about the whole chalice-carrying gig. When your Moogle says "I'm tired" or "It's your turn to carry the chalice," have him set it down so you can carry it for a little while. If you don't, the Moogle will move slowly and have a hard time keeping up with you. After he is rested (which doesn't take very long), he will say "Let me carry the chalice," at which point you can give it back to him. If you're going to one of the hot dungeons listed below, cut his hair first. If you're going to a cold dungeon, leave it long. Proper grooming will keep him in high spirits.

HOT DUNGEONS	
KILANDA	
LYNARI DESERT	

COLD DUNGEONS	
TIDA	CONALL CURACH
SELEPATION CAVE	REBENA TE RA
VEO LU SLUICE	MOUNT VELLENGE

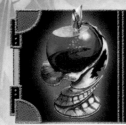

How to Battle

From magic to melee to making the most of multiplayer battles . . . everything you need to know about brawling is contained in these pages.

Melee Attacks and Combos

If you press the A Button with the Attack command selected, you will strike with your equipped weapon. If you press the button three times with proper timing (a slight pause between each press) you will unleash a combo attack.

Defense

If you press the A Button with the Defend command selected, your character will ward off enemy attacks. Your character's defense ability depends on his or her race.

Clavat and Lilty Defense

Clavats and Lilties have a defensive pose that leaves them vulnerable from behind. They can also be struck by magic.

Yuke and Selkie Defense

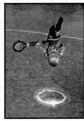

Yukes and Selkies enjoy a more advanced defensive posture. When defending, they are invulnerable to all attacks, including magic.

Magic

Magic works like a Focus Attack. Once you equip a ball of Magicite or a Magic Ring in your command list, you must press and hold the A Button to make the ring appear. When you release A, the magic will be cast.

Focus Attacks

If you press and hold A with Attack selected, a targeting ring will appear. When you release A, you will use one of the following Focus Attacks (depending on your weapon):

Move-Type Focus Attack

If an enemy hits you while your attack is charging, the attack will be disrupted. If you touch a foe in midair (after releasing the button but before you reach the targeting ring), you will strike that enemy instead.

Charge-Type Focus Attack

The attack can't be interrupted while charging, and touching an enemy in midair has no effect. The attack will have a knock-back effect on the target, forcing it backward.

Leaping-Type Focus Attack

The attack cannot be interrupted while charging. If you touch an enemy in midair, the attack will strike that enemy instead.

Unstoppable-Type Focus Attack

The attack cannot be interrupted while charging. If you strike enemies in midair, the attack will reach the targeting ring, damaging both the enemy targeted and the one who got in your way.

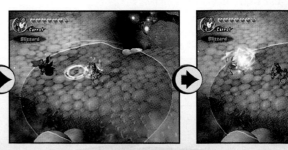

Single-Player Spell Fusion

Spell Fusion by Yourself

To fuse spells, place two or more compatible pieces of Magicite next to each other in the command list and select Fuse. You can fuse up to three magics together. The order makes a difference—Life on top of Blizzard will make Slow, but Blizzard on top of Life will make Holy. You can also fuse Magicite with your weapon if you want to use elemental-based attacks like Firestrike and Icestrike. To do so, take a spare weapon from your inventory and place it beneath the spell in the command list, then fuse them together.

Spell Fusion with Your Moogle

Another way to fuse spells is with your Moogle. When the Moogle says "Hang in there, Kupo!" he is ready to cast a spell. Have him drop the chalice, then hold the A Button to prepare your spell—the Moogle will place his targeting ring over yours. The timing is the same as spell fusion in multiplayer mode.

Multiplayer Spell Fusion

In multiplayer mode, you fuse magic by placing multiple targeting rings in the same spot and casting spells with the proper timing. There are five different timings—the magic appendix at the end of the book lists which type you must use to make a spell. The timing takes a lot of practice, so be patient!

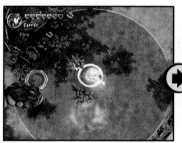

Timing Structures for Fusing Magic

Type A	Type B	Type C	Type D	Type E
Type A is the easiest timing of them all—once the rings are together, all players release the A Button at the same time. You may want to practice with a "one, two, three" count to get it down, but that is impractical during battle. It's much more efficient to agree that everyone will cast the spell the moment that the rings come together.	Type B is slightly trickier than Type A. After the first player releases the A Button, two or more players release their buttons after a pause of about one second. When you're casting spells that require different timing for multiple players, determine in advance the order of release. It's helpful for players to go in the same order each time.	To create a Type C spell, the first two players release the A Button at the same time, then other players release their buttons after a slight pause. While learning how long to pause is mostly a matter of practice, you can also listen for a slight hum that emits from the ring, and watch for it to change color slightly.	The type D spell seems difficult at first, but once you learn the timing it's actually pretty easy. All players release the A Button with a fairly long pause between each spell. Type D spells are hard to pull off in a hectic battle because they take a long time to set up, but they're some of the most powerful spells around.	Type E spells are similar to Type D ones, but each player's pause before releasing the A Button is shorter for a Type E. Fusing magic is one of the most enjoyable parts of a multiplayer game, but it's also the trickiest by far. Practice and patience are the best ways to become spell fusion masters.

Status Changes

Some enemy attacks will cause a status change in your character. In addition to the nasty effects listed on this page, you can also suffer from Stun (which renders you immobile) and Knock Back (which interrupts your attack). Time is the only cure for both.

Burning

When you're on fire, your Defense will drop and your movement will slow. You can recover by casting Clear on yourself, or by waiting for the flames to go out.

Frozen

You can't move when frozen. If a monster strikes you with a physical attack, it will do twice the damage. To recover, cast Clear or wiggle the Control Stick back and forth.

Paralysis

The Paralysis effect will occur if you're struck by a Thunder spell. Your character will become immobile for a short period of time. You can remove the effect with a Clear spell or by moving the Control Stick back and forth.

Slow

Slow will cause your movement to drop by half—including the time it takes to charge up a Focus Attack or magic spell. To recover, cast Clear or Haste, or wait for it to wear off.

Stasis

A Stasis attack will freeze your character in place. The only way to regain your senses is by casting Clear or just waiting for the spell to wear off.

Haste

Haste is a good thing when it's cast on you. Your movement will be increased, and you can use Focus Attacks and magic in half the time. If you want to remove the spell for some reason, Clear, Stop and Slow will all do the job. Haste will wear off naturally.

Poison

When poisoned, you will lose half of a heart every five seconds. To stop the toxin in its tracks, cast Clear. It will take away approximately three hearts before wearing off.

Petrification

Similar to Stasis, Petrification freezes you in place. While petrified, your character will be extremely vulnerable to physical and Gravity attacks. You can recover by using Clear or waiting.

Curse

A cursed character will have all of his or her abilities (Strength, Magic, Defense) drop by half—not a good thing at all. Remove the curse quickly by using Clear, or tough it out until the spell wears off.

Death

Sometimes you just can't win. If your character is killed, you can revive him or her with a Phoenix Down or the spells Life or Full-Life. In single-player, you must have the Phoenix Down in your command list for it to take effect.

Resisting Status Changes

Certain pieces of armor and accessories have a built-in resistance to status ailments. When you build one of the items listed below, it's a good idea to hang on to it so you can equip it when necessary. If you're going to Kilanda, for example, you'll want Burning resistance.

RESIST BURNING	RACE
BADGE OF THE FLAME	ALL
FLAME ARMLETS	LILTY
FLAME HELM	YUKE
FLAME MAIL	ALL
FLAME SASH	SELKIE
FLAME SHIELD	CLAVAT

RESIST SLOW	RACE
ACCURATE WATCH	ALL
TIME HELM	YUKE
TIME MAIL	ALL

RESIST CURSE	RACE
SAINTLY MAIL	ALL
SAINTLY SHIELD	CLAVAT
WHITE MISANGA	ALL

RESIST FREEZING	RACE
BADGE OF THE FROST	ALL
FROST ARMLETS	LILTY
FROST MAIL	ALL
FROST SASH	SELKIE
FROST SHIELD	CLAVAT

RESIST STASIS	RACE
ETERNAL HELM	YUKE
ETERNAL MAIL	ALL
UNFALTERING WATCH	ALL

RESIST PETRIFICATION	RACE
GOLD ARMLETS	LILTY
GOLD NECKLACE	ALL

RESIST PARALYSIS	RACE
BADGE OF THE STORM	ALL
STORM ARMLETS	LILTY
STORM HELM	YUKE
STORM MAIL	ALL
STORM SHIELD	CLAVAT

RESIST POISON	RACE
BLESSED MAIL	ALL
BLESSED SASH	SELKIE
BLUE MISANGA	ALL

The Art of War

Organized Labor

Don't just throw magic and items into your command list willy-nilly. Put spells that you use a lot, such as Cure, at the bottom of the list. That way you can switch from Attack to the spell with one tap of the L Button. Remove unwanted spells and items from the command list so you don't have to cycle through them.

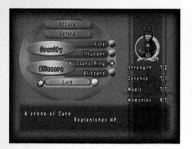 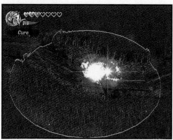

Holy Gravity!

Two of your more specialized spells are Gravity and Holy (and their upgraded versions). Use Gravity to force flying enemies to the ground (where they are more susceptible to damage) and use Holy to make transparent creatures appear. Holy is perhaps the best spell in the game—hardly any monsters have a resistance to it.

 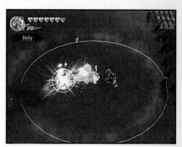

Know Your Role

In multiplayer mode, it's important to divide the work before you enter a dungeon. Figure out which characters will press the attack with their weapons and which will use magic from the rear. Also assign a healer for the party, and know in what order you will cast spells when trying to fuse magic.

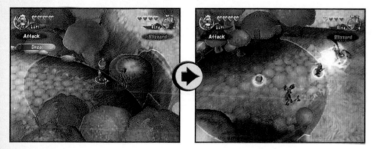

Head for the Hills

Keep an eye on your health meter in the top left-hand corner of the screen. If it starts to run low or if you get in a fight with multiple enemies, run to a safe spot and restore your health with Cure or some food. It's easy to get overwhelmed by enemies and taken out before you know what hit you.

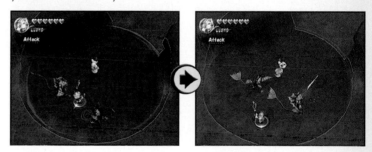

Stick and Move, Stick and Move

Learning a monster's attack pattern is essential for success. The vast majority of monsters will approach you, perform some kind of windup, then strike. Wait until the monster is in the windup, then retreat to a safe distance. As soon as it swings and misses, move in and hit it with whatever attack you like.

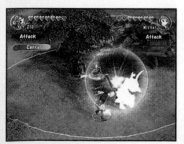 

Mano a Mano

Don't fight multiple enemies if you can avoid it—take them on one at a time. You can get pretty close to a monster before it spots you, but there's not much need to do so. Hit it from afar with a magic spell, then switch to close-range combat if it charges. If you're dealing with many enemies, retreat and take out those who follow.

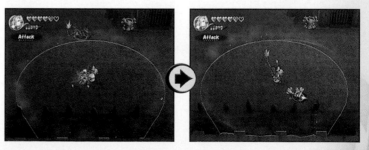

Breaking the Crockery

Use urns to your advantage while inside a dungeon. If you throw an oil-filled urn on the ground, cast Fire on the puddle to create a more powerful spell. If you break open an urn full of water, cast Blizzard or Thunder on the wet stuff. It's an easy way to nail multiple enemies with a single spell.

Sneak Attacks

Plan ahead before you press the attack. If you run up to a monster while waving your sword wildly in the air, it will see you coming and launch an attack. If, however, you sneak up behind a monster, you can often catch it unawares. Many monsters will let you get close enough to touch them if you approach from behind.

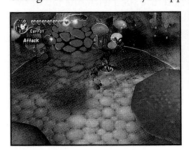
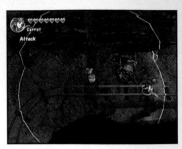

Pantry Provisions

When you have a Cure spell at the ready, it's easy to overlook the food in your inventory—but don't let it happen. Since food takes effect the moment you use it, it's perfect for restoring health in the middle of a tough fight. Most food will also temporarily raise your Strength, Magic or Defense by a couple of points.

Arise from Your Grave!

Phoenix Down is a solo adventurer's best friend. If you have a Phoenix Down set in your command list, you'll use it automatically if you're killed in battle. The item will also work if you are playing a multiplayer game. If only one character has a Life spell, give him or her a Phoenix Down also in case the player meets a bad end.

Mind the Gap

Use your brain—it's what separates you from the beasts. Monsters aren't the smartest critters around, and they usually take the shortest path to their intended victim. If you can get something in between you and an enemy—a gap, box or other obstacle—you can hang out on the other side and hit the foe with magic.

Stuck in a Moment

Magic can be effective even if it doesn't deal a lot of damage. If you cast Thunder, you can paralyze an enemy. If you cast Blizzard, you can freeze it in place. If you're fighting multiple foes, freeze or paralyze one of them, then attack the other while its buddy is immobile.

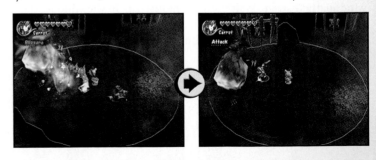

The Bonus-Point System

Each time you enter a dungeon, you will earn or lose bonus points based on how well you satisfy a certain bonus condition (all the possible conditions are listed below). The more bonus points you earn, the better your chances of receiving the best artifacts. You'll be sitting pretty if you earn 200 points, but it's possible to earn 300 points or more.

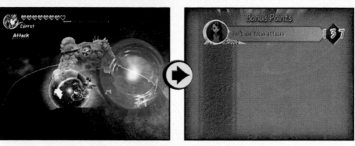

You won't get bonus points unless you defeat a a boss (you don't have to collect Myrrh to get the points). Once you win the battle, a screen that shows your points will appear. The points are based on your success with the bonus condition, plus a couple of other factors (see page 22 for more info).

To see your bonus condition, plug a GBA into the GCN and look at the bottom portion of the screen.

Bonus Conditions

PICK UP ITEMS	If you pick up any items except gil, you will earn bonus points. You can't earn points for picking up the chalice or for dropping items and then picking them up again.
PICK UP MONEY	Any time you pick up gil, you will earn bonus points. The amount of money doesn't affect the number of points. You won't get points if you drop money and then pick it up.
DEFEAT ENEMIES WITH SPELL FUSION	When you defeat an enemy with a fused spell (Blizzara, Fira, etc.) you'll get points. You won't receive points for damaging a monster, only for striking the finishing blow—so you can whittle it down with melee attacks if you want.
DEFEAT ENEMIES WITH FOCUS ATTACKS	If you defeat an enemy with a Focus Attack, you'll get points. You won't get any points for damaging your foe, only for striking the finishing blow—so you can use magic to wear it down without penalty.
DEFEAT ENEMIES WITH SPELLS	When you defeat an enemy by using any magic spell, you'll get points. As for the two conditions above, you won't get points for damaging enemies, only for striking the finishing blow.
OPEN TREASURE CHESTS	Any time you open a treasure chest, you'll be rewarded with bonus points. You'll even get points if the treasure chest turns out to be a Mimic.
INFLICT DAMAGE	When you deal damage to an enemy, you'll earn points. The amount of damage doesn't affect the points, so it's possible to earn a ton of points by using weak attacks, if you're so inclined.
TAKE PHYSICAL DAMAGE	If an enemy strikes you with a physical attack, it's your lucky bonus point day. The amount of damage doesn't matter, and suffering a magic attack won't add to your point total.
TAKE MAGICAL DAMAGE	You must be damaged by spells to earn points. Only spells that hurt you will count for points—magic such as Slow, Haste or Stop won't add to your point total.
AVOID DAMAGE	You'll start with a set number of points. Whenever you take damage of any kind, you will lose some of those points. Avoid being hit at all costs.
DON'T CAST SPELLS	You'll start with a set number of points. If you use a magic spell of any type, you'll lose a few. You won't lose points, however, if friends cast a spell on you in a multiplayer game.
DON'T USE FOCUS ATTACKS	You'll start with a set number of points. Any time you use a Focus Attack, your point total will fall. It doesn't matter if the attack fells the foe.
DON'T USE PHYSICAL ATTACKS	You'll start with a set number of points. If you hit an enemy with a physical attack, your points will diminish. You'll lose the same number of points whether you damage or finish off an enemy.
DON'T HEAL YOURSELF	You'll start with a set number of points. Once you take damage and cure yourself—whether with a spell or an item—some of your hard-won points will vanish.
DON'T PICK ANYTHING UP	You'll start with a set number of points. Any time you pick up gil or items, you'll lose points. The only exception is money that friends drop in a multiplayer game—you can pick it up without penalty.

Calculating Bonus Points

In the case of the first nine conditions, you start the level with zero points and earn them by performing an action. For the remaining conditions, you begin the level with 100 points and lose some each time you perform an action. (Note that the dungeons have different point penalties and bonuses.) You can receive a maximum of 100 points for fulfilling a condition. Your final point total (which will almost always be more than 100) is figured by taking the points you earned for meeting the bonus condition and adding that number to the number of enemies you defeated and the number of items that you picked up (for that dungeon only, not the entire game).

	RIVER BELLE PATH	GOBLIN WALL	THE MUSHROOM FOREST	THE MINE OF CATHURIGES	TIDA	MOSCHET MANOR	VEO LU SLUICE	DAEMON'S COURT	SELEPATION CAVE	KILANDA	CONALL CURACH	REBENA TE RA	LYNARI DESERT
PICK UP ITEMS	+5	+4	+5	+5	+3	+8	+7	+5	+3	+5	+2	+3	+3
PICK UP MONEY	+7	+7	+7	+7	+5	+10	+10	+7	+5	+7	+4	+5	+5
DEFEAT ENEMIES WITH SPELL FUSION	+5	+5	+5	+5	+4	+7	+6	+5	+5	+6	+5	+5	+5
DEFEAT ENEMIES WITH FOCUS ATTACKS	+5	+5	+5	+5	+4	+7	+6	+5	+5	+6	+5	+5	+5
DEFEAT ENEMIES WITH SPELLS	+5	+5	+5	+5	+4	+7	+6	+5	+5	+6	+5	+5	+5
OPEN TREASURE CHESTS	+15	+8	+10	+8	+8	+15	+20	+10	+9	+17	+5	+7	+10
INFLICT DAMAGE	+1	+1	+1	+1	+1	+1	+1	+1	+1	+1	+1	+1	+1
TAKE PHYSICAL DAMAGE	+2	+2	+2	+2	+2	+2	+2	+2	+2	+2	+2	+2	+2
TAKE MAGICAL DAMAGE	+10	+10	+10	+7	+4	+10	+6	+6	+6	+6	+5	+5	+6
AVOID DAMAGE	-1	-1	-1	-1	-1	-1	-1	-1	-1	-1	-1	-1	-1
DON'T CAST SPELLS	-5	-5	-5	-5	-5	-5	-5	-5	-5	-5	-5	-5	-5
DON'T USE FOCUS ATTACKS	-5	-5	-5	-5	-5	-5	-5	-5	-5	-5	-5	-5	-5
DON'T USE PHYSICAL ATTACKS	-5	-5	-5	-5	-5	-5	-5	-5	-5	-5	-5	-5	-5
DON'T HEAL YOURSELF	-2	-2	-2	-2	-2	-2	-2	-2	-2	-2	-2	-2	-2
DON'T PICK ANYTHING UP	-1	-1	-1	-1	-1	-1	-1	-1	-1	-1	-1	-1	-1

Artifact Sets

You can find and pick up a total of four artifacts in a dungeon (with the exception of levels in the Abyss). When you defeat a boss, it will drop four additional treasures. At the end of the level, you can take one.

The four items dropped by the boss are called an Artifact Set. There are eight possible sets over the three cycles of a dungeon—which one you get depends on bonus points, the number of players and the cycle. After all factors are considered, a set is dropped (see page 27 for more details).

In multiplayer games, the player with the most points will choose an artifact first, followed by the other players in descending order. Once an artifact is chosen, it cannot be taken by another player. Don't be an artifact hog—you want all players to have strong characters.

The Walk-through

World Map

The world of Crystal Chronicles is divided into nine distinct areas. They are kept separated by distance, water and Miasma Streams.

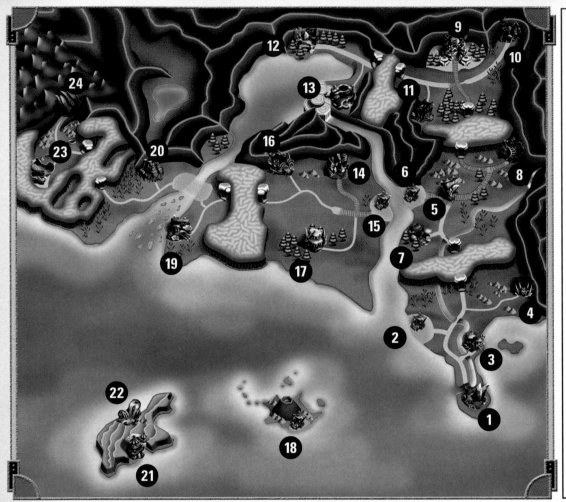

Miasma Streams

Miasma Streams are large expanses of Miasma that are infused with a certain elemental type. If your chalice's elemental type doesn't match the stream's, you can't pass through it. The stream's elemental type will change from year to year, so you'll have to adapt. Once you get the mysterious element, you can pass through any stream.

MIASMA'S ELEMENTAL CYCLE

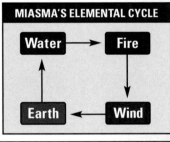

Water → Fire
Fire → Wind
Wind → Earth
Earth → Water

Inaccessible Areas

Sometimes you won't be able to get to a certain area. Whatever the problem, don't worry—by year eight you should be home free.

The charts on this page show when you can (and can't) access areas. Most will be inaccessible because of the Miasma Stream—you simply won't be able to make your chalice the proper elemental type to pass through. Other times, the Jegon River will dry up. Areas listed in tan boxes are accessible. Those in gray are inaccessible because of Miasma, and those in blue are inaccessible because of the river.

First Year

You can enter only two areas in the first year—Tipa Peninsula and Iron Mine Downs. Don't worry—there's more than enough there to keep your adventure hopping and your pockets filled with items and treasures.

AREA & ACCESSIBILITY	
TIPA PENINSULA	KILANDA ISLANDS
IRON MINE DOWNS	REBENA PLAINS
VALE OF ALFITARIA	LYNARI ISLE
VEO LU	THE ABYSS
PLAINS OF FUM	

Second Year

In the second year, things start to get interesting. You can visit four areas of the world, including two brand-new ones. Additionally, a new dungeon appears—the Goblin Wall emerges in the northeast corner of Tipa Peninsula.

AREA & ACCESSIBILITY	
TIPA PENINSULA	KILANDA ISLANDS
IRON MINE DOWNS	REBENA PLAINS
VALE OF ALFITARIA	LYNARI ISLE
VEO LU	THE ABYSS
PLAINS OF FUM	

Third Year

You can enter five areas in the third year. To reach the Plains of Fum, you'll have to go to the Jegon River and take a boat across the watery expanse. The ferryman will charge you a slight fee, but it's not unreasonable.

AREA & ACCESSIBILITY	
TIPA PENINSULA	KILANDA ISLANDS
IRON MINE DOWNS	REBENA PLAINS
VALE OF ALFITARIA	LYNARI ISLE
VEO LU	THE ABYSS
PLAINS OF FUM	

Fourth Year

Your first chance to hit the ocean waves comes during year four. The same ferryman who takes you across the Jegon River will carry your party to Mt. Kilanda—a small rock composed entirely of a very active volcano.

AREA & ACCESSIBILITY	
TIPA PENINSULA	KILANDA ISLANDS
IRON MINE DOWNS	REBENA PLAINS
VALE OF ALFITARIA	LYNARI ISLE
VEO LU	THE ABYSS
PLAINS OF FUM	

Fifth Year

During year five, the Jegon River will dry up, leaving you unable to access many of the areas. If you want to take care of the problem right away, go to Lynari Isle and equip your chalice with the mysterious element, then head for Veo Lu Sluice and bring the flowers back to life.

AREA & ACCESSIBILITY	
TIPA PENINSULA	KILANDA ISLANDS
IRON MINE DOWNS	REBENA PLAINS
VALE OF ALFITARIA	LYNARI ISLE
VEO LU	THE ABYSS
PLAINS OF FUM	

Sixth & Seventh Years

If you take care of the Jegon River problem during year five, you can go almost anywhere you like. If not, the areas marked in blue will be inaccessible. The Abyss will be forbidden until you get the mysterious element form Lynari Desert.

AREA & ACCESSIBILITY	
TIPA PENINSULA	KILANDA ISLANDS
IRON MINE DOWNS	REBENA PLAINS
VALE OF ALFITARIA	LYNARI ISLE
VEO LU	THE ABYSS
PLAINS OF FUM	

Eighth Year

The Jegon River will fill with water automatically after year seven, leaving you free to explore the entire world. Note that The Abyss is protected by an unknown Miasma Stream—if you don't equip your chalice with the unknown element, you won't be able to enter the area.

AREA & ACCESSIBILITY	
TIPA PENINSULA	KILANDA ISLANDS
IRON MINE DOWNS	REBENA PLAINS
VALE OF ALFITARIA	LYNARI ISLE
VEO LU	THE ABYSS
PLAINS OF FUM	

Using the Walk-through

You're through the appetizer . . . now it's time for the main course!
Learn to read the walk-through pages before starting your adventure.

This box shows the Miasma Stream's elemental type from year to year. After the fourth year, it will start anew from year one.

This is an example of a town page. If there are shops or blacksmiths in the town, we tell you what goods are sold in the shop and what gear the smith will construct. If there is a boat launch in the town, we show you where you can go, list the fares and tell you how to get a discount, if applicable.

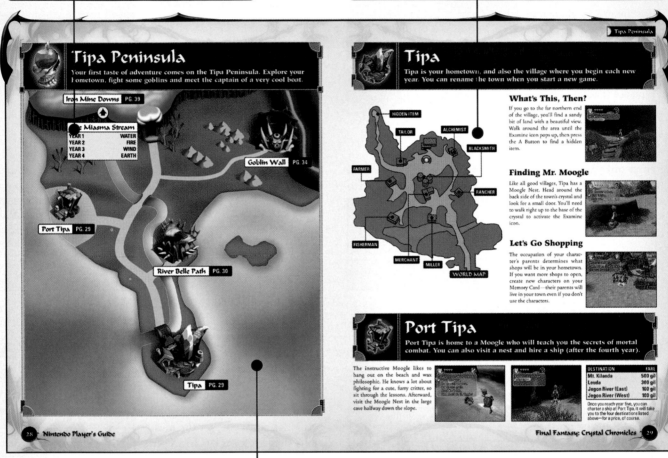

Tipa Peninsula

Your first taste of adventure comes on the Tipa Peninsula. Explore your hometown, fight some goblins and meet the captain of a very cool boat.

Iron Mine Downs PG. 39

The Miasma Stream

YEAR 1	WATER
YEAR 2	FIRE
YEAR 3	WIND
YEAR 4	EARTH

Goblin Wall PG. 34

Port Tipa PG. 29

River Belle Path PG. 30

Tipa PG. 29

Tipa

Tipa is your hometown, and also the village where you begin each new year. You can rename the town when you start a new game.

HIDDEN ITEM
TAILOR
ALCHEMIST
BLACKSMITH
FARMER
RANCHER
FISHERMAN
MERCHANT
MILLER
WORLD MAP

What's This, Then?
If you go to the far northern end of the village, you'll find a sandy bit of land with a beautiful view. Walk around the area until the Examine icon pops up, then press the A Button to find a hidden item.

Finding Mr. Moogle
Like all good villages, Tipa has a Moogle Nest. Head around the back side of the town's crystal and look for a small door. You'll need to walk right up to the base of the crystal to activate the Examine icon.

Let's Go Shopping
The occupation of your character's parents determines what shops will be in your hometown. If you want more shops to open, create new characters on your Memory Card—their parents will live in your town even if you don't use the characters.

Port Tipa

Port Tipa is home to a Moogle who will teach you the secrets of mortal combat. You can also visit a nest and hire a ship (after the fourth year).

The instructive Moogle likes to hang out on the beach and wax philosophic. He knows a lot about fighting for a cute, furry critter, so sit through the lessons. Afterward, visit the Moogle Nest in the large cave halfway down the slope.

DESTINATION	FARE
Mt. Kilanda	500 gil
Leuda	300 gil
Jegon River (East)	100 gil
Jegon River (West)	100 gil

Once you reach year five, you can charter a ship at Port Tipa. It will take you to the four destinations listed above—for a price, of course.

Each time you reach a new area in the walk-through, a map of it will appear. The numbers to the right of the dungeon names will direct you to pages that cover the level in detail.

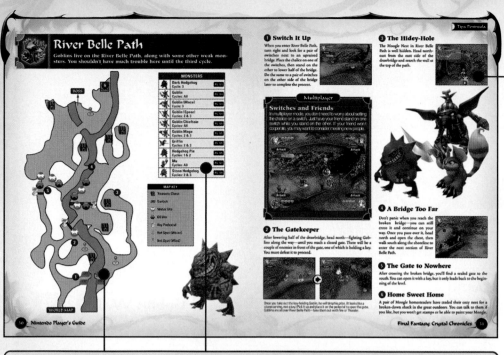

All screenshots and tips assume that you are playing through the first cycle of a dungeon, unless otherwise noted. Any tip specific to multiplayer games will be called out in a special box.

Icons on the dungeon map show the locations of treasure chests, switches, urns, pedestals and hot spots (where you can change the chalice's elemental type). The numbers on the map correspond to the numbered tips in the walk-through. Finally, the box on the right-hand side of the page lists all monsters in the dungeon, and in which cycle(s) they will be present. If you want specific information on a monster, turn to the page number listed next to its name.

This box lists the artifacts, scrolls and materials that you can get from a monster (represented by numbers) or a treasure chest (represented by letters). All of the numbers and letters correspond to numbers and letters on the closest map. Note that while the chart shows what you *can* get from a monster or chest, you won't *always* get it—you may end up with gil or an everyday item like a Phoenix Down instead.

The boss box shows how to beat the level's boss, and also what elemental resistances the boss has. A small number means that the boss is weaker against that elemental type, while a large number means that the boss is strong against it. So if a boss has a Fire rating of three and a Holy rating of zero, it is nearly impervious to Fire but very weak against Holy attacks.

Bosses will become more difficult during the second and third cycles. Tips for fighting a boss during those cycles appear to the right of the main boss box. If you return to an area after the third cycle, the boss and monsters will remain the same.

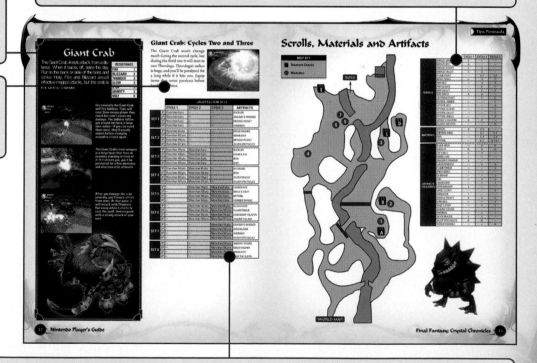

This chart lists the items that the boss drops. (A boss drops four items at a time, which is called a set.) Which set you get is determined by the cycle, the number of players and the number of bonus points you have. Once you meet a certain criterion, the game will select one of the sets that matches that criterion. For example, assume that you get one set by having more than zero bonus points, and another for having more than 140 points. If you earn 149 points, you might receive the same set that you would if you had five points. If you have five bonus points, however, you won't be able to get the 149-point set. For multiplayer games, add your points together and compare them to the part of the chart that shows the number of players you have.

Tipa Peninsula

Your first taste of adventure comes on the Tipa Peninsula. Explore your hometown, fight some goblins and meet the captain of a very cool boat.

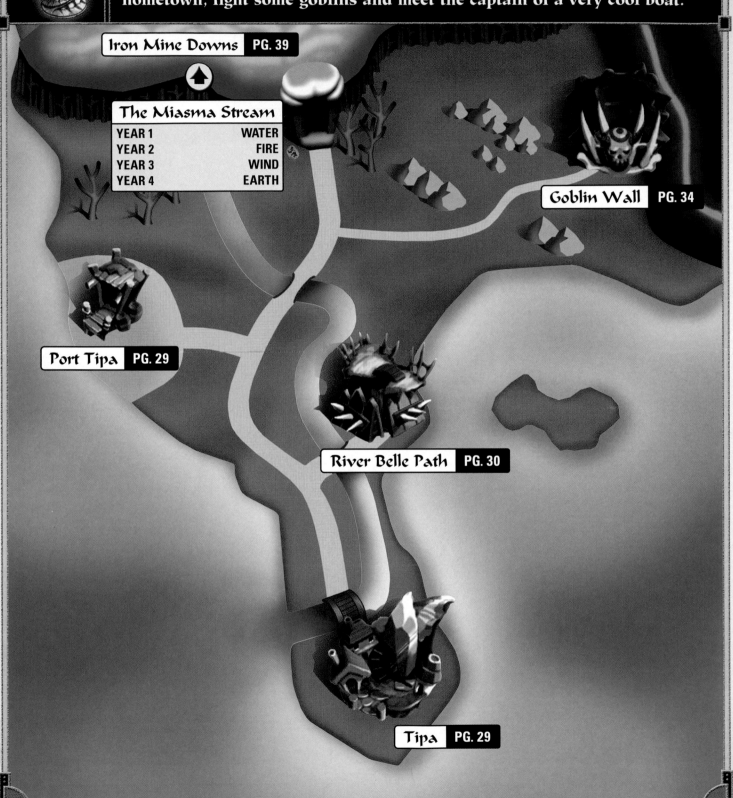

Iron Mine Downs PG. 39

The Miasma Stream

YEAR 1	WATER
YEAR 2	FIRE
YEAR 3	WIND
YEAR 4	EARTH

Goblin Wall PG. 34

Port Tipa PG. 29

River Belle Path PG. 30

Tipa PG. 29

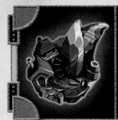

Tipa

Tipa is your hometown, and also the village where you begin each new year. You can rename the town when you start a new game.

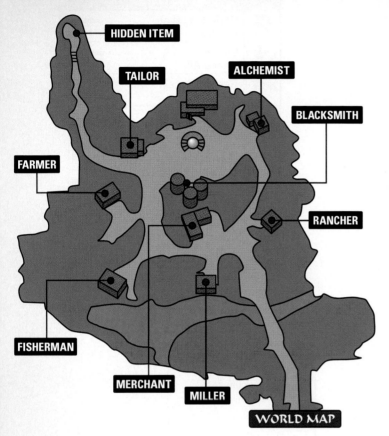

What's This, Then?

If you go to the far northern end of the village, you'll find a sandy bit of land with a beautiful view. Walk around the area until the Examine icon pops up, then press the A Button to find a hidden item.

Finding Mr. Moogle

Like all good villages, Tipa has a Moogle Nest. Head around the back side of the town's crystal and look for a small door. You'll need to walk right up to the base of the crystal to activate the Examine icon.

Let's Go Shopping

The occupation of your character's parents determines what shops will be in your hometown. If you want more shops to open, create new characters on your Memory Card—their parents will live in your town even if you don't use the characters.

Port Tipa

Port Tipa is home to a Moogle who will teach you the secrets of mortal combat. You can also visit a nest and hire a ship (after the fourth year).

The instructive Moogle likes to hang out on the beach and wax philosophic. He knows a lot about fighting for a cute, furry critter, so sit through the lessons. Afterward, visit the Moogle Nest in the large cave halfway down the slope.

DESTINATION	FARE
Mt. Kilanda	500 gil
Leuda	300 gil
Jegon River (East)	100 gil
Jegon River (West)	100 gil

Once you reach year five, you can charter a ship at Port Tipa. It will take you to the four destinations listed above—for a price, of course.

River Belle Path

Goblins live on the River Belle Path, along with some other weak monsters. You shouldn't have much trouble here until the third cycle.

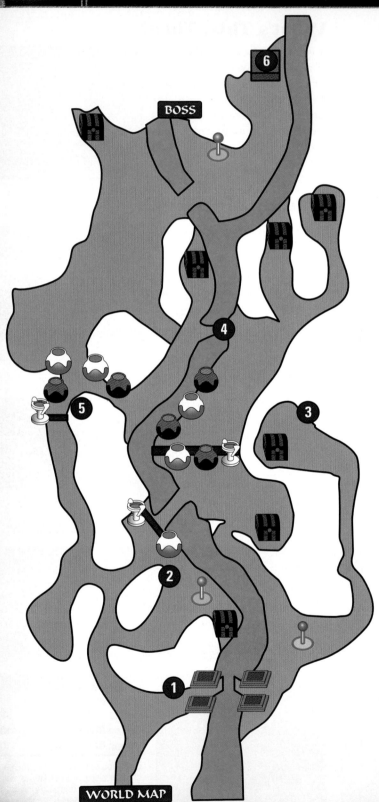

BOSS

WORLD MAP

MONSTERS		
Dark Hedgehog Cycle: 3		PG. 123
Goblin Cycles: All		PG. 124
Goblin (Mace) Cycle: 3		PG. 124
Goblin (Spear) Cycles: 2 & 3		PG. 124
Goblin Chieftain Cycles: All		PG. 125
Goblin Mage Cycles: 2 & 3		PG. 125
Griffin Cycles: 2 & 3		PG. 125
Hedgehog Pie Cycles: 1 & 2		PG. 125
Mu Cycles: All		PG. 127
Stone Hedgehog Cycles: 2 & 3		PG. 129

MAP KEY	
	Treasure Chest
	Switch
	Water Urn
	Oil Urn
	Key Pedestal
	Hot Spot (Water)
	Hot Spot (Wind)

① Switch It Up

When you enter River Belle Path, turn right and look for a pair of switches next to an upraised bridge. Place the chalice on one of the switches, then stand on the other to lower half of the bridge. Do the same to a pair of switches on the other side of the bridge later to complete the process.

③ The Hidey-Hole

The Moogle Nest in River Belle Path is well hidden. Head northeast from the east side of the drawbridge and search the wall at the top of the path.

Multiplayer

Switches and Friends

In multiplayer mode, you don't need to worry about setting the chalice on a switch. Just have your friend stand on one switch while you stand on the other. If your friend won't cooperate, you may want to consider meeting new people.

② The Gatekeeper

After lowering half of the drawbridge, head north—fighting Goblins along the way—until you reach a closed gate. There will be a couple of enemies in front of the gate, one of which is holding a key. You must defeat it to proceed.

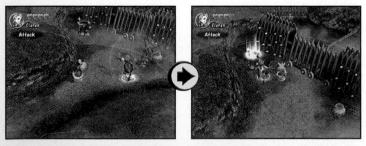

Once you take out the key-holding Goblin, he will drop his prize. (It looks like a stone carving, not a key.) Pick it up and place it on the pedestal to open the gate. Goblins are all over River Belle Path—take them out with Fire or Thunder.

④ A Bridge Too Far

Don't panic when you reach the broken bridge—you can still cross it and continue on your way. Once you pass over it, head north and open the chest, then walk south along the shoreline to enter the next section of River Belle Path.

⑤ The Gate to Nowhere

After crossing the broken bridge, you'll find a sealed gate to the south. You can open it with a key, but it only leads back to the beginning of the level.

⑥ Home Sweet Home

A pair of Moogle homesteaders have traded their cozy nest for a broken-down shack in the great outdoors. You can talk to them if you like, but you won't get stamps or be able to paint your Moogle.

Giant Crab

The Giant Crab likes to attack from a distance. When it backs off, seize the day. Run to the back or side of the boss and strike. Holy, Fire and Blizzard are all effective magical attacks, but the crab is immune to Thunder.

RESISTANCE	
FIRE	1
BLIZZARD	2
THUNDER	3
SLOW	3
STOP	3
GRAVITY	2
HOLY	0

Occasionally the Giant Crab will fire bubbles. They will cast Slow on any player they touch but won't cause any damage. The bubbles follow you around but have a large turn radius—if you can avoid them once, they'll usually vanish before swinging around to attack again.

The Giant Crab's main weapon is a large laser that fires at enemies standing in front of it. If it strikes you, you'll be paralyzed for a few moments and also lose a bit of health.

After you damage the crab severely, you'll knock off its front arms. At that point, it will attack with Thundara. Run away when it starts to cast the spell, then respond with a strong attack of your own.

Giant Crab: Cycles Two and Three

The Giant Crab won't change much during the second cycle, but during the third one it will start to cast Thundaga. Thundaga's radius is huge, and you'll be paralyzed for a long while if it hits you. Equip items that resist paralysis before battling the boss.

DROPPED ITEM SETS					
		CYCLE 1	CYCLE 2	CYCLE 3	ARTIFACTS
SET 1	1P	More than 0 pts.	—	—	BUCKLER
	2P	More than 0 pts.	—	—	DRAGON'S WHISKER
	3P	More than 0 pts.	—	—	MOOGLE POCKET
	4P	More than 0 pts.	—	—	SHURIKEN
SET 2	1P	More than 95 pts.	—	—	MAGE MASHER
	2P	More than 102 pts.	—	—	MANEATER
	3P	More than 116 pts.	—	—	MOOGLE POCKET
	4P	More than 127 pts.	—	—	SILVER SPECTACLES
SET 3	1P	More than 119 pts.	More than 0 pts.	—	BUCKLER
	2P	More than 128 pts.	More than 0 pts.	—	DOUBLE AXE
	3P	More than 146 pts.	More than 0 pts.	—	IRON
	4P	More than 160 pts.	More than 0 pts.	—	KRIS
SET 4	1P	More than 149 pts.	More than 95 pts.	—	ICE BRAND
	2P	More than 160 pts.	More than 102 pts.	—	IRON
	3P	More than 182 pts.	More than 116 pts.	—	SILVER BRACER
	4P	More than 200 pts.	More than 127 pts.	—	SILVER SPECTACLES
SET 5	1P	—	More than 119 pts.	More than 0 pts.	LOADED DICE
	2P	—	More than 128 pts.	More than 0 pts.	MAGE'S STAFF
	3P	—	More than 146 pts.	More than 0 pts.	MYTHRIL
	4P	—	More than 160 pts.	More than 0 pts.	WONDER BANGLE
SET 6	1P	—	More than 149 pts.	More than 95 pts.	BLACK HOOD
	2P	—	More than 160 pts.	More than 102 pts.	FLAMETONGUE
	3P	—	More than 182 pts.	More than 116 pts.	LEGENDARY WEAPON
	4P	—	More than 200 pts.	More than 127 pts.	SASUKE'S BLADE
SET 7	1P	—	—	More than 119 pts.	DRAGON'S WHISKER
	2P	—	—	More than 128 pts.	ORICHALCUM
	3P	—	—	More than 146 pts.	SHURIKEN
	4P	—	—	More than 160 pts.	SILVER SPECTACLES
SET 8	1P	—	—	More than 149 pts.	ANCIENT SWORD
	2P	—	—	More than 160 pts.	MAGE MASHER
	3P	—	—	More than 182 pts.	MANEATER
	4P	—	—	More than 200 pts.	SAVE THE QUEEN

Scrolls, Materials and Artifacts

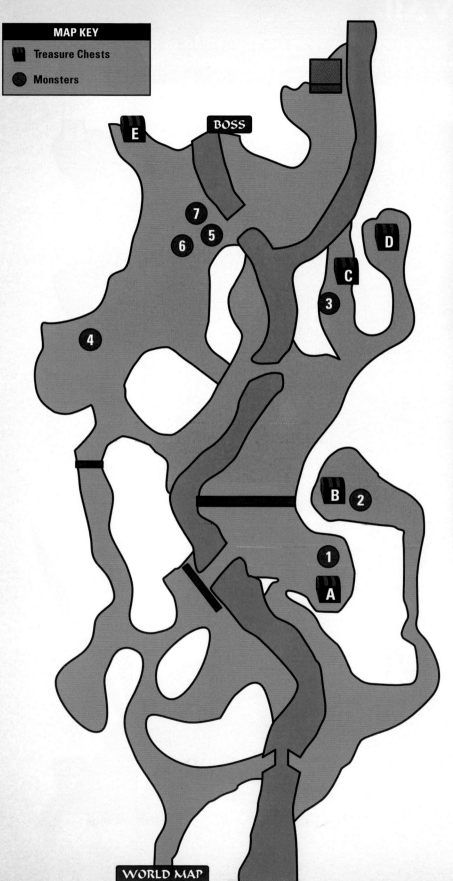

MAP KEY

🗃	Treasure Chests
⚫	Monsters

		CYCLE 1	CYCLE 2	CYCLE 3
SCROLLS	BRONZE ARMOR	E	E	—
	BRONZE BELT	A	—	—
	BRONZE GLOVES	C	C	—
	BRONZE SALLET	C	C	—
	FLAME CRAFT	—	6, 7	6, 7
	FROST CRAFT	—	D	D
	IRON BELT	—	A	A
	IRON GLOVES	—	C	C
	IRON SALLET	—	C	C
	IRON SHIELD	A	A	—
	LIGHTNING CRAFT	—	E	E
	MYTHRIL ARMOR	—	—	E
	MYTHRIL BELT	—	—	A
	MYTHRIL GLOVES	—	—	C
	MYTHRIL SALLET	—	—	C
	MYTHRIL SHIELD	—	—	A
	NOVICE'S WEAPON	D	D	—
	VALIANT WEAPON	—	—	D

		CYCLE 1	CYCLE 2	CYCLE 3
MATERIALS	BRONZE	3	2, 3	—
	GRIFFIN'S WING	—	6, 7	6, 7
	IRON	—	2, 3	2, 3
	MYTHRIL	—	6, 7	2, 3, 6, 7

		CYCLE 1	CYCLE 2	CYCLE 3
ARTIFACTS (TREASURES)	BLACK HOOD	—	B	B
	BUCKLER	B	B	B
	CAT'S BELL	4	4	—
	DOUBLE AXE	1	1	—
	DRAGON'S WHISKER	4	—	—
	EARTH PENDANT	—	5	5
	FLAMETONGUE	—	1	1
	GREEN BERET	1	1	—
	ICE BRAND	—	1	1
	KRIS	—	4	4
	LOADED DICE	—	—	1
	MAGE MASHER	4	—	—
	MAGE'S STAFF	—	—	4
	MANEATER	1	—	—
	MOOGLE POCKET	5	5	5
	RUNE BELL	—	—	4
	SAGE'S STAFF	—	4	4
	SASUKE'S BLADE	—	—	1
	SHURIKEN	1	—	—
	SILVER BRACER	4	4	—
	SILVER SPECTACLES	B	B	—
	WONDER BANGLE	—	—	B

Goblin Wall

The Goblin-infested mine pops into view on the world map only after you complete your first year. When it emerges, plunder its depths.

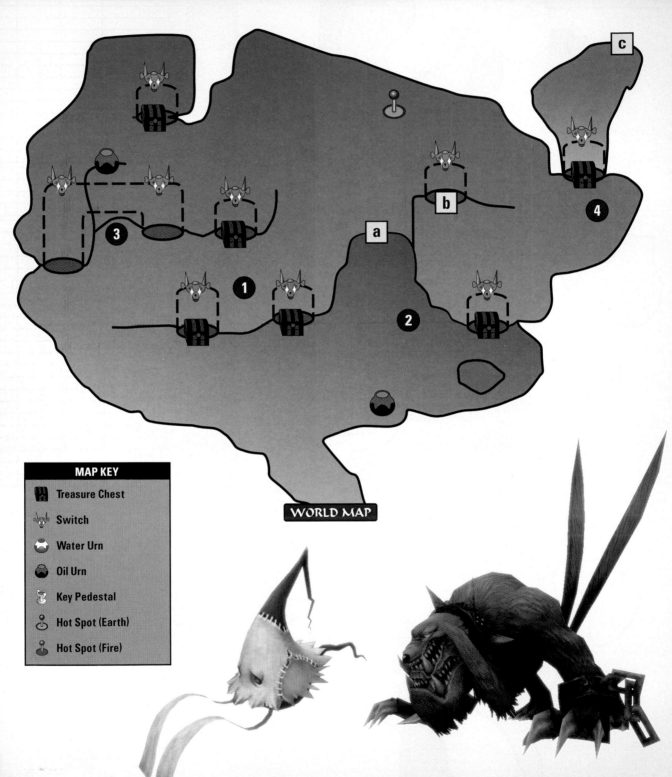

WORLD MAP

MAP KEY

- Treasure Chest
- Switch
- Water Urn
- Oil Urn
- Key Pedestal
- Hot Spot (Earth)
- Hot Spot (Fire)

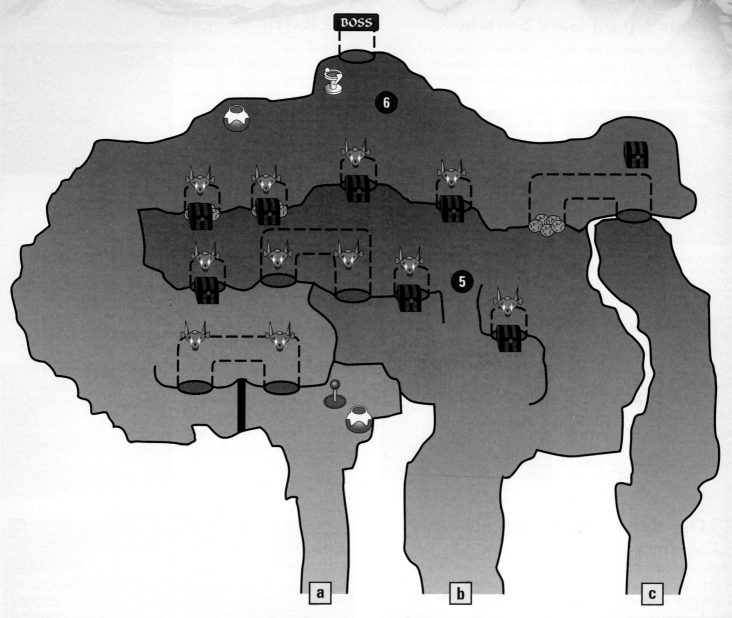

BOSS

6

5

a

b

c

MONSTERS			
Bat Cycles: All	PG. 122	**Goblin** Cycles: All	PG. 124
Cerberus Cycles: 2 & 3	PG. 123	**Goblin (Mace)** Cycles: 2 & 3	PG. 124
Electric Jellyfish Cycles: All	PG. 124	**Goblin (Spear)** Cycles: 2 & 3	PG. 124
Flan Cycles: All	PG. 124	**Goblin Chieftain** Cycles: All	PG. 125
Ghost Cycles: 2 & 3	PG. 124	**Goblin Mage** Cycles: All	PG. 125

① Bone Up on Gate Switches

The Goblins use gates to bar passage into many tunnels and chest-bearing alcoves. You'll find the skull switch that opens each gate on the ledge above it. To strike the switch, shift into Attack mode and whack it with your weapon—spells won't work.

You'll usually find several gates next to each other. Don't open and pass through each gate separately. Strike all of the switches on the ledge above, then return to the floor below to explore the whole series of opened alcoves and passages.

② Bring Bats Down to Earth

Goblin Wall's bats are pesky. They're fliers that take quick bites from your health. Use Gravity to immobilize a bat, then strike the fiend. If you can't cast Gravity, use regular attacks to hit one—Focus Attacks do just as little damage but take much longer to prep.

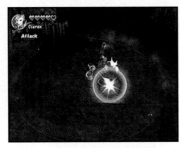

③ Dig Deep for the Moogle Nest

To reach the Moogle Nest, you'll need to open the gates at either end of a seemingly pointless tunnel. Enter the nest and get your Mog Stamp, then paint your Moogle red to increase your chances of getting him to add Fire to your repertoire—great for Goblin-slaying.

Some Moogle Nests are hidden in obvious locations marked by an object. The Goblin Wall nest isn't one of them. It's tucked in the darkness at the left side of the double-gated tunnel. Nose around until you see the telltale Examine option.

④ The Long Haul in Later Cycles

When you return for Goblin Wall's second drop of Myrrh, you'll see that the Goblins have cleared the rocks from a tunnel collapse (near tip 5 on the map). At the end of the cleared tunnel is a gate switch. Hit it then make the long trek back to the gate for its chest.

⑤ Electric Boogaloo

To knock the lights out of the Electric Jellyfish, use Blizzard-powered spells—the monsters are vulnerable to cold. Whatever your method, keep a distance from them, or else they'll headbutt you to deliver a jolt that'll knock you to your knees for a moment.

⑥ Clear the Crowd on Your Terms

The toothy entrance to the Goblin King's cave can be opened only by placing a key in the pedestal, and one of the nearby creatures has it. Don't let the enemies gang up on you. Try to attract the attention of one of the monsters, then lure it away for some private time.

Multiplayer

Start a Goblin Bonfire

Goblins are weakest against Fire spells, so join with other players to create the most powerful Fire-based spell possible. If only two members of your team have Fire, take the extra casting time you need to create Firaga, not Fira.

Goblin King

The Goblin King waits behind a double-locked gate. Defeat the entry-area Goblins to get the two keys. As you attack the king, Goblin duos will often storm the scene. Position yourself so both Goblins stop and strike at once, then beat a hasty retreat and power up a felling blow against both as they advance in tandem.

RESISTANCE	
FIRE	2
BLIZZARD	2
THUNDER	2
SLOW	3
STOP	3
GRAVITY	2
HOLY	0

The king is most vulnerable when he's casting a spell—you'll have several seconds to strike him. Steer clear when he's not conjuring, or he'll hit you with his staff.

Run to the far side of the cave when you see murk swirl near you—it's a sign that the king is about to complete his poison spell. The resulting cloud has an obnoxiously wide range.

The king teleports to four spots. When he vanishes, watch where his life meter floats. Run to the spot then power up and position a spell or Focus Attack before he reappears.

Goblin King: Cycles Two and Three

Starting with your second-cycle romp, the Goblin King will smell trouble when you reenter his lair; he'll add lots of Fira and some Thundara to his bag of tricks. To help shrug off the spells' aftereffects, equip Paralysis- and Burning-resistant items for Thundara and Fira, respectively.

		DROPPED ITEM SETS			
		CYCLE 1	CYCLE 2	CYCLE 3	ARTIFACTS
SET 1	1P	More than 0 pts.	—	—	DOUBLE AXE
	2P	More than 0 pts.	—	—	EARTH PENDANT
	3P	More than 0 pts.	—	—	SPARKLING BRACER
	4P	More than 0 pts.	—	—	WINGED CAP
SET 2	1P	More than 110 pts.	—	—	EARTH PENDANT
	2P	More than 119 pts.	—	—	KAISER KNUCKLES
	3P	More than 135 pts.	—	—	SPARKLING BRACER
	4P	More than 148 pts.	—	—	WONDER WAND
SET 3	1P	More than 138 pts.	More than 0 pts.	—	ASHURA
	2P	More than 148 pts.	More than 0 pts.	—	FAERIE RING
	3P	More than 169 pts.	More than 0 pts.	—	HELM OF ARAI
	4P	More than 185 pts.	More than 0 pts.	—	MOOGLE POCKET
SET 4	1P	More than 172 pts.	More than 110 pts.	—	DARK MATTER
	2P	More than 186 pts.	More than 119 pts.	—	FANG CHARM
	3P	More than 211 pts.	More than 135 pts.	—	MOOGLE POCKET
	4P	More than 232 pts.	More than 148 pts.	—	SPARKLING BRACER
SET 5	1P	—	More than 138 pts.	More than 0 pts.	ANCIENT POTION
	2P	—	More than 148 pts.	More than 0 pts.	HELM OF ARAI
	3P	—	More than 169 pts.	More than 0 pts.	MJOLLNIR
	4P	—	More than 185 pts.	More than 0 pts.	RED SLIPPERS
SET 6	1P	—	More than 172 pts.	More than 110 pts.	ENGETSURIN
	2P	—	More than 186 pts.	More than 119 pts.	HELM OF ARAI
	3P	—	More than 211 pts.	More than 135 pts.	NOAH'S LUTE
	4P	—	More than 232 pts.	More than 148 pts.	ORICHALCUM
SET 7	1P	—	—	More than 138 pts.	CANDY RING
	2P	—	—	More than 148 pts.	DIAMOND BELT
	3P	—	—	More than 169 pts.	FANG CHARM
	4P	—	—	More than 185 pts.	WONDER BANGLE
SET 8	1P	—	—	More than 172 pts.	CURSED CROOK
	2P	—	—	More than 186 pts.	GALATYN
	3P	—	—	More than 211 pts.	GREEN BERET
	4P	—	—	More than 232 pts.	SPARKLING BRACER

Scrolls, Materials and Artifacts

WORLD MAP

MAP KEY

🎁	Treasure Chest
⬤	Monster

BOSS

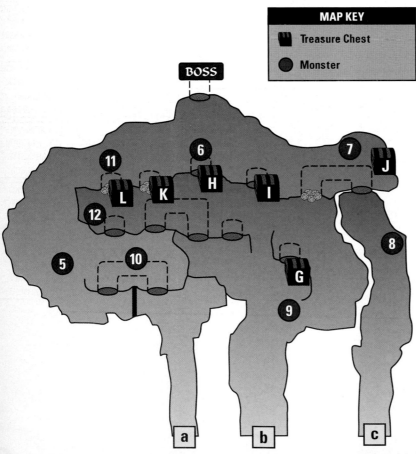

	CYCLE 1	CYCLE 2	CYCLE 3
SCROLLS			
FLAME GLOVES	–	–	C
FLAME SHIELD	–	–	C
GOLD GLOVES	–	–	K
HOLY ARMOR	–	–	H
HOLY SHIELD	–	–	K
IRON ARMOR	H	H	–
IRON BELT	I	–	–
IRON GLOVES	C	–	–
IRON SALLET	I	–	–
IRON SHIELD	C	–	–
LIGHTNING BELT	–	I	I
LIGHTNING GLOVES	–	K	K
LIGHTNING SALLET	–	I	I
LIGHTNING SHIELD	–	K	K
MASTER'S WEAPON	D	D, F, L	F, L
MIGHTY WEAPON	–	L	D, F, L
MYTHRIL ARMOR	H	H	H
MYTHRIL BELT	I	I	–
MYTHRIL GLOVES	C	C, K	C
MYTHRIL SALLET	I	I	–
MYTHRIL SHIELD	C	C, K	C
PURE ARMOR	–	–	H
PURE BELT	–	–	I
SECRETS OF WISDOM	–	–	B
TIME ARMOR	–	H	H
TIME SALLET	–	–	I
TOME OF WISDOM	B	B	B
VALIANT WEAPON	–	–	D, F, L
VICTORIOUS WEAPON	–	D, F	D, F, L
WARRIOR'S WEAPON	D	D, L	–
MATERIALS			
ALLOY	–	2, 3, 5, 6	2, 3, 5, 6
BLUE SILK	–	9, 10, 11, 12*	–
BRONZE	2, 3, 5, 6, B	–	–
CERBERUS'S FANG	–	1	1, 4
CRYSTAL BALL	7, 8	7, 8	–
DIAMOND ORE	–	9, 10, 11, 12*	9, 10, 11, 12*
IRON	2, 3, 5, 6, B	1, 2, 3, 5, 6, B	–
JADE	–	7, 8	7, 8
MYTHRIL	–	1	1, 2, 3, 4, 5, 6
RUBY	–	7, 8	7, 8
SHINY SHARD	7, 8	–	–
THUNDERBALL	7, 8	7, 8	7, 8
WHITE SILK	–	–	9, 10, 11, 12*
ARTIFACTS (TREASURES)			
BLACK HOOD	–	G	G
BUCKLER	G	–	–
CAT'S BELL	J	J	–
DOUBLE AXE	E	E	–
DRAGON'S WHISKER	J	–	–
EARTH PENDANT	A	A	A
FLAMETONGUE	–	E	E
GREEN BERET	E	E	–
ICE BRAND	–	E	E
KRIS	–	J	J
LOADED DICE	–	–	E
MAGE MASHER	J	–	–
MAGE'S STAFF	–	–	J
MANEATER	E	–	–
MOOGLE POCKET	A	A	A
RUNE BELL	–	–	J
SAGE'S STAFF	–	J	J
SASUKE'S BLADE	–	–	E
SHURIKEN	E	–	–
SILVER BRACER	J	J	–
SILVER SPECTACLES	G	G	–
WONDER BANGLE	–	–	G

*The monster emerges only when three or four characters are playing.

Iron Mine Downs

In your first year, you won't be able to cross the northern Miasma Stream, so shake down the forest and the mines to top off your chalice.

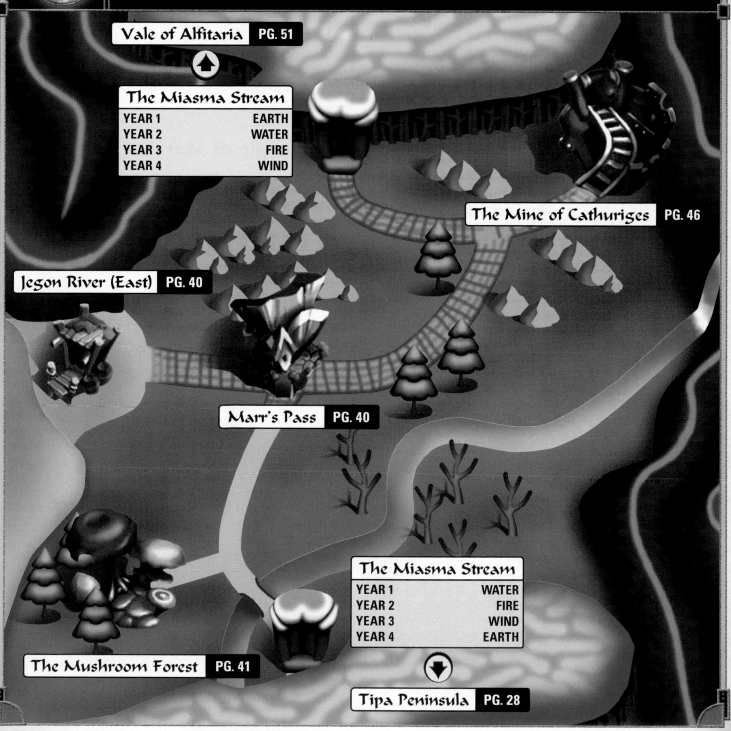

Vale of Alfitaria PG. 51

The Miasma Stream

YEAR 1	EARTH
YEAR 2	WATER
YEAR 3	FIRE
YEAR 4	WIND

The Mine of Cathuriges PG. 46

Jegon River (East) PG. 40

Marr's Pass PG. 40

The Miasma Stream

YEAR 1	WATER
YEAR 2	FIRE
YEAR 3	WIND
YEAR 4	EARTH

The Mushroom Forest PG. 41

Tipa Peninsula PG. 28

Marr's Pass

The two blacksmiths in Marr's Pass will craft weapons and armor for a small fee—if you have the scrolls and materials.

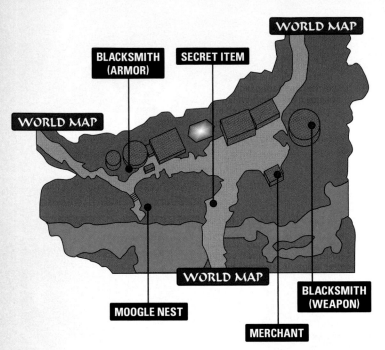

WORLD MAP

BLACKSMITH (ARMOR)

SECRET ITEM

WORLD MAP

WORLD MAP

MOOGLE NEST

BLACKSMITH (WEAPON)

MERCHANT

A Wellside Secret

You can often find hidden items in towns if you search every nook and cranny. In Marr's Pass, there's an item beside the well at the town's entrance. Once you find a secret item, it won't appear again until you get a drop of Myrrh.

The Moogle of Marr's Pass

South of the armor blacksmith's shop is a wooden staircase. Go down it, then examine the cliffside to find the Moogle Nest. Inside, you can get your stamp and paint your Moogle companion.

Strike a Deal

When you visit Marr's Pass during an odd-numbered year, a pair of traveling Selkie peddlers will have a shop. They sell an assortment of scrolls and materials—the peddlers' wares and prices are displayed to the left.

Cecil B. Here

A man named Cecil hangs out in the center of town. Talk to him, then speak to Leu Tipa in Leuda. After that conversation, go to Tipa and find a letter in a tree. Show the letter to both people, then return to Tipa in the next year to see the end of a sad story.

SELKIE PEDDLERS			
BRONZE	300	MYTHRIL ARMOR	300
IRON	500	MYTHRIL SHIELD	250
MYTHRIL	5,000	IRON GLOVES	100
BRONZE SHARD	100	MYTHRIL GLOVES	250
IRON SHARD	100	IRON SALLET	100
ALLOY	250	MYTHRIL SALLET	250
WARRIOR'S WEAPON	300	IRON BELT	100
IRON ARMOR	150	MYTHRIL BELT	250

Jegon River (East)

Tristan runs a small ferry business on the eastern shore of Jegon River. Hop aboard his vessel to visit new and exciting areas.

Tristan's fares are a bit steep, but he's running the only ferry business around. Before you can board his ship, you must tell him where you wish to go and pay up front. If you give him Kilanda Sulfur or a Cactus Flower, you can ride the ferry at a 20 percent discount. If you give him both of the items, he'll reward you with half-price ferry rides. After two years of paying the discounted ferry fee, Tristan will offer to sell you a lifetime ferry pass for 50,000 gil.

DESTINATION	FARE
Jegon River (West)	50 gil
Mt. Kilanda	500 gil
Leuda	300 gil
Port Tipa	100 gil

In the third year, Tristan will open his ferry business. You can ride the ferry to each of the areas listed above—Mt. Kilanda and Leuda will be off-limits until Year 4.

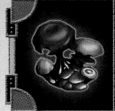

The Mushroom Forest

A winding forest of giant mushrooms lies before the caravan. Fire-based spells will work wonders against nearly all the enemies.

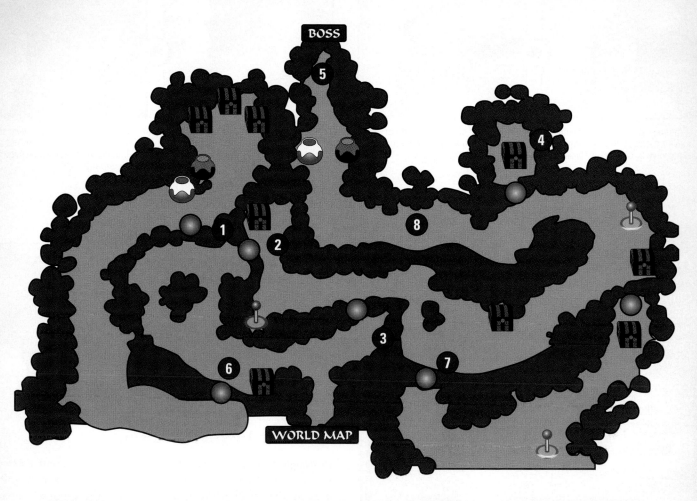

MONSTERS					
	Ahriman Cycles: All	PG. 122		**Ice Ahriman** Cycles: 2 & 3	PG. 125
	Carrion Worm Cycle: 3	PG. 123		**Ochu** Cycles: 2 & 3	PG. 127
	Dark Hedgehog Cycle: 3	PG. 123		**Stone Hedgehog** Cycle: 3	PG. 129
	Gremlin Cycles: All	PG. 125		**Stone Plant** Cycles: 2 & 3	PG. 129
	Hedgehog Pie Cycles: All	PG. 125		**Tiny Worm** Cycles: All	PG. 130
	Hell Plant Cycles: All	PG. 125			

MAP KEY	
	Treasure Chest
	Water Urn
	Oil Urn
	Hot Spot (Water)

1 Toadstool Springs

Not only are the fungi in the Mushroom Forest enormous, but some of them are bouncy—hop on to the springy toadstools to reach new areas. The springy mushrooms won't work until you, your Moogle and the Crystal Chalice are all ready to go. If one is left behind, the mushroom will remain dormant.

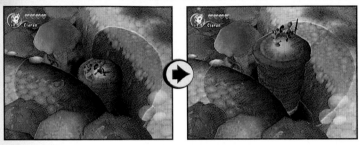

Most (but not all) of the bouncy platforms stay in place after you use them—so you can't backtrack across them if you miss something. If you need to return to an area you've already been through, you must circle around.

2 Grounded by Gravity

Most flying monsters, such as Ahrimans and Griffins, have stronger defense while in the air. Use Gravity to knock them out of the sky and stun them temporarily. Ahrimans are especially weak to physical attacks once they're grounded—a few hits with your weapon after a dose of Gravity will do in the flying beasts.

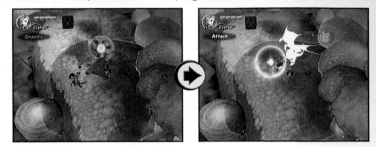

How you create Gravity differs slightly depending on whether you're flying solo or playing with friends. In multiplayer mode, you and a friend must each cast a different elemental spell (Fire, Thunder or Blizzard) to create Gravity (see page 142). In single-player mode, simply fuse two different elemental spells.

Multiplayer

All Aboard!

One of the more challenging aspects of playing Crystal Chronicles with your pals is remembering to watch each other's backs. When you're traveling through the Mushroom Forest in multiplayer mode, stick together! Every player will need to step onto the springy mushroom platforms at the same time to make them work.

3 'Shroom Shortcut

The mushroom platform at point 3 will take you to the Mushroom Forest entrance. If you're ever overwhelmed by the enemies, use the platform—some areas are easier to tackle after you've upgraded your equipment and raised your stats.

4 Nest beside a Chest

A Moogle Nest is hidden near the treasure chest at point 4. After you defeat the enemies nearby and collect the treasure, examine the area around the small white mushrooms on the ground. Enter the Moogle Nest to collect your stamp.

Moogle Nests are often camouflaged and difficult to find. When you suspect that a Moogle Nest might be near, search around the area until the word "Examine" appears on your screen, then press B to reveal the nest.

❺ Caught in the Crossfire

Sometimes enemies will surround you. When that happens, take out mobile enemies first, then focus on the stationary ones. At point 5, you'll be assaulted by two Hell Plants and a mobile enemy that changes depending on the cycle. Run beyond the Hell Plants' range to take care of the wandering foe, then eliminate the plants.

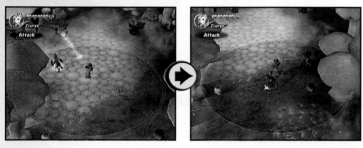

In cycles two and three, the mobile enemy that appears at point five is a massive Ochu. The plantlike menace is very weak against Fire magic, so nail it with Flamestrike or a fused Fire-based magic spell. You can also use Slow on the Ochu to gain the upper hand.

❻ New-Growth Mushrooms

The Mushroom Forest changes a little as the years go by. During the second cycle, a new cluster of mushrooms will appear at point 6. Use the newly formed path to reach the west area—a branch of the forest that you could not reach previously.

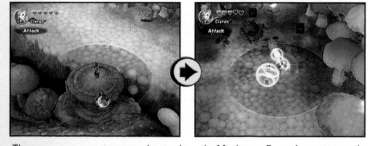

There are some new treasure chests along the Mushroom Forest's western path. In cycle two, you can cross the newly grown mushrooms at point 6 to discover new goodies. Also during the second and third cycles, another part of the forest will be blocked off by newly grown thorny mushrooms. Don't panic—they won't prevent you from getting any goodies.

❼ Through the Motions Thrice

If you return during the cycle 3, you'll have access to the forest's southeastern path. Use the mushroom platform at point 7 to reach the new area. You'll be rewarded with an untouched treasure chest.

❽ Cast Away the Shadows

You'll also encounter new enemies during the Mushroom Forest's third cycle. One of the new arrivals is the Dark Hedgehog. The foe has high weapon and magic resistances while in its shrouded form, and you won't be able to attack one until you've used Holy to reveal it.

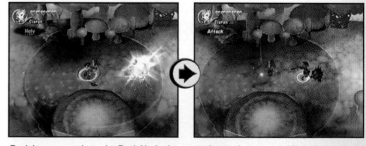

Dark beasts, such as the Dark Hedgehogs, are impervious to any kind of attack while they are in their transparent form. Force your dark foes to appear by casting Holy on them, then close in and finish them off with magic or your weapon.

Malboro

Malboro's breath is definitely worse than its bite. Attack the massive beast by striking its sides, trying to avoid its poisonous breath and lashing tentacles. Team up with your Moogle pal in single-player mode, or with a friend in multi-player mode, to use Flamestrike—it will lower Malboro's defensive power.

RESISTANCES	
FIRE	1
BLIZZARD	2
THUNDER	2
SLOW	3
STOP	3
GRAVITY	2
HOLY	0

During your battle with Malboro, it will attack with foul, poisonous breath. When the putrid beast exhales, either back up or keep moving to the side to avoid the cloud. In multiplayer mode, it's helpful to equip one player with Clear to cure party members who become poisoned.

Malboro will try to snare you by casting the time-altering spell Slowga, which affects a wide area. When you see Malboro charging up Slowga, quickly run beyond the spell's range. If you become slowed, back away until the condition wears off.

When Malboro inhales, it will pull you close. Your instinct may be to run the other way, but let yourself be drawn in instead. You can use the opportunity to attack your foe while it's preoccupied.

Malboro: Cycles Two and Three

Starting with cycle two, Malboro will cast Blizzaga. The spell has a wide area of effect and will freeze anyone it hits. Before you take on the boss, equip yourself with an item that raises your resistance to Ice magic, such as the Frost Mail or Frost Badge.

DROPPED ITEM SETS				
	CYCLE 1	**CYCLE 2**	**CYCLE 3**	**ARTIFACTS**
SET 1 1P	More than 0 pts.	—	—	SHURIKEN
2P	More than 0 pts.	—	—	DRAGON'S WHISKER
3P	More than 0 pts.	—	—	BUCKLER
4P	More than 0 pts.	—	—	EARTH PENDANT
SET 2 1P	More than 108 pts.	—	—	FLAMETONGUE
2P	More than 116 pts.	—	—	MAGE MASHER
3P	More than 132 pts.	—	—	SILVER SPECTACLES
4P	More than 145 pts.	—	—	MOOGLE POCKET
SET 3 1P	More than 135 pts.	More than 0 pts.	—	MANEATER
2P	More than 145 pts.	More than 0 pts.	—	SAGE'S STAFF
3P	More than 165 pts.	More than 0 pts.	—	BUCKLER
4P	More than 181 pts.	More than 0 pts.	—	EARTH PENDANT
SET 4 1P	More than 169 pts.	More than 108 pts.	—	DOUBLE AXE
2P	More than 182 pts.	More than 116 pts.	—	SILVER BRACER
3P	More than 207 pts.	More than 132 pts.	—	BLACK HOOD
4P	More than 227 pts.	More than 145 pts.	—	MOOGLE POCKET
SET 5 1P	—	More than 135 pts.	More than 0 pts.	SASUKE'S BLADE
2P	—	More than 145 pts.	More than 0 pts.	CAT'S BELL
3P	—	More than 165 pts.	More than 0 pts.	WONDER BANGLE
4P	—	More than 181 pts.	More than 0 pts.	ANCIENT POTION
SET 6 1P	—	More than 169 pts.	More than 108 pts.	GREEN BERET
2P	—	More than 182 pts.	More than 116 pts.	MAGE'S STAFF
3P	—	More than 207 pts.	More than 132 pts.	WONDER BANGLE
4P	—	More than 227 pts.	More than 145 pts.	ORICHALCUM
SET 7 1P	—	—	More than 135 pts.	DOUBLE AXE
2P	—	—	More than 145 pts.	SILVER BRACER
3P	—	—	More than 165 pts.	MOOGLE POCKET
4P	—	—	More than 181 pts.	DIAMOND ARMOR
SET 8 1P	—	—	More than 169 pts.	ASHURA
2P	—	—	More than 182 pts.	CAT'S BELL
3P	—	—	More than 207 pts.	EARTH PENDANT
4P	—	—	More than 227 pts.	MALBORO SEED

Scrolls, Materials and Artifacts

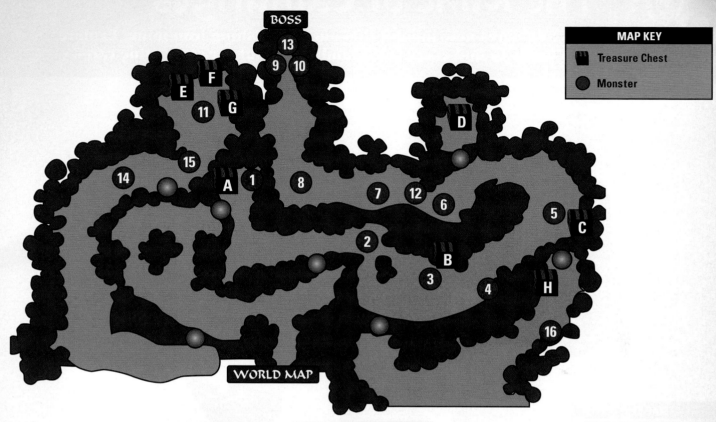

MAP KEY

- Treasure Chest
- Monster

SCROLLS		CYCLE 1	CYCLE 2	CYCLE 3
	BRONZE ARMOR	9	9	—
	BRONZE BELT	8	8	—
	BRONZE GLOVES	6	6	—
	BRONZE SALLET	8	8	—
	DAEMON KIT	—	—	F, H
	FIEND KIT	—	F	2, 7, F, H
	GOLD GLOVES	—	—	6, G
	HOLY ARMOR	—	—	9
	HOLY SHIELD	—	—	G
	IRON BELT	—	E	—
	IRON GLOVES	—	G	—
	IRON SALLET	—	E	—
	IRON SHIELD	—	G	—
	MAGIC SHIELD	—	—	6
	MASTER'S WEAPON	—	10	10
	MIGHTY WEAPON	—	—	10
	MYTHRIL ARMOR	—	9	9
	MYTHRIL BELT	—	8, E	8, E
	MYTHRIL GLOVES	—	6, G	6, G
	MYTHRIL SALLET	—	8, E	8, E
	MYTHRIL SHIELD	—	6, G	6, G
	NOVICE'S WEAPON	10	10	—
	PURE ARMOR	—	—	9
	PURE BELT	—	—	8, E
	TIME SALLET	—	—	8, E
	TOME OF SPEED	—	—	2, 7
	VALIANT WEAPON	—	10	10
	VICTORIOUS WEAPON	—	—	10

MATERIALS		CYCLE 1	CYCLE 2	CYCLE 3
	ALLOY	—	—	4, 5
	ANGEL'S TEAR	—	—	14, 15*
	BRONZE	6, 8, 9, 10	6	—
	CHILLY GEL	—	14, 15*	14, 15*
	CRYSTAL BALL	2, 5, 7	2, 5, 7, 12	12
	DIAMOND ORE	—	—	4, 5
	FAERIE'S TEAR	—	14, 15*	—
	GOLD	2, 5, 7	2, 5, 7, 12	12
	IRON	—	1, 3	—
	JADE	—	—	2, 4, 5, 7
	MYTHRIL	—	13	11, 13, 16**
	RUBY	—	—	2, 4, 5, 7
	SILVER	2, 5, 7	2, 5, 7, 12	12
	TINY CRYSTAL	—	11, 13	11, 13

ARTIFACTS (TREASURES)		CYCLE 1	CYCLE 2	CYCLE 3
	BLACK HOOD	—	A	A
	BUCKLER	A	—	—
	CAT'S BELL	B	B	—
	DOUBLE AXE	C	C	—
	DRAGON'S WHISKER	B	—	—
	EARTH PENDANT	D	D	D
	FLAMETONGUE	—	C	C
	GREEN BERET	C	C	—
	ICE BRAND	—	C	C
	KRIS	—	B	B
	LOADED DICE	—	—	C
	MAGE MASHER	B	—	—
	MAGE'S STAFF	—	—	B
	MANEATER	C	—	—
	MOOGLE POCKET	D	—	D
	RUNE BELL	—	—	B
	SAGE'S STAFF	—	B	B
	SASUKE'S BLADE	—	—	C
	SHURIKEN	C	—	—
	SILVER BRACER	B	B	—
	SILVER SPECTACLES	A	A	—
	WONDER BANGLE	—	—	A

*The monster emerges only in multiplayer mode.

**The monster emerges only when three or four characters are playing.

The Mine of Cathuriges

Orcs and ogres now inhabit this once-flourishing iron mine. Explore both levels to find every chest, and watch out for stray mine carts.

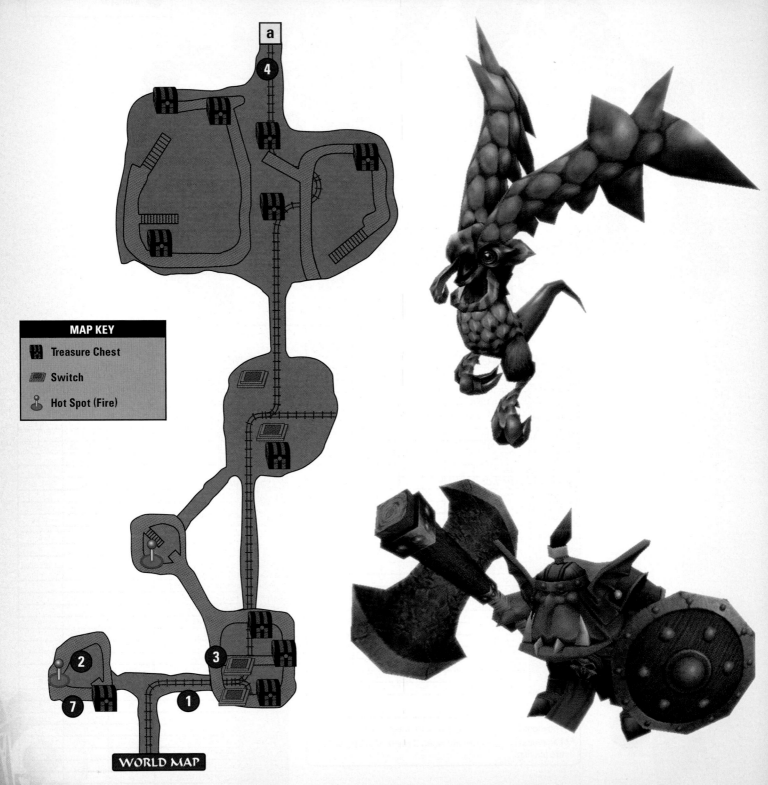

MAP KEY

- 🗃 Treasure Chest
- ▨ Switch
- ⚲ Hot Spot (Fire)

WORLD MAP

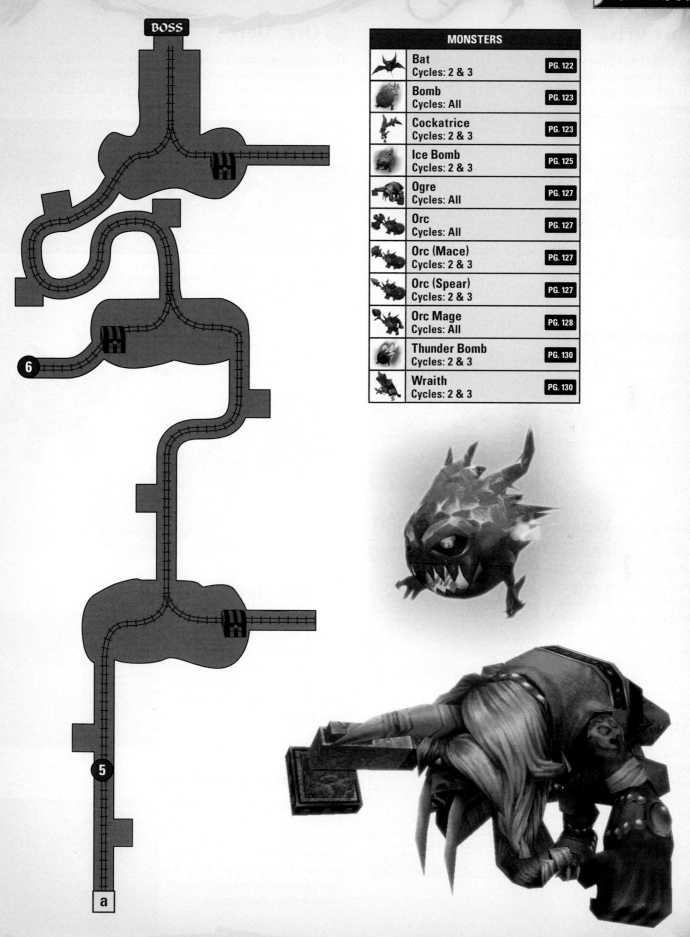

BOSS

MONSTERS		
Bat Cycles: 2 & 3		PG. 122
Bomb Cycles: All		PG. 123
Cockatrice Cycles: 2 & 3		PG. 123
Ice Bomb Cycles: 2 & 3		PG. 125
Ogre Cycles: All		PG. 127
Orc Cycles: All		PG. 127
Orc (Mace) Cycles: 2 & 3		PG. 127
Orc (Spear) Cycles: 2 & 3		PG. 127
Orc Mage Cycles: All		PG. 128
Thunder Bomb Cycles: 2 & 3		PG. 130
Wraith Cycles: 2 & 3		PG. 130

1 Cart Crisis

Wooden boxes block your path throughout the mine. Strike the cart at the mine's entrance with your weapon to get it moving along the tracks. It will smash the wooden boxes and open up new areas.

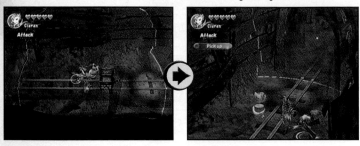

Select Attack in your command list and whack the mine cart to move it a short distance. Hit it twice to break through the first barrier. Be careful not to hit it a third time until you've activated the correct switch (see tip 3).

2 Bomb Shelter

Head left from the entrance to meet your first set of enemies. Bombs don't fight very aggressively, but they go out with a bang when you strike the final blow. Take cover, and watch as the explosion damages other enemies.

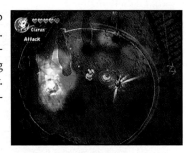

3 Stay on Track

You'll have to change the alignment of the tracks twice to move the cart in the right direction. After the first barrier is broken, step on the northernmost switch before you strike the cart to send it north.

4 An Ogre Holds the Key

Ogres and Orcs are slow, but they pack a punch. Use their sluggishness against them by charging up spells or Focus Attacks. Take down the Ogre to the north to obtain the key to the next area.

5 Orc Alert

The narrow path can be treacherous if you are not careful—monsters are hiding around many corners. Use a Fire-based spell to take care of the Orcs. In cycles two and three, cast Holy to make the Wraiths vulnerable, then hit them with everything you've got.

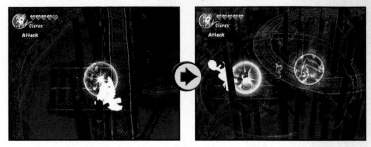

Orc Mages look like regular Orcs but can attack from a distance. Wait for them to charge a spell, then move out of the way and use a Fire spell or strike with your weapon to take them out.

6 Mooglemania!

What seems like a dead end is really a Moogle Nest. When the Examine icon appears, press B to enter. The friendly Moogle will stamp your card and allow you to paint your Moogle. Blazin' Caravans, here we come!

7 Explore Upstairs

The wide-open areas make it difficult to find every treasure. The mine's upper levels will give you a broader view of each room. Be sure to revisit the upper levels on the second and third cycles—new treasure chests will appear.

Orc King

You can defeat the Orc King by using either magic or weapon attacks. In single-player mode, fuse Blizzara in your command list and attack from a distance to damage the Orc King while freezing the pesky Orcs around him. Attacking with physical attacks will also work if your Defense is high enough.

RESISTANCE	
FIRE	1
BLIZZARD	2
THUNDER	2
SLOW	3
STOP	3
GRAVITY	2
HOLY	0

The Orc King will perform a dizzying spin attack if you stay in close range for too long. Use it to your advantage by attacking or charging up a spell when your foe is disoriented. In multiplayer, one person can act as bait while the others charge up an attack and fuse Fira or Firaga.

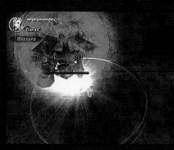

Fire spells are the Orc King's attacks of choice. Stay at a medium distance and find the right rhythm to avoid the boss's spells while casting spells of your own.

When you've depleted the Orc King's energy by three-quarters, he will begin to glow. You'll have a short amount of time to finish the job before the king self-destructs. Use your fiercest attacks—the Orc King will not fight back. If you cannot defeat him in time, run to the corner to avoid suffering significant damage.

Orc King: Cycles Two and Three

In the second and third cycles, both the Orc King and his Orc minions will be stronger and faster. You'll have very limited time to charge up spells, so make them count. When the Orc King begins to self-destruct, cast Cure on yourself and run to the corner.

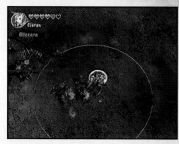

DROPPED ITEM SETS				
		CYCLE 1	CYCLE 2	CYCLE 3	ARTIFACTS
SET 1	1P	More than 0 pts.	—	—	SHURIKEN
	2P	More than 0 pts.	—	—	DRAGON'S WHISKER
	3P	More than 0 pts.	—	—	BUCKLER
	4P	More than 0 pts.	—	—	EARTH PENDANT
SET 2	1P	More than 116 pts.	—	—	LOADED DICE
	2P	More than 125 pts.	—	—	MAGE MASHER
	3P	More than 142 pts.	—	—	SILVER SPECTACLES
	4P	More than 156 pts.	—	—	MOOGLE POCKET
SET 3	1P	More than 145 pts.	More than 0 pts.	—	MANEATER
	2P	More than 156 pts.	More than 0 pts.	—	RUNE BELL
	3P	More than 178 pts.	More than 0 pts.	—	BUCKLER
	4P	More than 195 pts.	More than 0 pts.	—	EARTH PENDANT
SET 4	1P	More than 181 pts.	More than 116 pts.	—	DOUBLE AXE
	2P	More than 196 pts.	More than 125 pts.	—	SILVER BRACER
	3P	More than 222 pts.	More than 142 pts.	—	BLACK HOOD
	4P	More than 244 pts.	More than 156 pts.	—	MOOGLE POCKET
SET 5	1P	—	More than 145 pts.	More than 0 pts.	SASUKE'S BLADE
	2P	—	More than 156 pts.	More than 0 pts.	CAT'S BELL
	3P	—	More than 178 pts.	More than 0 pts.	WONDER BANGLE
	4P	—	More than 195 pts.	More than 0 pts.	LEGENDARY WEAPON
SET 6	1P	—	More than 181 pts.	More than 116 pts.	GREEN BERET
	2P	—	More than 196 pts.	More than 125 pts.	MAGE'S STAFF
	3P	—	More than 222 pts.	More than 142 pts.	WONDER BANGLE
	4P	—	More than 244 pts.	More than 156 pts.	ORICHALCUM
SET 7	1P	—	—	More than 145 pts.	KAISER KNUCKLES
	2P	—	—	More than 156 pts.	FAERIE RING
	3P	—	—	More than 178 pts.	ULTIMATE POCKET
	4P	—	—	More than 195 pts.	ORC BELT
SET 8	1P	—	—	More than 181 pts.	ONION SWORD
	2P	—	—	More than 196 pts.	WINGED CAP
	3P	—	—	More than 222 pts.	EARTH PENDANT
	4P	—	—	More than 244 pts.	MURASAME

Scrolls, Materials and Artifacts

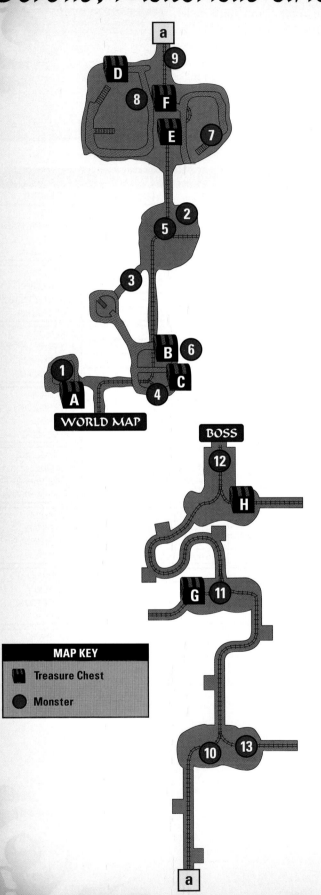

WORLD MAP

BOSS

MAP KEY

- 🎁 Treasure Chest
- ⬤ Monster

		CYCLE 1	CYCLE 2	CYCLE 3
SCROLLS	BRONZE ARMOR	—	4	—
	FLAME ARMOR	—	—	1, 3, 8
	FLAME CRAFT	—	1, 3, 8	1, 3, 8
	FROST ARMOR	—	—	10, 13*
	FROST CRAFT	—	10, 13*	10, 13*
	LIGHTNING ARMOR	—	—	11
	MASTER'S WEAPON	—	4	4, 6
	MYTHRIL ARMOR	—	4	4, 6
	SECRETS OF SPEED	—	-	B, C
	TOME OF SPEED	—	B, C	B, C
MATERIALS	ALLOY	—	12, A, D, E, F	12
	BRONZE	1, 3, 8	—	—
	BRONZE SHARD	1, 3, 8	—	—
	CHILLY GEL	—	10, 13*	10, 13*
	COCKATRICE SCALE	—	5, 7	5, 7
	CRYSTAL BALL	—	5, 7	—
	DIAMOND ORE	—	—	5, 7, A, D, E, F
	IRON	1, 3, 8	1, 3, 4, 8, 10, 11, 12, 13*	—
	IRON SHARD	1, 3, 8	1, 3, 8, 10, 11, 13*	—
	MAGMA ROCK	—	1, 3, 8	1, 3, 8
	MYTHRIL	—	5, 7, A, D, E, F	4, 5, 6, 7, 12, A, D, E, F
	OGRE FANG	—	12	12
	SHINY SHARD	—	D, E, F	—
	THUNDERBALL	—	11	11
	TINY CRYSTAL	—	—	A, D, E, F
ARTIFACTS (TREASURES)	BLACK HOOD	—	G	G
	BUCKLER	G	—	—
	CAT'S BELL	9	9	—
	DOUBLE AXE	2	2	—
	DRAGON'S WHISKER	9	—	—
	EARTH PENDANT	H	H	H
	FLAMETONGUE	—	2	2
	GREEN BERET	2	2	—
	ICE BRAND	—	2	2
	KRIS	—	9	9
	LOADED DICE	—	—	2
	MAGE MASHER	9	—	—
	MAGE'S STAFF	—	—	9
	MANEATER	2	—	—
	MOOGLE POCKET	—	H	H
	RUNE BELL	—	—	9
	SAGE'S STAFF	—	9	9
	SASUKE'S BLADE	—	—	2
	SHURIKEN	2	—	—
	SILVER BRACER	9	9	—
	SILVER SPECTACLES	G	G	—
	WONDER BANGLE	—	—	G

*The monster emerges only when three or four characters are playing.

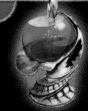

Vale of Alfitaria

A mansion filled with Tonberry Chefs, a creepy ghost town and a bustling city await you as your adventure continues into the Vale of Alfitaria.

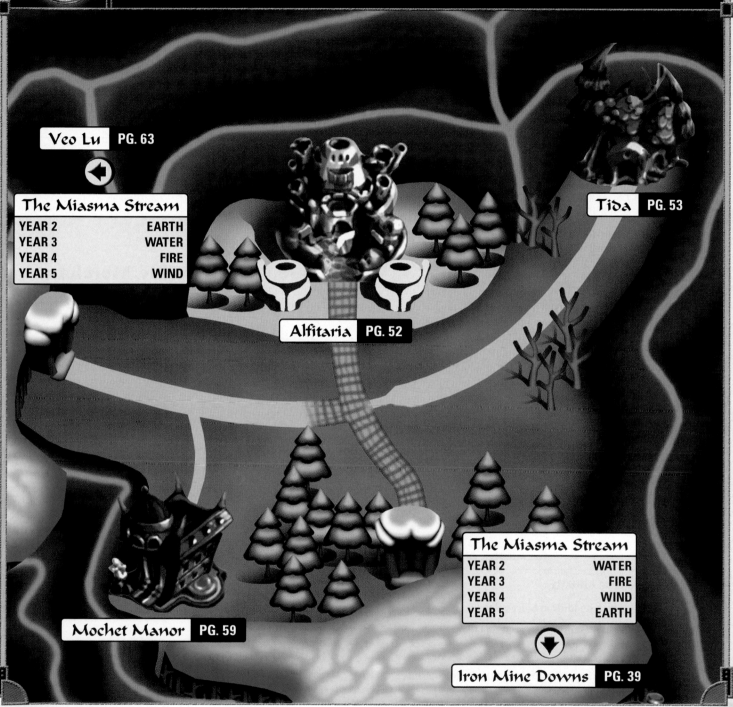

Veo Lu PG. 63

The Miasma Stream	
YEAR 2	EARTH
YEAR 3	WATER
YEAR 4	FIRE
YEAR 5	WIND

Tida PG. 53

Alfitaria PG. 52

The Miasma Stream	
YEAR 2	WATER
YEAR 3	FIRE
YEAR 4	WIND
YEAR 5	EARTH

Mochet Manor PG. 59

Iron Mine Downs PG. 39

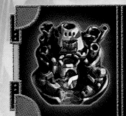

Alfitaria

Lilties intended to make the city into the capital of an empire. Instead, it turned out to be a serviceable stop where you can gear up mightily.

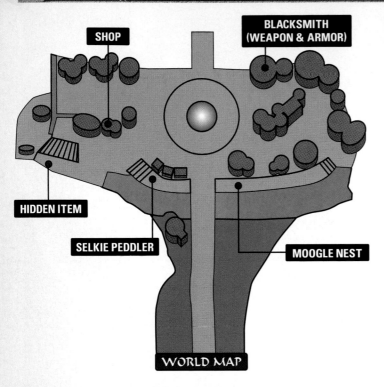

SHOP

BLACKSMITH
(WEAPON & ARMOR)

HIDDEN ITEM

SELKIE PEDDLER

MOOGLE NEST

WORLD MAP

SELKIE PEDDLER			
BRONZE	300	MYTHRIL ARMOR	300
IRON	500	MYTHRIL SHIELD	250
MYTHRIL	5,000	IRON GLOVES	100
BRONZE SHARD	100	MYTHRIL GLOVES	250
IRON SHARD	100	IRON SALLET	100
ALLOY	250	MYTHRIL SALLET	250
WARRIOR'S WEAPON	300	IRON BELT	100
IRON ARMOR	150	MYTHRIL BELT	250

SHOP	
MEAT	40
FISH	40
SPRING WATER	20
MILK	20

Even-Tempered Selkie Merchant

When you visit the city on an even-numbered year, you'll find a Selkie along the left canal. He carries a range of metals and scrolls. If you check in with the local blacksmith and find that you're short on materials for item creation, the Selkie can be a lifesaver.

Royal Story, Rich Payoff

When you enter Alfitaria, hunt down the city's chamberlain, Knocfelna, to start a story sequence that will give you insights into the life of Alfitaria's reluctant princess. You won't be able to complete the cycle until at least the sixth year.

1 Talk to Knocfelna in Alfitaria.

2 Speak to Te Odow, a peddler in Marr's Pass.

3 Bump into the disguised princess at Jegon River.

4 Encounter Knocfelna at Jegon River.

5 Speak to the princess and Knocfelna in the Fields of Fum.

6 Encounter the princess and Knocfelna in Leuda.

7 Exit Leuda by land to watch a movie about the princess.

8 Enter Alfitaria to watch the final movie sequence.

You must complete the steps in sequence, and you may need to collect Myrrh to advance each step. The final payoff is immense—100,000 gil!

Sniff Out the Hidden Item

If you haven't scared up a hidden item since your last Myrrh gain, you'll find one wedged in a spot to the side of the stairs on the left side of Alfitaria. You'll need to nose into the tight space until you see the Examine option pop up on the screen.

Squeaky-Clean Moogles

Follow the right branch of the canal to its end, where you'll find a water outlet. It's also the entrance to a Moogle Nest. Enter and get your Mog Stamp, then consider your next dungeon destination and paint Mog a color that will grant a favorable radar.

Tida

When Tida's crystal failed, its citizens fell to the Miasma. But the dead village still bustles—with many highly combustible monsters.

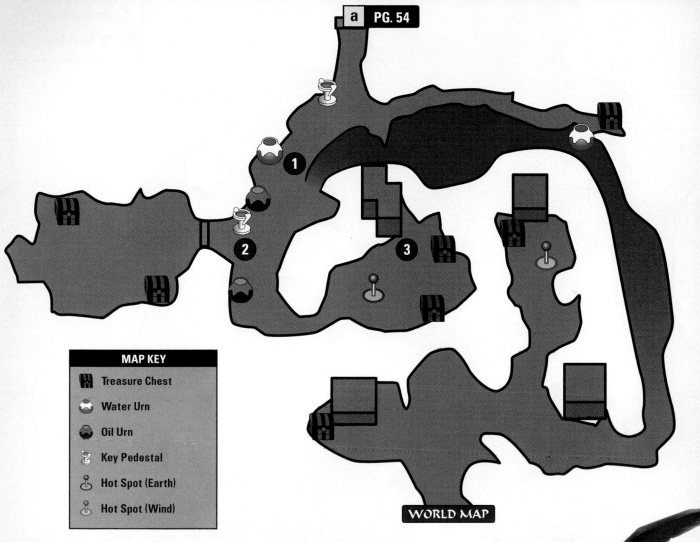

a PG. 54

WORLD MAP

MAP KEY

🗄	Treasure Chest
🏺	Water Urn
🏺	Oil Urn
⚱	Key Pedestal
⚲	Hot Spot (Earth)
⚲	Hot Spot (Wind)

MONSTERS

	Abaddon Cycles: 2 & 3	PG. 122		Skeleton Cycles: 2 & 3	PG. 128
	Bomb Cycles: All	PG. 123		Skeleton (Mace) Cycles: 2 & 3	PG. 128
	Carrion Worm Cycles: All	PG. 123		Skeleton (Spear) Cycles: 2 & 3	PG. 129
	Gremlin Cycles: All	PG. 125		Skeleton Mage Cycles: All	PG. 129
	Hell Plant Cycles: All	PG. 125		Stone Plant Cycles: 2 & 3	PG. 129
	Magic Plant Cycles: 2 & 3	PG. 126			

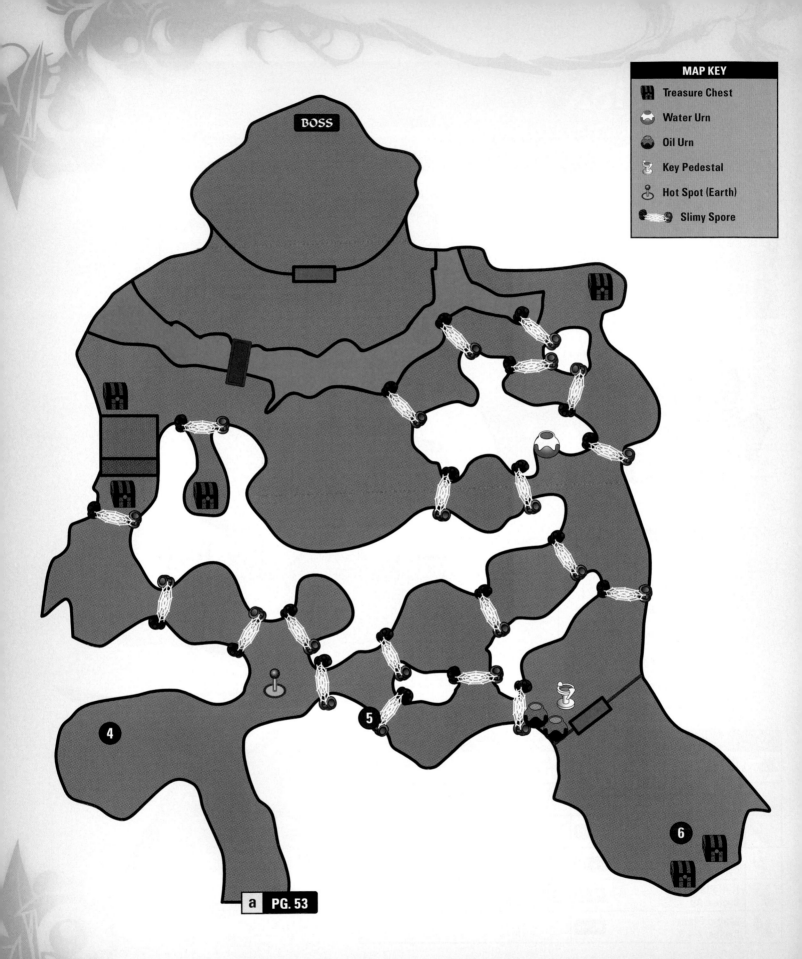

MAP KEY

Treasure Chest

Water Urn

Oil Urn

Key Pedestal

Hot Spot (Earth)

Slimy Spore

BOSS

4

5

6

a PG. 53

1 Have the Last Laugh

The flaming Bomb isn't particularly difficult to defeat in combat (you can snuff it out most quickly with Blizzard magic), but its departure can cause a lot of grief. When you whack it down to zero health, run for cover; it will explode almost instantly. Fortunately, you can turn its blast against its compadres.

When the Bomb explodes, it will damage all creatures in its blast radius. Before you deliver the felling blow, lure nearby foes toward the Bomb then linger just long enough to ensure that they take the blast damage, instead of you.

2 An Incendiary Entrance

One of the monsters that loiters near the gate holds the key that fits into the pedestal. You can't drop the key onto the pedestal, however, until you've cleared the vines from it—the key will slide off the vines and hit the ground. Scare up some Fire magic, then burn away the vines and fit the key into place.

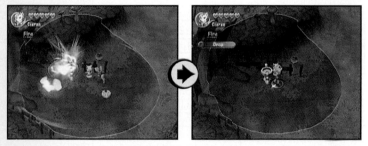

Two treasure chests lie on the other side of the gate, but you won't be able to use the key pedestal until you possess Fire magic. If you don't have any, explore other areas until you gain the Magicite, then return to burn the vines.

3 Tida's Happiest Resident

Tida might be a shadow of its former self, but there's one happy home that still holds a warm fireplace. You'll find a Moogle Nest tucked in the wreckage of one house. Enter to get your stamp, then paint Mog red to force your GBA radar into Monster Radar mode. Tida's full of evil beings; don't let any sneak up on you.

The ruined house behind the Hot Spot hides the Moogle Nest. Walk up to its front door to make the Examine option appear, then enter the house to nab another Mog Stamp and paint your Moogle.

4 The Saddest Story Ever Told

If you've spoken to Cecil in Marr's Pass and Leu Tipa in Leuda (after year five), you'll find a torn-up letter in the tree trunk. If you show the note to each of them later, you'll find them at the tree, along with a second letter.

5 The Secret Life of Slimy Spores

Slimy spores grow throughout Tida, blocking passages by slinging a filmy tendril to a nearby stone urn. The fastest way to break through its tendril is to use a Fire-based spell. The tendril will grow back many times if you use Fire. If you use Fira, it will grow back only once. It won't grow back at all if you use Firaga. If you don't have any Fire Magicite, you can use two interesting methods to move onward.

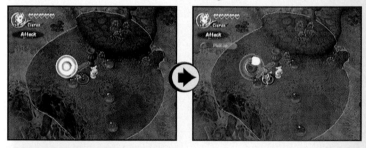

 The slimy spore isn't impervious to weapon attacks. If you repeat your strikes on its tendril long enough, you'll destroy the filmy irritant. Also, if you have no Fire in your inventory, you can hit the larger spore until it spits out several pieces of Fire Magicite. Use the technique to gear up for Firaga spellcasting.

6 Fighting with Wild Abaddon

When you return to Tida for its second drop of Myrrh (and each time thereafter), you'll find many flying Abaddons. The bumbling monster has powerful attacks and many hit points. You don't have a hope of defeating it until you bring down the blimp with Gravity.

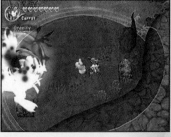

You'll dish out nothing but nicks and scratches against the floating monstrosity if you attack it while it's flying. Cast Gravity to bring the beast down to earth, then strike it with powerful attacks before it takes to the sky again.

Armstrong

It takes a village to raise a good boss, and Tida's big boy seems to be made of ruins and mold. Holy- and Fire-based spells work best against him. Thunder spells won't touch him. If you exploited Tida's slimy spores for Fire Magicite, you'll have Firaga at your command. Use it to strong-arm Armstrong.

RESISTANCE	
FIRE	1
BLIZZARD	2
THUNDER	3
SLOW	3
STOP	3
GRAVITY	2
HOLY	0

Don't linger around Armstrong for too long—especially around its feet—or else the colossus will swipe its single arm at you. It's a powerful punch. Steer clear.

Armstrong will also issue a purple haze that will put you in a Slow funk. When you see the haze emerge, run away before you're caught in the cloud.

If you retreat too far, the boss will fire a quick burst from its cannon. During your first encounter with the creature, it will fire shots that will take a chunk out of your health. In later cycles, it will add status effects to its arsenal.

Armstrong: Cycles Two and Three

When you face Armstrong on your second Myrrh-run to Tida, the boss will add a projectile to its cannon, one that inflicts a Stop condition. On your third encounter with the beast, it will throw yet another projectile that causes Curse into the mix.

		DROPPED ITEM SETS			
		CYCLE 1	CYCLE 2	CYCLE 3	ARTIFACTS
SET 1	1P	More than 0 pt.	—	—	TWISTED HEADBAND
	2P	More than 0 pt.	—	—	DRAGON'S WHISKER
	3P	More than 0 pt.	—	—	SILVER SPECTACLES
	4P	More than 0 pt.	—	—	CHOCOBO POCKET
SET 2	1P	More than 155 pt.	—	—	SHURIKEN
	2P	More than 167 pt.	—	—	KRIS
	3P	More than 190 pt.	—	—	SPARKLING BRACER
	4P	More than 208 pt.	—	—	MOOGLE POCKET
SET 3	1P	More than 193 pt.	More than 0 pt.	—	MANEATER
	2P	More than 208 pt.	More than 0 pt.	—	SILVER BRACER
	3P	More than 237 pt.	More than 0 pt.	—	ELVEN MANTLE
	4P	More than 260 pt.	More than 0 pt.	—	CHOCOBO POCKET
SET 4	1P	More than 241 pt.	More than 155 pt.	—	POWER WRISTBAND
	2P	More than 260 pt.	More than 167 pt.	—	CAT'S BELL
	3P	More than 295 pt.	More than 190 pt.	—	SPARKLING BRACER
	4P	More than 325 pt.	More than 208 pt.	—	SASUKE'S BLADE
SET 5	1P	—	More than 193 pt.	More than 0 pt.	GIANT'S GLOVE
	2P	—	More than 208 pt.	More than 0 pt.	FLAMETONGUE
	3P	—	More than 237 pt.	More than 0 pt.	WONDER BANGLE
	4P	—	More than 260 pt.	More than 0 pt.	ANCIENT POTION
SET 6	1P	—	More than 241 pt.	More than 155 pt.	RUNE BELL
	2P	—	More than 260 pt.	More than 167 pt.	GOLD HAIRPIN
	3P	—	More than 295 pt.	More than 190 pt.	WONDER BANGLE
	4P	—	More than 325 pt.	More than 208 pt.	ORICHALCUM
SET 7	1P	—	—	More than 193 pt.	POWER WRISTBAND
	2P	—	—	More than 208 pt.	SILVER BRACER
	3P	—	—	More than 237 pt.	CHOCOBO POCKET
	4P	—	—	More than 260 pt.	LEGENDARY WEAPON
SET 8	1P	—	—	More than 241 pt.	GREEN BERET
	2P	—	—	More than 260 pt.	CAT'S BELL
	3P	—	—	More than 295 pt.	BRIGANDOLOGY
	4P	—	—	More than 325 pt.	DWEOMER SPORE

Scrolls, Materials and Artifacts

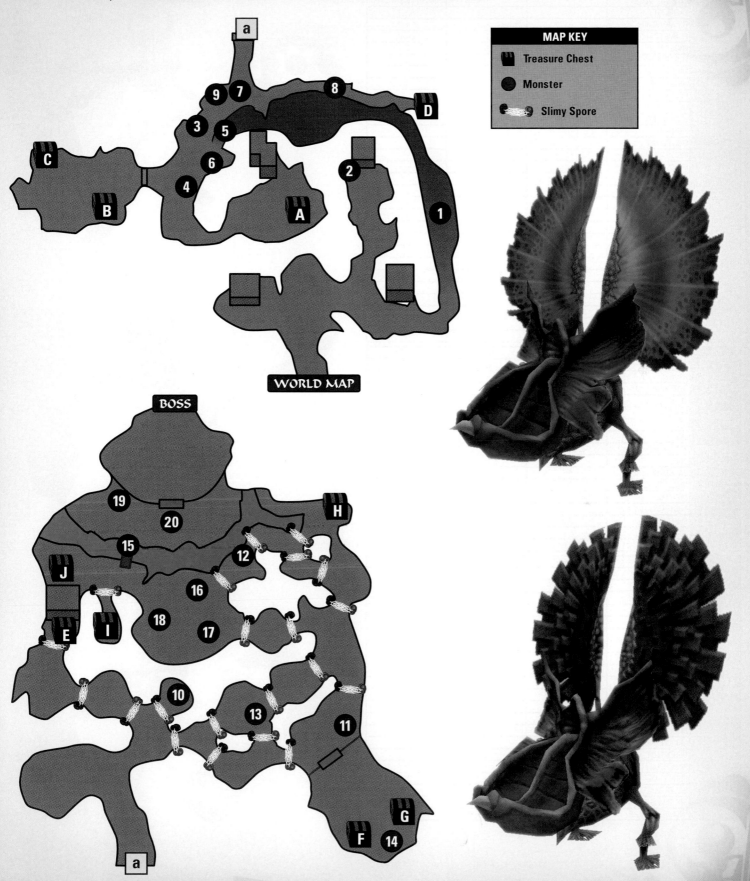

MAP KEY

🗃	Treasure Chest
⬤	Monster
🦠	Slimy Spore

a

9 7 8 D

3 5

C 6

4 2

B A 1

WORLD MAP

BOSS

19 H

20

15

J 12

16

18 17

E I

10

13

11

G

F 14

a

	CYCLE 1	CYCLE 2	CYCLE 3
SCROLLS			
ANGEL KIT	–	–	15, E, I
ETERNAL SALLET	–	–	G
FAERIE KIT	E, I	15, E, I	15, E, I
FLAME ARMOR	–	–	3, 6, 11
FLAME CRAFT	–	3, 6, 11	3, 6, 11
FROST BELT	–	G	G
FROST GLOVES	–	J	J
FROST SALLET	–	G	G
FROST SHIELD	–	J	J
GOLD GLOVES	–	J	–
HOLY ARMOR	–	–	A
IRON ARMOR	A	A	–
IRON BELT	G	–	–
IRON GLOVES	J	–	–
IRON SALLET	G	–	–
IRON SHIELD	J	–	–
MAGIC SHIELD	–	–	J
MASTER'S WEAPON	B	B	B
MIGHTY WEAPON	–	–	B
MYTHRIL ARMOR	A	A	A
MYTHRIL BELT	G	G	–
MYTHRIL GLOVES	J	J	–
MYTHRIL SALLET	G	G	–
MYTHRIL SHIELD	J	J	–
PURE ARMOR	–	–	A
TIME ARMOR	–	A	A
VALIANT WEAPON	–	–	B
VICTORIOUS WEAPON	–	B	B
WARRIOR'S WEAPON	B	B	–
WIND BELT	–	–	G
MATERIALS			
ALLOY	–	16, 17	16, 17
BLUE SILK	–	2, 4	2, 4
BRONZE	3, 6, 11	–	–
BRONZE SHARD	2, 3, 4, 6, 11	–	–
CRYSTAL BALL	2, 4	–	–
DIAMOND ORE	–	–	14, 16, 17, 18, 19, 20
GEAR	5, 8, 13	5, 8, 13	5, 8, 13
IRON	1, 3, 6, 7, 10, 11, 12	1, 3, 6, 7, 9, 10, 11, 12	–
IRON SHARD	2, 3, 4, 6, 11	2, 3, 4, 6, 11	–
JADE	–	–	2, 4
JAGGED SCYTHE	–	14, 19	14, 18, 19, 20
MAGMA ROCK	–	3, 6, 11	3, 6, 11
MYTHRIL	–	14, 16, 17, 19	14, 16, 17, 18, 19, 20
RUBY	–	2, 4	2, 4
SHINY SHARD	2, 4	2, 4	–
TINY CRYSTAL	–	–	2, 4, 16, 17
WORM ANTENNA	1, 7, 10, 12	1, 7, 9, 10, 12	1, 7, 9, 10, 12
ARTIFACTS (TREASURES)			
ASHURA	C	–	–
CAT'S BELL	H	H	–
CHOCOBO POCKET	F	F	F
DRAGON'S WHISKER	H	–	–
ELVEN MANTLE	–	D	D
ENGETSURIN	–	–	C
FANG CHARM	–	C	C
HELM OF ARAI	D	D	–
ICE BRAND	C	C	–
KAISER KNUCKLES	C	C	–
KRIS	–	H	H
MAGE MASHER	H	–	–
MAGE'S STAFF	–	–	H
MANEATER	C	–	–
MJOLLNIR	–	–	C
MOOGLE POCKET	F	F	F
OGREKILLER	–	C	C
RUNE BELL	–	–	H
RUNE STAFF	–	–	D
SILVER BRACER	H	H	–
SPARKLING BRACER	D	–	–
WONDER BANGLE	–	–	D

Moschet Manor

Avoid the courtyard Gargoyles until you can cast Gravity. Raid rooms for Magicite and artifacts—and to provoke a fight with the Gigas Lord.

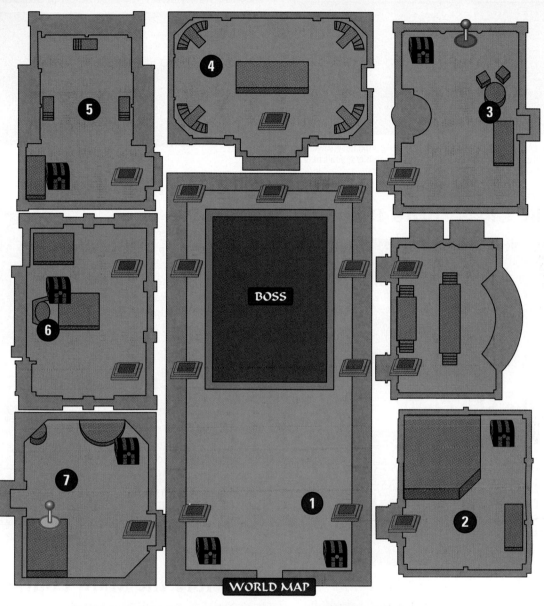

MONSTERS		
Coeurl Cycles: All		PG. 123
Gargoyle Cycles: All		PG. 124
Gremlin Cycles: All		PG. 125
Ochu Cycle: 3		PG. 127
Tonberry Chef Cycles: All		PG. 130

MAP KEY	
	Treasure Chest
	Switch
	Hot Spot (Fire)
	Hot Spot (Water)

① Open-Door Policy

The doors that connect the courtyard to the perimeter rooms are all keyed to the four character races. If you stand on the pad in front of a door when your race's symbol (see page 3) is shown on its surface, the door will swing open. Don't fret if your race isn't shown, the pad will soon change its symbol.

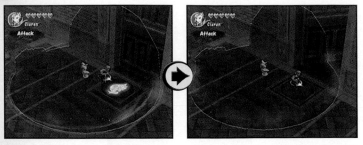

Loiter a while if the pad doesn't show your race's symbol. Approximately every 10 seconds, the symbol will change. After the correct symbol appears, you'll need to stand on the pad for several seconds to open the door.

② Delay the Gigas Lord's Dinner

The manor boss has ordered his Tonberry Chefs to make a meal, and he'll show up if you eliminate them all. Start in the southeast room, then proceed counterclockwise—you'll find the manor's scarce Magicite early in the process.

③ Skewer the Shy Chef

You'll need to flush out every Tonberry Chef to trigger the Gigas Lord's dramatic entrance. The chef in the northwest room is hard to spot, and he won't reveal himself unless you come close to his position. Approach the north end of the bed to scare him out.

④ Rough Up the Statuary

Gargoyles abound in the manor. Gravity will clip their wings for a few moments, and they won't use their powers while on the ground. If you've plundered rooms in a counterclockwise fashion, you'll probably have the Magicite to cast Gravity. Whack the Gargoyles in the north room several times before they take to the air, then ground 'em with Gravity before you continue your attacks.

⑤ Quick History Lesson

Knowledge is power, especially since citizens become more forgetful as the years progress. After you've purged the library of foes, stand on each of the three platforms to read books. You'll get a few insights into the connection between Myrrh and Miasma.

⑥ Moogle Infestation

Approach the west side of the table to see the entrance to the Moogle Nest. Collect your stamp, then paint Mog a color that will up your chances of getting Mog to match your elemental spellcasting (see page 15). You'll need powerful spells to defeat the Gigas Lord.

⑦ Before the Main Course

Eliminate two distractions before you clear the last chef from the room with the Moogle Nest. First, clear the courtyard of foes to rack up more bonus points. Second, visit Maggie in her boudoir. You can't hurt the Lamia, but you can ravage the room and get treasure.

Gigas Lord

After you destroy the last chef, the Gigas Lord will meet you in the courtyard. When you first score a hit, Maggie, the boss's lady Lamia, will come to his rescue with Slowga spells. Prevent her participation by casting Thunder- or Blizzard-based spells until she flees the scene, then hit the Gigas Lord with Fire-based magic.

RESISTANCE	
FIRE	1
BLIZZARD	2
THUNDER	3
SLOW	3
STOP	3
GRAVITY	2
HOLY	0

If you get too close to the Gigas Lord, he'll pounce on you. You may be able to avoid a direct hit, but the move sends out shockwaves that are hard to avoid even if you use Defend.

While Maggie is on the field, the Gigas Lord will strike a macho pose that heals them both fully. Strike Maggie with heavy attacks quickly to break their dangerous liaison.

The Gigas Lord will steamroller you with his attacks if Maggie hits you with Slowga. If you can't interrupt her casting, run far away from the wide-area effect.

Gigas Lord: Cycles Two and Three

The Gigas Lord is a big beast, but Maggie is the linchpin. Without her support, he'll eventually fall to your attacks. Starting with the second cycle, Maggie will add Stop spells to her partner-protecting repertoire—all the more reason to take her out of the picture.

DROPPED ITEM SETS					
		CYCLE 1	CYCLE 2	CYCLE 3	ARTIFACTS
SET 1	1P	More than 0 pts.	—	—	FLAMETONGUE
	2P	More than 0 pts.	—	—	RUNE STAFF
	3P	More than 0 pts.	—	—	BUCKLER
	4P	More than 0 pts.	—	—	CHOCOBO POCKET
SET 2	1P	More than 84 pts.	—	—	GREEN BERET
	2P	More than 91 pts.	—	—	RED SLIPPERS
	3P	More than 103 pts.	—	—	SILVER SPECTACLES
	4P	More than 113 pts.	—	—	EARTH PENDANT
SET 3	1P	More than 105 pts.	More than 0 pts.	—	FANG CHARM
	2P	More than 113 pts.	More than 0 pts.	—	BOOK OF LIGHT
	3P	More than 129 pts.	More than 0 pts.	—	BLACK HOOD
	4P	More than 141 pts.	More than 0 pts.	—	MOON PENDANT
SET 4	1P	More than 132 pts.	More than 84 pts.	—	KAISER KNUCKLES
	2P	More than 142 pts.	More than 91 pts.	—	FAERIE RING
	3P	More than 161 pts.	More than 103 pts.	—	HELM OF ARAI
	4P	More than 177 pts.	More than 113 pts.	—	CHOCOBO POCKET
SET 5	1P	—	More than 105 pts.	More than 0 pts.	ICE BRAND
	2P	—	More than 113 pts.	More than 0 pts.	SAGE'S STAFF
	3P	—	More than 129 pts.	More than 0 pts.	CHOCOBO POCKET
	4P	—	More than 141 pts.	More than 0 pts.	MOON PENDANT
SET 6	1P	—	More than 132 pts.	More than 84 pts.	MASQUERADE
	2P	—	More than 142 pts.	More than 91 pts.	MAGE'S STAFF
	3P	—	More than 161 pts.	More than 103 pts.	WONDER BANGLE
	4P	—	More than 177 pts.	More than 113 pts.	ORICHALCUM
SET 7	1P	—	—	More than 105 pts.	POWER WRISTBAND
	2P	—	—	More than 113 pts.	CHOCOBO POCKET
	3P	—	—	More than 129 pts.	LEGENDARY WEAPON
	4P	—	—	More than 141 pts.	LORD'S ROBE
SET 8	1P	—	—	More than 132 pts.	GEKKABIJIN
	2P	—	—	More than 142 pts.	CANDY RING
	3P	—	—	More than 161 pts.	CHOCOBO POCKET
	4P	—	—	More than 177 pts.	LEGENDARY SHIELD

Scrolls, Materials and Artifacts

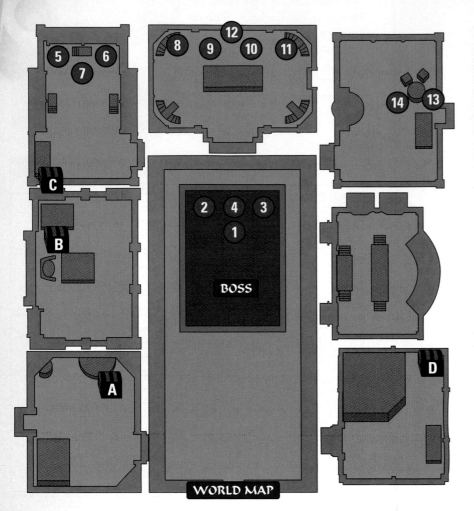

		CYCLE 1	CYCLE 2	CYCLE 3
SCROLLS	FASHION KIT	A	A	A
	LADY'S ACCESSORIES	A	A	A
MATERIALS	ALLOY	2, 3, 8, 11	2, 3 ,8, 11	2, 3, 8, 11
	COEURL'S WHISKER	7*	7*, 12, 14*	7*, 12, 14*
	HOLY WATER	7*	—	7*, 12, 14*
	IRON	2, 3, 8, 11	—	—
	MYTHRIL	—	—	2, 3, 4, 8, 11
	RUBY	7*	7*, 12, 14*	7*, 12, 14*
	SILVER	7*	7*, 12, 14*	7*, 12, 14*
	TINY CRYSTAL	—	—	4
	YELLOW FEATHER	—	—	5, 6, 9, 10, 13
ARTIFACTS (TREASURES)	ASHURA	B	—	—
	CANDY RING	—	C	C
	CHOCOBO POCKET	1	—	—
	DARK MATTER	—	—	C
	EARTH PENDANT	1	1	1
	ELVEN MANTLE	—	D	D
	ENGETSURIN	—	—	B
	FAERIE RING	C	—	—
	FANG CHARM	—	B	B
	FLAMETONGUE	B	B	—
	HELM OF ARAI	D	D	—
	KAISER KNUCKLES	B	B	—
	MJOLLNIR	—	—	B
	MOON PENDANT	—	—	1
	NOAH'S LUTE	—	—	C
	OGREKILLER	—	B	B
	RED SLIPPERS	—	C	C
	RUNE STAFF	C	—	—
	SHURIKEN	B	—	—
	SPARKLING BRACER	D	—	—
	WINGED CAP	C	C	—
	WONDER BANGLE	—	—	D
	WONDER WAND	C	C	—

*The monster emerges only when three or four characters are playing.

MAP KEY

🗂 Treasure Chest

🔴 Monster

Veo Lu

A visit to magic-savvy Shella is profitable at any time, but push through to Veo Lu by your fifth year to exploit a fleeting problem with the sluice.

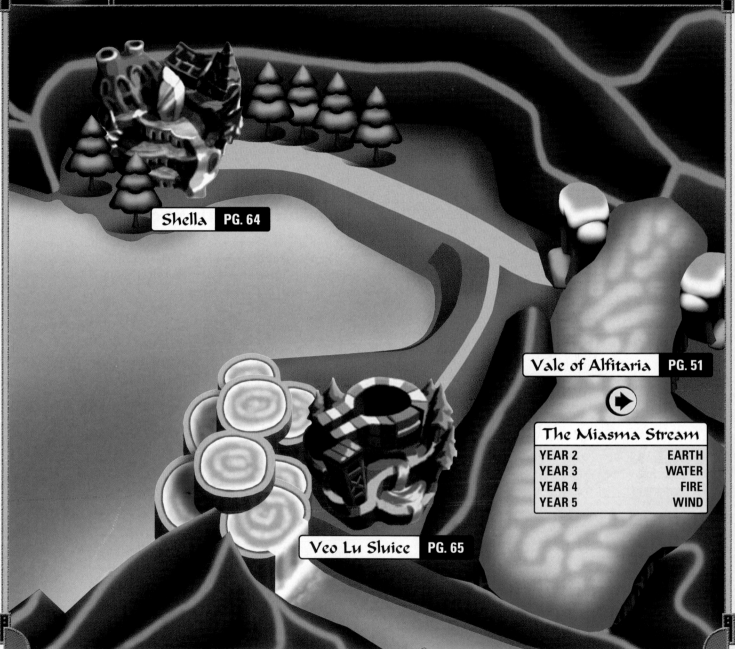

Shella PG. 64

Vale of Alfitaria PG. 51

Veo Lu Sluice PG. 65

The Miasma Stream	
YEAR 2	EARTH
YEAR 3	WATER
YEAR 4	FIRE
YEAR 5	WIND

Shella

If you're a Yuke you'll have an easy time entering Shella, a town full of rich lore. If not, you may need to quest for a special key.

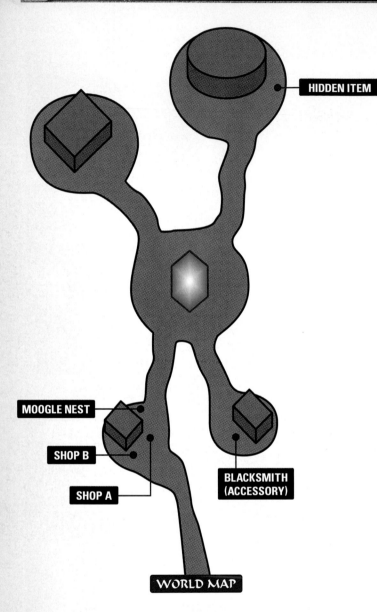

- HIDDEN ITEM
- MOOGLE NEST
- SHOP B
- SHOP A
- BLACKSMITH (ACCESSORY)
- WORLD MAP

Bypass the Yuke Bouncer

An elder Yuke protects Shella's entrance from riffraff. Speak to the Yuke if you have a Shella Mark or if you're a Yuke. The elder will then summon a bridge that spans the rushing waters. If you need a Shella Mark, head into nearby Veo Lu Sluice—you may find one.

Accessorize with Shella Style

If your home village doesn't have a tailor, you can have accessories made only by the blacksmith in Shella. If you don't have any scrolls that contain accessory patterns, visit the Yukes who sell their wares just inside the entrance to the town.

Make a Pen Pal

When you enter Shella, you can talk to a Selkie who's researching Miasma. After your meeting, he'll leave Shella and occasionally send you letters. After he sends you nine letters, you can get his Worn Bandanna as the spoils from a monster fight in Conall Curach.

Hidden and Precious

Approach the two barrels on the right side of the grand house at Shella's northernmost point. If you haven't found a hidden item since your last Myrrh harvest, you'll see the Examine option pop up onscreen.

Hollow-Stump Moogle Nest

You can enter a Moogle Nest via a stump on the right side of the house near Shella's entrance. Get your Mog Stamp, then paint your Moogle red if you're going to Veo Lu Sluice next—having the monster radar on your GBA will help you watch your back.

SHOP A	
FLAME CRAFT	100
FROST CRAFT	100
LIGHTNING CRAFT	100
CLOCKWORK	100
NEW CLOCKWORK	100
BLUE YARN	100
WHITE YARN	100
GOLD CRAFT	100
SHELLA MARK	50

SHOP B	
STRANGE LIQUID	20
SHELLA MARK	50

Veo Lu Sluice

Visit the sluice often when it's broken, from Year 5 through Year 8, to dredge up all possible artifacts. Bring friends to nab the strongest ones.

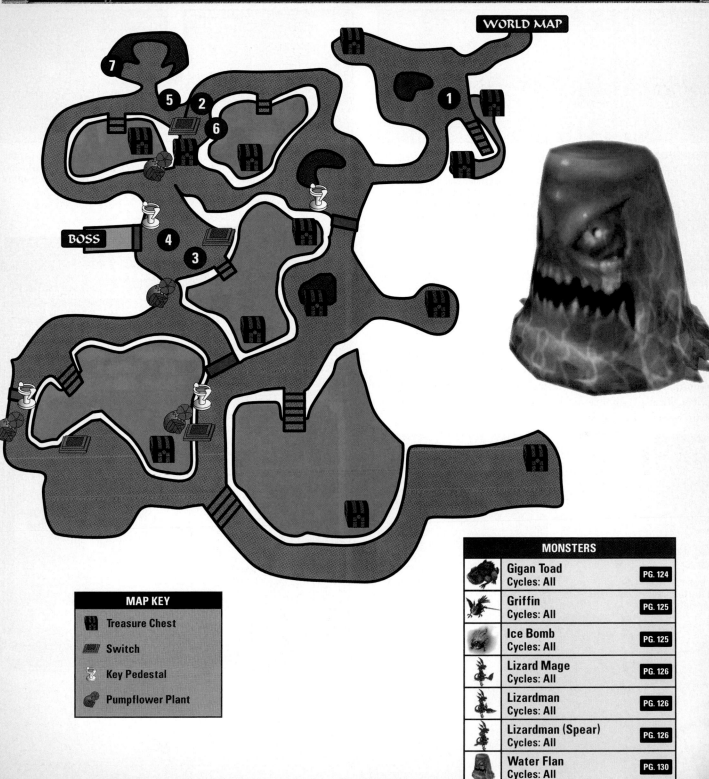

WORLD MAP

BOSS

MAP KEY

🗃	Treasure Chest
🔲	Switch
⚱	Key Pedestal
🌿	Pumpflower Plant

MONSTERS		
Gigan Toad Cycles: All		PG. 124
Griffin Cycles: All		PG. 125
Ice Bomb Cycles: All		PG. 125
Lizard Mage Cycles: All		PG. 126
Lizardman Cycles: All		PG. 126
Lizardman (Spear) Cycles: All		PG. 126
Water Flan Cycles: All		PG. 130

① A Prosperous Dry Spell

Veo Lu Sluice channels water from nearby Lake Shella into the Jegon River. When it's operating normally, the sluice's pools are filled. In Year 5 the sluice will malfunction, resulting in low pool levels. While the levels are low, you can enter the shallows to reach more enemies and treasure chests—take full advantage of the problem while it lasts.

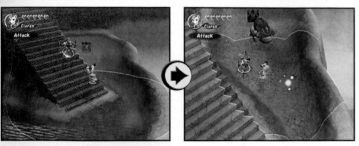

From Year 5 through Year 8, you can tromp down the stairs to battle more monsters and open chests that may contain great artifacts. Plunder the area repeatedly during the four-year span—you'll never get another chance.

② Flush Out the Pedestal Keys

You won't collect pedestal keys from fallen enemies in Veo Lu Sluice. They've been dropped down holes. To get the keys to appear, step on a wooden pad. Water will gush from a nearby hole and lift the key into view. Drop the chalice on the pad to maintain water pressure, then run over to grab the key.

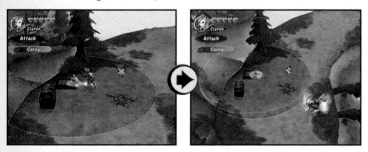

You may need to run outside of your chalice's protective field to reach the key. A second after you grab the key, the Miasma will hit you hard, causing you to drop the key. Return to pick it up once you have the chalice back in hand.

③ Risky Miasma Maneuver

The key for the final key pedestal is the hardest to get without taking Miasma damage. You'll need to drop the chalice on the wooden pad to trigger the key's appearance—as detailed in tip 2—but you'll need to run through much more Miasma to reach the key. Have a Cure spell handy.

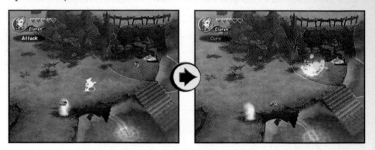

Drop the chalice on the wooden pad, then dash for the resulting geyser to get the pedestal key. After you carry it away, a Miasma shock will hit you, causing you to drop the item. Leave it behind and run for the protective field. Heal yourself with a Cure spell, then use the chalice's protection to nab the key safely.

Multiplayer

Fair Share of the Burden

Wresting the keys from holes is far safer in a multiplayer game. One hero can stand on the pad while a second runs for the key as it's borne up by the water. Once the second hero takes the key, another player can grab the chalice and run toward the out-of-bounds player to bring him within the chalice's protective field before Miasma damage occurs.

④ Shella among the Spoils

You won't be able to enter nearby Shella unless you're a Yuke or you possess the Shella Mark—the gatekeeper won't open the magical path. If you need a key, rampage through Veo Lu Sluice and defeat monsters until one of them drops a Shella Mark. Most often you'll obtain the town key from foes on the western side of the sluice.

After you grab a Shella Mark from a fallen foe, head back to Shella and speak with the guardian who stands on the outskirts of the town. He'll summon a magical bridge that spans the waters around Shella.

⑤ Sluice Moogle

You'll find a hole in the wall near the northwest point of the sluice. Collect the stamp, then paint Mog a color that will increase the odds that he'll help you power up a stronger Fire-, Thunder- or Blizzard-based spell for your upcoming boss battle.

⑥ Green Thumb for the Pumps

The pads won't trigger the water gush if there's no underground flow. When the sluice has problems in Year 5 through Year 8, the giant plants that leech water from the reservoirs will be dead. Cast a Life spell on a bulbous root while standing in the pool below it or on the ledge next to it—you'll have it functioning in no time.

If you don't have Life Magicite, put Phoenix Down in your command list, then use it to target the plant with its life-restoring power. After you revive the plant, go to the nearby wooden pad and use it to flush out the key.

⑦ Blizzard—Anytime, Anywhere

Monsters in the northwest corner of the sluice will often drop the Blizzard Ring, one of the most useful artifacts in Veo Lu Sluice. It lets you start an area with Blizzard magic, which can lead to Blizzara and Blizzaga casting earlier in a dungeon run—powerful stuff.

Golem

The metallic Golem that protects Veo Lu Sluice is immune to Freeze and Paralysis status effects, but it's vulnerable to Blizzard- and Thunder-based damage, as well as Fire spells and other magic. With one Magicite, the Blizzard Ring and some help from Mog, you should be able to cast Blizzaga. Unleash a winter storm.

RESISTANCE	
FIRE	2
BLIZZARD	2
THUNDER	2
SLOW	3
STOP	3
GRAVITY	2
HOLY	0

Golem will reel back and fire off his fists for two rocket-powered punches. If you see him gear up for his wallop, stand between his fists or run to the side to avoid impact.

When the boss's eyes gleam with blue energy, run a good distance away before he blasts his immediate area with lasers that inflict a Freeze condition on targets.

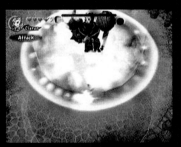

When Golem loses half of his health, he'll fire a red laser beam that etches a red perimeter, which he'll then hit with an inferno. Run outside the ring to avoid the pain.

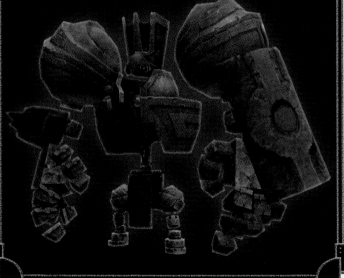

Golem: Cycle Three

When you visit Golem during your third Myrrh mission, he'll transform into a whirling dervish. When you see the boss reconfigure his parts so his fists are pointed to the sides, run far away. He'll spin and bash everything around him.

DROPPED ITEM SETS		CYCLE 1	CYCLE 2	CYCLE 3	ARTIFACTS
SET 1	1P	More than 0 pts.	—	—	ICE BRAND
	2P	More than 0 pts.	—	—	SILVER BRACER
	3P	More than 0 pts.	—	—	BUCKLER
	4P	More than 0 pts.	—	—	RING OF BLIZZARD
SET 2	1P	More than 92 pts.	—	—	GREEN BERET
	2P	More than 99 pts.	—	—	SAGE'S STAFF
	3P	More than 112 pts.	—	—	SILVER SPECTACLES
	4P	More than 123 pts.	—	—	MOON PENDANT
SET 3	1P	More than 115 pts.	More than 0 pts.	—	FANG CHARM
	2P	More than 124 pts.	More than 0 pts.	—	CAT'S BELL
	3P	More than 140 pts.	More than 0 pts.	—	ELVEN MANTLE
	4P	More than 154 pts.	More than 0 pts.	—	MOON PENDANT
SET 4	1P	More than 143 pts.	More than 92 pts.	—	SHURIKEN
	2P	More than 155 pts.	More than 99 pts.	—	FAERIE RING
	3P	More than 176 pts.	More than 112 pts.	—	SPARKLING BRACER
	4P	More than 193 pts.	More than 123 pts.	—	RING OF BLIZZARD
SET 5	1P	—	More than 115 pts.	More than 0 pts.	HEAVY ARMBAND
	2P	—	More than 124 pts.	More than 0 pts.	WONDER WAND
	3P	—	More than 140 pts.	More than 0 pts.	RAT'S TAIL
	4P	—	More than 154 pts.	More than 0 pts.	MOON PENDANT
SET 6	1P	—	More than 143 pts.	More than 92 pts.	LOADED DICE
	2P	—	More than 155 pts.	More than 99 pts.	NOAH'S LUTE
	3P	—	More than 176 pts.	More than 112 pts.	RING OF BLIZZARD
	4P	—	More than 193 pts.	More than 123 pts.	ORICHALCUM
SET 7	1P	—	—	More than 115 pts.	GREEN BERET
	2P	—	—	More than 124 pts.	WINGED CAP
	3P	—	—	More than 140 pts.	DIAMOND HELM
	4P	—	—	More than 154 pts.	GREEN SPHERE
SET 8	1P	—	—	More than 143 pts.	FANG CHARM
	2P	—	—	More than 155 pts.	CANDY RING
	3P	—	—	More than 176 pts.	TAOTIE MOTIF
	4P	—	—	More than 193 pts.	DIAMOND ARMOR

Scrolls, Materials and Artifacts

WORLD MAP

MAP KEY

🏰 Treasure Chest

⬤ Monster

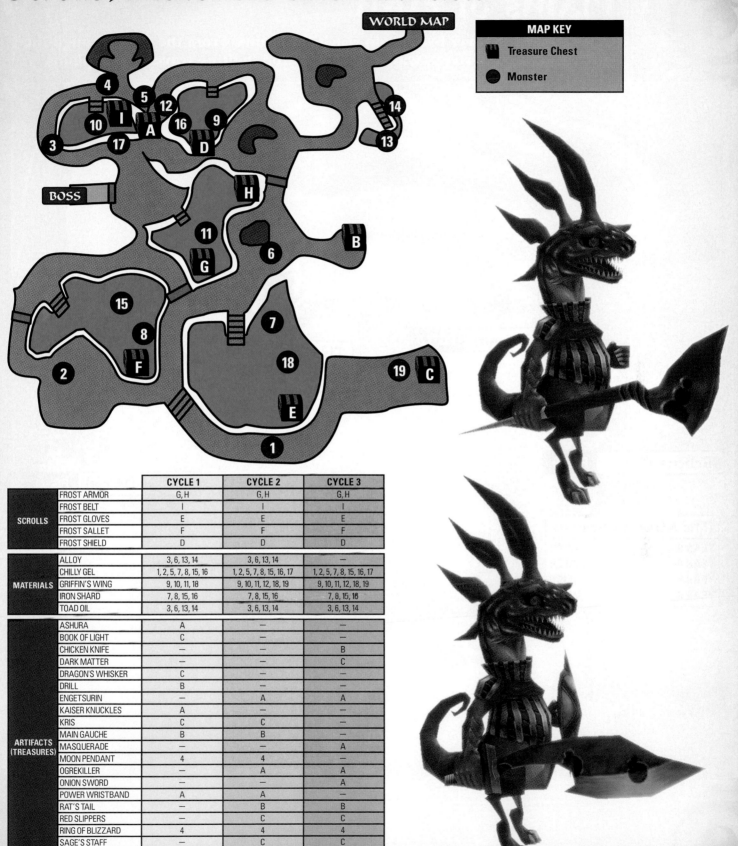

		CYCLE 1	CYCLE 2	CYCLE 3
SCROLLS	FROST ARMOR	G, H	G, H	G, H
	FROST BELT	I	I	I
	FROST GLOVES	E	E	E
	FROST SALLET	F	F	F
	FROST SHIELD	D	D	D
MATERIALS	ALLOY	3, 6, 13, 14	3, 6, 13, 14	—
	CHILLY GEL	1, 2, 5, 7, 8, 15, 16	1, 2, 5, 7, 8, 15, 16, 17	1, 2, 5, 7, 8, 15, 16, 17
	GRIFFIN'S WING	9, 10, 11, 18	9, 10, 11, 12, 18, 19	9, 10, 11, 12, 18, 19
	IRON SHARD	7, 8, 15, 16	7, 8, 15, 16	7, 8, 15, 16
	TOAD OIL	3, 6, 13, 14	3, 6, 13, 14	3, 6, 13, 14
ARTIFACTS (TREASURES)	ASHURA	A	—	—
	BOOK OF LIGHT	C	—	—
	CHICKEN KNIFE	—	—	B
	DARK MATTER	—	—	C
	DRAGON'S WHISKER	C	—	—
	DRILL	B	—	—
	ENGETSURIN	—	A	A
	KAISER KNUCKLES	A	—	—
	KRIS	C	C	—
	MAIN GAUCHE	B	B	—
	MASQUERADE	—	—	A
	MOON PENDANT	4	4	—
	OGREKILLER	—	A	A
	ONION SWORD	—	—	A
	POWER WRISTBAND	A	A	—
	RAT'S TAIL	—	B	B
	RED SLIPPERS	—	C	C
	RING OF BLIZZARD	4	4	4
	SAGE'S STAFF	—	C	C
	SILVER BRACER	C	C	—
	TOME OF ULTIMA	—	—	C
	TWISTED HEADBAND	A	A	—

Plains of Fum

Cross the Jegon River by ferry to reach the plains. From the fifth through the seventh years, the river's water level will drop, halting travel to the plains.

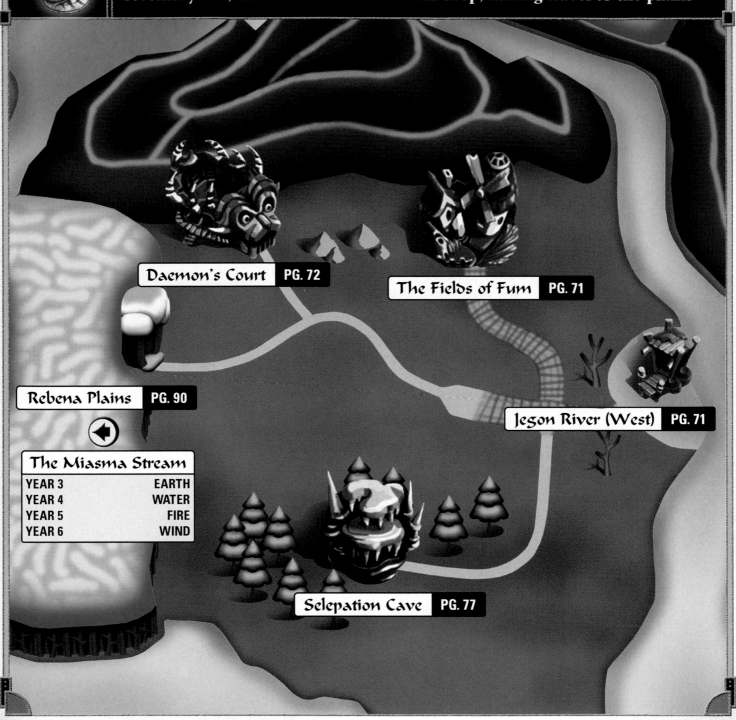

Daemon's Court PG. 72

The Fields of Fum PG. 71

Rebena Plains PG. 90

Jegon River (West) PG. 71

The Miasma Stream	
YEAR 3	EARTH
YEAR 4	WATER
YEAR 5	FIRE
YEAR 6	WIND

Selepation Cave PG. 77

The Fields of Fum

Striped Apple orchards and lush meadows make up The Fields of Fum, where you can purchase a wide array of fresh veggies from local farmers.

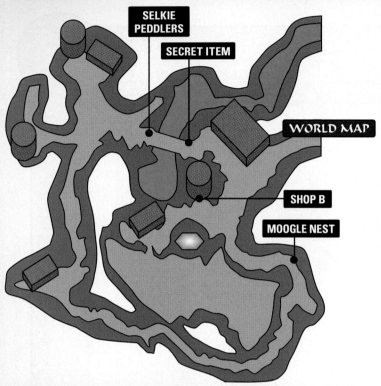

Riveting Cow Races

Morris Ranch features a very special event—cow racing! Talk to Morris to start the races and bet on your favorite cow. Speak with Morris's wife, Mileu, to purchase a cow for your family. The cow will be sent to your hometown automatically.

Finders Keepers

Someone dropped an item near the bridge in town. Examine the area around the bridge to find the secret item, assuming you haven't found another one since your last Myrrh trip.

East-Side Moogle

The resident Moogle lives on the east side of The Fields of Fum. Follow the southern road around to the southeast and search for the nest.

Selkie Sales

During odd-numbered years, Selkie peddlers will visit The Fields of Fum. The merchants sell scrolls and materials needed to forge weapons and armor.

SELKIE PEDDLERS			
BRONZE	300	MYTHRIL ARMOR	300
IRON	500	MYTHRIL SHIELD	250
MYTHRIL	5,000	IRON GLOVES	100
BRONZE SHARD	100	MYTHRIL GLOVES	250
IRON SHARD	100	IRON SALLET	100
ALLOY	250	MYTHRIL SALLET	250
WARRIOR'S WEAPON	300	IRON BELT	100
IRON ARMOR	150	MYTHRIL BELT	250

SHOP	
STRIPED APPLE	40
CHERRY CLUSTER	40
RAINBOW GRAPES	40
STAR CARROT	40
GOURD POTATO	40
ROUND CORN	40

Jegon River (West)

Tristan will ferry you back across the Jegon River, as well as to a few other locations, from the river's western bank.

Tristan's ferry service travels across the Jegon River when the water is at its highest point. From the fifth through the seventh years, the water level will be low. There is a Moogle Nest on Jegon River's western bank, near the exit to the world map. Search for a hole in the side of a hill to find the nest, then jump in the hole to visit the riverside Moogle.

DESTINATION	FAIR
Jegon River (East)	50
Mt. Kilanda	500
Leuda	300
Port Tipa	100

Mt. Kilanda will appear as a ferry destination from the fourth year on. Tristan's fares for his western Jegon River service are listed above.

Daemon's Court

Daemon's Court is swarming with savage lizards and other foes—
beware those who live within the fortress walls.

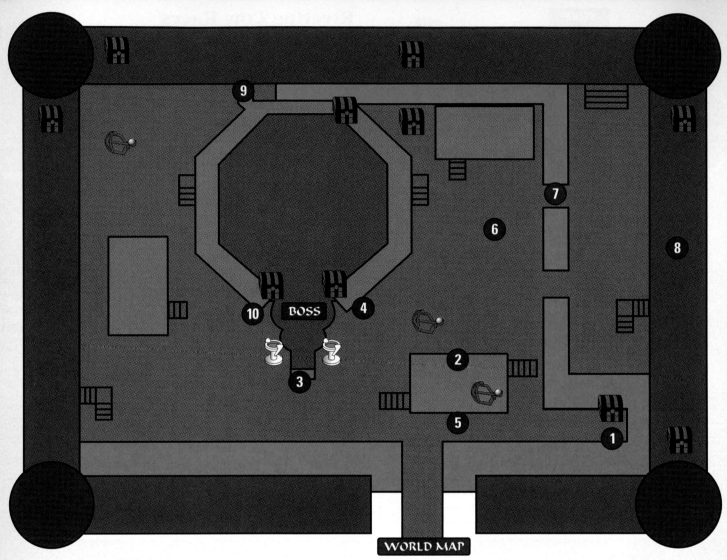

MAP KEY	
	Treasure Chest
	Key Pedestal
	Catapult

MONSTERS					
	Bomb Cycles: All	PG. 123		Lizard Soldier Cycles: All	PG. 126
	Coeurl Cycles: All	PG. 123		Lizard Warrior Cycles: All	PG. 126
	Killer Bee Cycles: All	PG. 125		Lizard Wizard Cycles: All	PG. 126
	Lizard Skirmisher Cycles: All	PG. 126		Wraith Cycles: All	PG. 130
	Lizard Skirmisher (Gold) Cycles: All	PG. 126			

❶ Gather the Elements

The treasure chest at point 3 contains a random Magicite—either Blizzard, Fire, Thunder or Cure. Open the chest as soon as you enter the dungeon. The reptilian foes are weak against Ice, so use Blizzard at every opportunity.

❷ Catapult Barrage

If you're quick, you can use the catapults scattered throughout the court to attack nearby enemies. Stand near a catapult and use the Attack command to launch its stone ammo. Be sure to lure an enemy in front of the catapult before you activate it, or you'll waste its powerful attack.

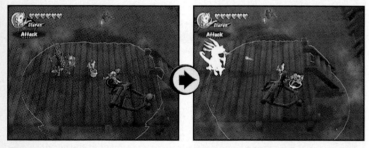

The catapults in Daemon's Court have only one round of ammo, so don't use them until you have the opportunity to clobber a foe. Aim true!

❸ Golden Key-Keepers

The gate to the Lizardman King is locked when you first enter the fortress. To reach him, you must find the two keys that fit onto the Key Pedestals in front of the central door. Two golden Lizard Skirmishers in the area usually hold the keys. Leave no reptile standing!

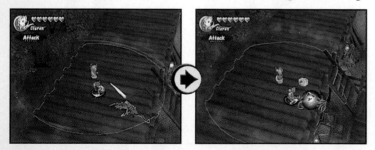

The golden Lizard Skirmishers have exactly the same stats and weaknesses as regular Skirmishers—the only difference is their color. The key-bearing enemies are usually surrounded by a few other reptilian baddies, so watch out!

❹ The Life Within

The treasure chest at point 4 contains a Life Magicite. Use Life to create Holy—you'll need it to attack the Wraiths that you'll encounter in Daemon's Court. As a bonus, the spell will both unveil the Wraiths and damage them.

❺ Snipe from Safety

You can attack some foes from a safe distance. Stand below the wooden platforms and cast attack magic at the enemies above you. The enemies can't hit you, and you can take your time defeating the unsuspecting monsters one by one.

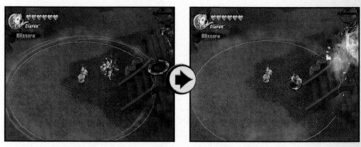

Blizzard is the best spell to use on the lizards in any situation, because it freezes them on the spot. You must move the targeting ring up the stairs to reach the foes on the platforms.

❻ Soften Up the Enemy

Before you attack, bring flying foes to the ground with Gravity and undead foes into sight with Holy. If you try to attack before weakening winged or undead foes, you will do little or no damage to them.

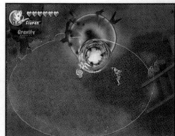

Reveal the Wraiths with Holy, then strike. Wraiths have low magic resistance, so Fire, Blizzard and Thunder will all finish them off.

Cast Gravity on the Killer Bees to knock them out of the air, then scorch them with Fire or squash them with your weapon.

7 Bomb Chain Reaction

If you destroy a bridge twice in Daemon's Court, you'll unlock a secret area in Conall Curach. Defeat the Bomb on the bridge at point 7, then leave the area and return (you must exit fully to the world map). When you destroy the bridge a second time the logs will create a path in the adjacent area—Conall Curach.

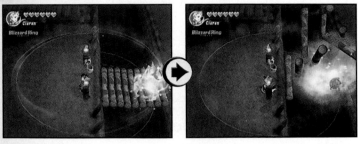

Bombs are vulnerable to Ice and Lightning magic. Stand on the shore just before or after the bridge and use Blizzard or Thunder to defeat the Bomb. When the Bomb explodes, it will destroy the bridge and send the logs downriver for you to use later.

8 Lizard Legion

There are five different types of lizards in Deamon's Court: Skirmishers, Gold Skirmishers, Soldiers, Warriors and Wizards. Both types of Skirmishers and the Soldiers have identical statistics, but the Wizards have lower strength and higher magic. The Warriors have more than double the HP of their brethren.

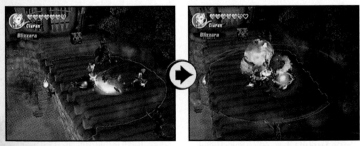

One of the best ways to deal with a group of lizards is with Blizzard or Blizzara. Cast the Ice-based spell in the center of the lizards—not only will you do tons of damage to them, but you'll freeze them in place.

9 That's One Brave Moogle

There's a Moogle living among the lizards in Daemon's Court. He must not get out very often because of all the danger outside, so pay the little guy a visit. Search the back wall of the fortress for a small hole. Then examine the spot to find the Moogle Nest.

10 Close Quarters

The narrow walkways along the east and west walls of the fortress are packed with enemies. If you rush ahead, you'll become overwhelmed. Maneuver around the monsters and take them out one by one as you progress. If you find yourself surrounded, back up to give yourself more space.

Ice- and Thunder-based spells incapacitate your enemies temporarily by paralyzing or freezing them. Don't forget the lone treasure chest at the end of the narrow walkway, at the end near the dungeon's entrance.

Lizardman King

The towering Lizardman King may pack quite a punch, but he's slow on his feet. If you take any damage during your battle with the king, you can easily dash away and cure yourself. Use the saw blades in the arena to your advantage by luring the Lizardman King over them when they pass.

RESISTANCES	
FIRE	3
BLIZZARD	2
THUNDER	2
SLOW	3
STOP	3
GRAVITY	2
HOLY	0

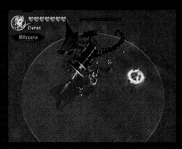

The Lizardman King brandishes a massive spear. If he hits you with the weapon, you'll suffer heavy damage. There's no way to block the spear strike, so avoid it at all costs. When your foe lunges at you with the weapon, you should have time to step to the side.

The Lizardman King's ranged attack shoots five arrows simultaneously in whatever direction he's facing. When you see the projectiles headed your way, quickly dodge to the side to avoid being skewered.

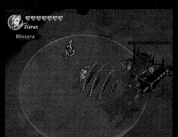

There are switches in the Lizardman King's arena. Whenever someone (including an enemy) steps on one of the switches, spinning saw blades will emerge and move along the ground. The saws will hurt anyone they touch, even the king.

Lizardman King: Cycles Two and Three

During the second cycle, the Lizardman King in Daemon's Court will use a Fire-based spell that will ignite you. On and after the third cycle through the fortress, he'll use an Ice-based spell that will freeze anyone it hits.

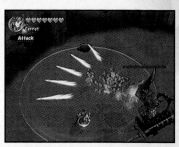

DROPPED ITEM SETS					
		CYCLE 1	CYCLE 2	CYCLE 3	ARTIFACTS
SET 1	1P	More than 0 pts.	—	—	LOADED DICE
	2P	More than 0 pts.	—	—	WINGED CAP
	3P	More than 0 pts.	—	—	BUCKLER
	4P	More than 0 pts.	—	—	CHOCOBO POCKET
SET 2	1P	More than 103 pts.	—	—	SHURIKEN
	2P	More than 111 pts.	—	—	WONDER WAND
	3P	More than 126 pts.	—	—	SILVER SPECTACLES
	4P	More than 138 pts.	—	—	MOON PENDANT
SET 3	1P	More than 128 pts.	More than 0 pts.	—	MANEATER
	2P	More than 138 pts.	More than 0 pts.	—	CANDY RING
	3P	More than 157 pts.	More than 0 pts.	—	RAT'S TAIL
	4P	More than 172 pts.	More than 0 pts.	—	CHOCOBO POCKET
SET 4	1P	More than 160 pts.	More than 103 pts.	—	DOUBLE AXE
	2P	More than 173 pts.	More than 111 pts.	—	DRAGON'S WHISKER
	3P	More than 197 pts.	More than 126 pts.	—	SPARKLING BRACER
	4P	More than 216 pts.	More than 138 pts.	—	MOON PENDANT
SET 5	1P	—	More than 128 pts.	More than 0 pts.	GIANT'S GLOVE
	2P	—	More than 138 pts.	More than 0 pts.	RUNE BELL
	3P	—	More than 157 pts.	More than 0 pts.	WONDER BANGLE
	4P	—	More than 172 pts.	More than 0 pts.	MOON PENDANT
SET 6	1P	—	More than 160 pts.	More than 103 pts.	OGREKILLER
	2P	—	More than 173 pts.	More than 111 pts.	DARK MATTER
	3P	—	More than 197 pts.	More than 126 pts.	CHOCOBO POCKET
	4P	—	More than 216 pts.	More than 138 pts.	ORICHALCUM
SET 7	1P	—	—	More than 128 pts.	FLAMETONGUE
	2P	—	—	More than 138 pts.	KRIS
	3P	—	—	More than 157 pts.	DIAMOND GLOVES
	4P	—	—	More than 172 pts.	KING'S SCALE
SET 8	1P	—	—	More than 160 pts.	ICE BRAND
	2P	—	—	More than 173 pts.	RED SLIPPERS
	3P	—	—	More than 197 pts.	AEGIS
	4P	—	—	More than 216 pts.	DIAMOND SHIELD

Scrolls, Materials and Artifacts

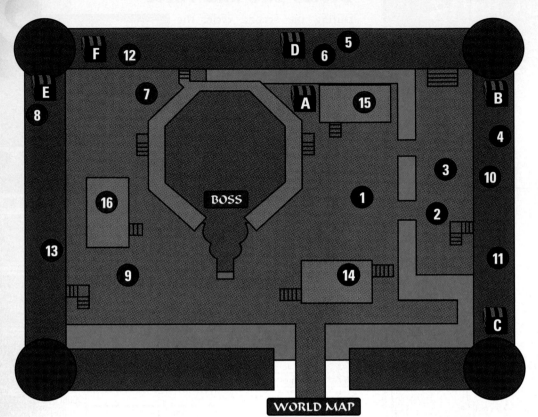

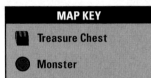

MAP KEY

🗄	Treasure Chest
⬤	Monster

WORLD MAP

		CYCLE 1	CYCLE 2	CYCLE 3
SCROLLS	DESIGNER GLASSES	–	–	A
	EYEWEAR TECHNIQUES	A	A	–
	MASTER'S WEAPON	F	F	F
	MIGHTY WEAPON	–	–	F
	VALIANT WEAPON	–	–	F
	VICTORIOUS WEAPON	–	F	F
	WARRIOR'S WEAPON	F	–	–
MATERIALS	ALLOY	–	–	4, 5, 6, 8, 10, 11, 12, 13
	COEURL'S WHISKER	1, 3, 7	1, 3, 7, 16	1, 3, 7, 16
	HEAVENLY DUST	2, 9	2, 9,15, 16	2, 9, 15, 16
	HOLY WATER	2, 9	2, 9, 14, 15	2, 9, 14, 15
	IRON	4, 5, 6, 8, 10, 11, 12, 13	–	–
	MYTHRIL	4, 5, 6, 8, 10, 11, 12, 13	4, 5, 6, 8, 10, 11, 12, 13	4, 5, 6, 8, 10, 11, 12, 13
ARTIFACTS (TREASURES)	BOOK OF LIGHT	C	–	C
	CAT'S BELL	C	C	–
	CHICKEN KNIFE	–	–	B
	CHOCOBO POCKET	E	E	E
	DRILL	B	–	–
	ENGETSURIN	D	D	–
	FAERIE RING	C	C	–
	FANG CHARM	D	–	–
	GIANT'S GLOVE	–	–	D
	GOLD HAIRPIN	–	C	C
	HEAVY ARMBAND	–	D	D
	MAGE'S STAFF	–	C	C
	MAIN GAUCHE	B	B	–
	MASQUERADE	–	D	D
	MOON PENDANT	E	E	E
	ONION SWORD	–	–	D
	NOAH'S LUTE	–	–	C
	POWER WRISTBAND	D	–	–
	RAT'S TAIL	–	B	B
	RUNE STAFF	C	–	–
	TOME OF ULTIMA	–	–	C
	TWISTED HEADBAND	D	D	–

Selepation Cave

The labyrinthine cavern contains a wealth of treasure. Though you can reach the area's boss easily, it pays to fight your way to every chest first.

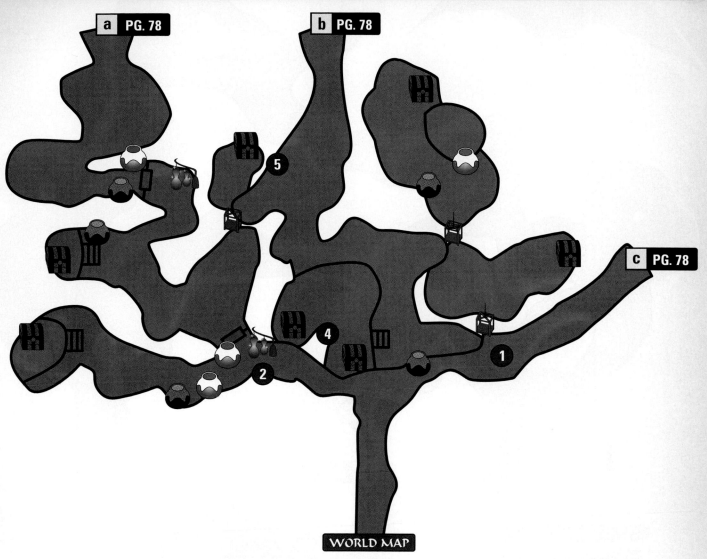

a PG. 78
b PG. 78
c PG. 78

WORLD MAP

MAP KEY	
	Treasure Chest
	Switch (Crystal)
	Water Urn
	Oil Urn
	Elevator

MONSTERS					
Blazer Beetle Cycles: All	PG. 123		Lizard Mage Cycles: All	PG. 126	
Cockatrice Cycles: All	PG. 123		Lizardman Cycles: All	PG. 126	
Electric Jellyfish Cycles: All	PG. 124		Lizardman (Mace) Cycle: 3	PG. 126	
Gigas Cycles: All	PG. 124		Lizardman (Spear) Cycles: 2 & 3	PG. 126	
Killer Bee Cycles: All	PG. 125		Sahagin Cycles: All	PG. 128	
Lizard Captain Cycles: All	PG. 126		Sonic Bat Cycles: 2 & 3	PG. 129	

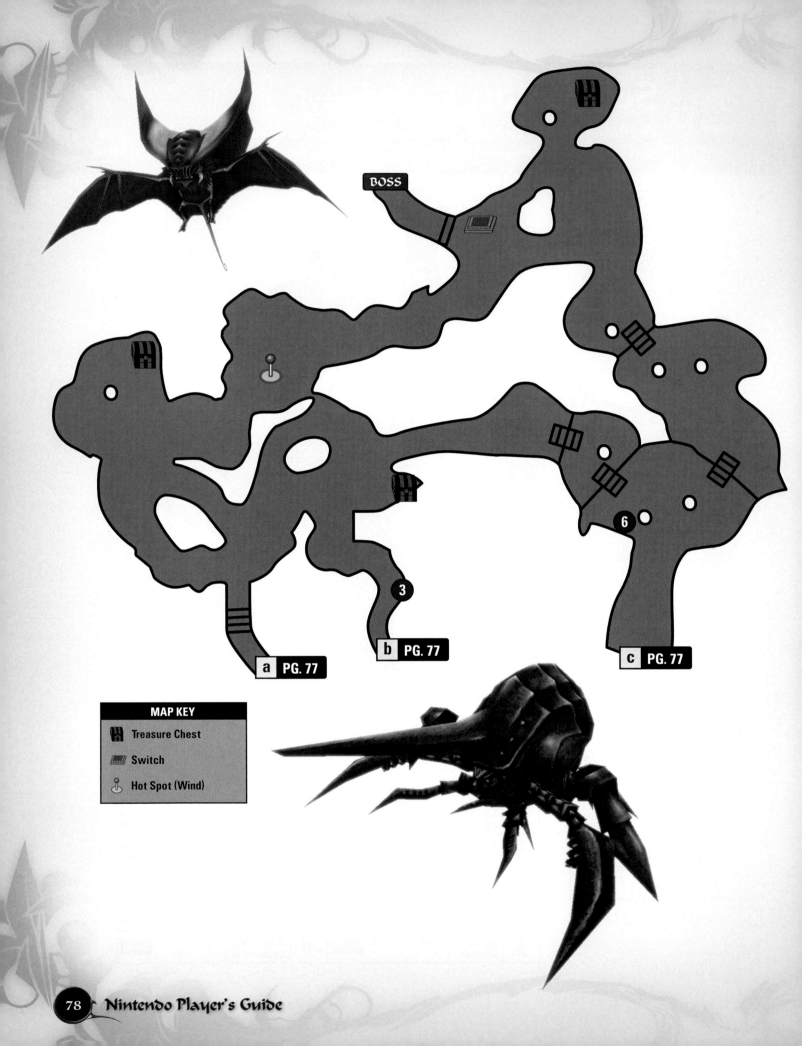

BOSS

a PG. 77

b PG. 77

c PG. 77

3

6

MAP KEY

Treasure Chest

Switch

Hot Spot (Wind)

Diligence Pays

The shortest path is the least rewarding in Selepation Cave. It leads directly to the boss, bypassing many of the treasure chests hidden deep within the cavern. You must use the three elevators in the cavern to reach some of the out-of-the-way chests.

Blazer Beetles in Numbers

The massive Blazer Beetles are some of Selepation Cave's toughest monsters. They have high HP, but they are very vulnerable to magic, especially Fire-, Ice- and Lightning-based spells.

Blazer Beetles are quick, despite their size. Attack them from a distance with magic, or maneuver around to their backsides to strike with your weapon. Avoid facing the armored giants head-on—their spells and lancelike horns are quite formidable.

Wrath of the Gigas

With their powerful fists and spells, Gigas are a force to be reckoned with. They have more HP than any other monster in Selepation Cave. Luckily, the Gigas have a weakness—Fire-based magic.

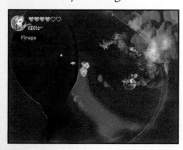

The lumbering Gigas move slowly, which makes it easier to attack them at range. The beasts have a natural resistance to Ice-based spells. If you choose to attack with a weapon, dodge your foe's fists when it swings.

❶ Magicite for All

The monsters near point 1 carry Blizzard, Cure and Thunder Magicite. Fuse Thunder and Blizzard to create Gravity—it'll come in handy when facing the pesky Killer Bees and Sonic Bats. The troublesome Electric Jellyfish, on the other hand, are vulnerable to Ice-based spells.

❷ Strike a Common Note

There are three wooden gates that won't open with any amount of force in the dungeon—you will have to use the crystal-like switches hanging near the gates to make them open. Stand between the crystals and strike them with your weapon. If you hit both at the same time, the door will open.

You don't have to hit the switches at exactly the same time to open the door, but it has to be pretty close. The best way to hit them is by using the third part of your combo move or a Focus Attack. Finally, you must use a physical attack—magic won't do the trick.

Multiplayer

Synchronized Symphony

When you're exploring Selepation Cave in multiplayer mode, three crystal switches control each gate. It takes teamwork to hit all three switches at once. Place one player in front of each switch and swing at them simultaneously to unlock the gate.

③ Paths Once Traveled

The middle section of Selepation Cave seems out of reach at first glance, but don't be fooled. To reach the middle area, enter the second section of the cave at point a, then circle back around to the first area via point b. You'll have access to most of the middle section—except that which must be reached via an elevator.

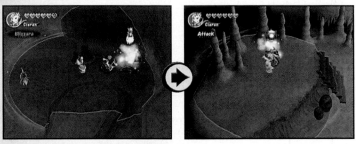

The only way to reach the elevators and some of the treasure chests in Selepation Cave's middle section is to take the back route. The majority of the artifacts are in the area, so it's worth your time.

④ Subterranean Living

You'd think Moogles would get tired of living in dungeons, but it doesn't seem to bother them. To find Selepation Cave's resident fuzzball, enter the middle section and walk south until you find a set of wooden stairs. Go up the stairs and down another set, then look for a hole in the wall.

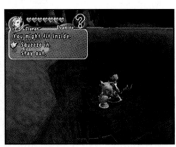

⑤ Search High and Low

The three elevators in Selepation Cave's middle section will lower you to platforms where many treasure chests and item-carrying monsters reside. To keep track of where you've been, clear out the entire upper half of the middle section before you take any elevator rides.

To operate an elevator, you must stand on it with both the Crystal Chalice and Mog. If you can't make the lift operate, try moving away and standing on it again—sometimes Mog will look like he's onboard when he really isn't. In a multiplayer game, everyone must stand on the elevator before it will move.

⑥ Sahagin Surprise

Sahagins are monsters that live in small water holes throughout Selepation Cave. When you approach one of their hiding spots, a Sahagin will leap out and attack. Sahagins are quick on their feet—but they're vulnerable to Fire-based magic and have relatively low HP.

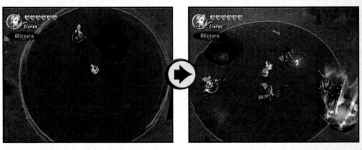

Some spots in Selepation Cave have several Sahagin water holes clustered together. Take your time and approach the holes one at a time.

Cave Worm

The Cave Worm won't pursue you around its arena, but it'll pivot on an axis, spewing harmful sand at anyone who dares to venture near it. Attack the cave-dweller close-up with weapons or at range with magic. Choose your spells wisely—the boss is heavily resistant to most elements, especially Ice. Holy magic is the most effective.

RESISTANCES	
FIRE	2
BLIZZARD	3
THUNDER	2
SLOW	3
STOP	3
GRAVITY	2
HOLY	0

The Cave Worm's most common attack is its sandstorm breath. Watch for the beast to slowly open its round mouth, then step to the side and continue the attack. The worm also uses a beam attack that will slow anyone it hits—look for the same tell-tale giveaway with the open mouth.

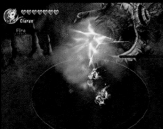

If you keep your distance from the Cave Worm, it will inhale and pull in everyone and everything around it. When that happens, run toward the beast and press the attack—you won't take any damage while the creature is inhaling.

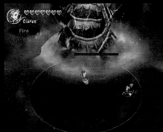

When the Cave Worm's health is low, it will perform a special attack. As you approach the boss, it will rear up and slam the ground with its entire body—if you get hit, you'll suffer a huge amount of damage. Dodge sideways and strike when it lands to deal the stunning blow.

Cave Worm: Cycles Two and Three

Unlike other areas' bosses, who gain new spells or abilities as the years pass, the Cave Worm's attacks remain the same every time you encounter it. What Selepation Cave's boss does gain, however, is increased stats—he'll be harder to beat each time.

		DROPPED ITEM SETS			
		CYCLE 1	CYCLE 2	CYCLE 3	ARTIFACTS
SET 1	1P	More than 0 pts.	—	—	OGREKILLER
	2P	More than 0 pts.	—	—	DRAGON'S WHISKER
	3P	More than 0 pts.	—	—	BUCKLER
	4P	More than 0 pts.	—	—	CHOCOBO POCKET
SET 2	1P	More than 158 pts.	—	—	ASHURA
	2P	More than 170 pts.	—	—	RUNE BELL
	3P	More than 193 pts.	—	—	SILVER SPECTACLES
	4P	More than 212 pts.	—	—	RING OF THUNDER
SET 3	1P	More than 197 pts.	More than 0 pts.	—	KAISER KNUCKLES
	2P	More than 212 pts.	More than 0 pts.	—	MAGE MASHER
	3P	More than 241 pts.	More than 0 pts.	—	SPARKLING BRACER
	4P	More than 265 pts.	More than 0 pts.	—	MOON PENDANT
SET 4	1P	More than 246 pts.	More than 158 pts.	—	POWER WRISTBAND
	2P	More than 266 pts.	More than 170 pts.	—	RUNE STAFF
	3P	More than 302 pts.	More than 193 pts.	—	TEDDY BEAR
	4P	More than 332 pts.	More than 212 pts.	—	RING OF THUNDER
SET 5	1P	—	More than 197 pts.	More than 0 pts.	SASUKE'S BLADE
	2P	—	More than 212 pts.	More than 0 pts.	KRIS
	3P	—	More than 241 pts.	More than 0 pts.	BLACK HOOD
	4P	—	More than 265 pts.	More than 0 pts.	DIAMOND ARMOR
SET 6	1P	—	More than 246 pts.	More than 158 pts.	TWISTED HEADBAND
	2P	—	More than 266 pts.	More than 170 pts.	GOLD HAIRPIN
	3P	—	More than 302 pts.	More than 193 pts.	MOON PENDANT
	4P	—	More than 332 pts.	More than 212 pts.	ORICHALCUM
SET 7	1P	—	—	More than 197 pts.	LOADED DICE
	2P	—	—	More than 212 pts.	SAGE'S STAFF
	3P	—	—	More than 241 pts.	RING OF THUNDER
	4P	—	—	More than 265 pts.	WIND CRYSTAL
SET 8	1P	—	—	More than 246 pts.	OGREKILLER
	2P	—	—	More than 266 pts.	WONDER WAND
	3P	—	—	More than 302 pts.	EARTH ARMOR
	4P	—	—	More than 332 pts.	RING OF PROTECTION

Scrolls, Materials and Artifacts

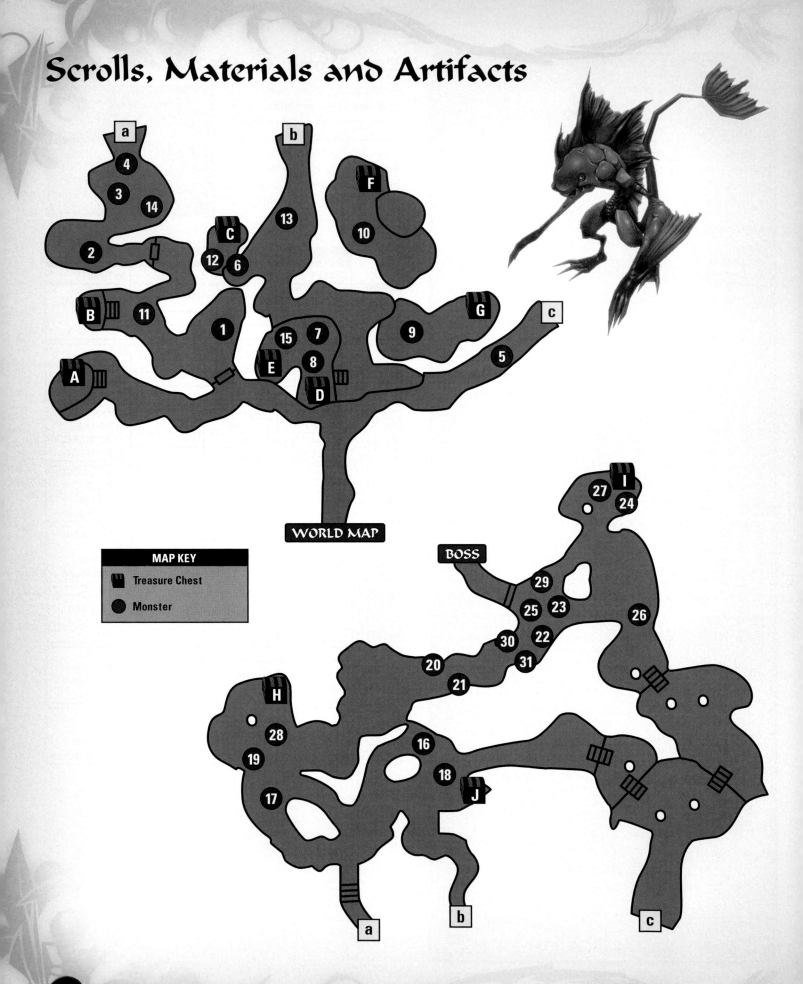

MAP KEY

▦ Treasure Chest

● Monster

WORLD MAP

BOSS

		CYCLE 1	CYCLE 2	CYCLE 3
SCROLLS	GOLD GLOVES	–	–	A
	HOLY ARMOR	–	–	C
	HOLY SHIELD	–	–	A
	IRON ARMOR	C	C	–
	IRON BELT	B	–	–
	IRON GLOVES	A	–	–
	IRON SALLET	B	–	–
	IRON SHIELD	A	–	–
	LIGHTNING BELT	–	B	B
	LIGHTNING GLOVES	–	A	A
	LIGHTNING SALLET	–	B	B
	LIGHTNING SHIELD	–	A	A
	MASTER'S WEAPON	J	J	J
	MIGHTY WEAPON	–	–	J
	MYTHRIL ARMOR	C	C	C
	MYTHRIL BELT	B	B	–
	MYTHRIL GLOVES	A	A	–
	MYTHRIL SALLET	B	B	–
	MYTHRIL SHIELD	A	A	–
	PURE ARMOR	–	–	C
	PURE BELT	–	–	B
	RING OF LIGHT	D, G	D, G	D, G
	TIME ARMOR	–	C	C
	TIME SALLET	–	–	B
	VALIANT WEAPON	–	J	J
	VICTORIOUS WEAPON	–	–	J
	WARRIOR'S WEAPON	J	J	–
MATERIALS	ALLOY	1, 2, 10	1, 2, 10	1, 2, 10
	COCKATRICE SCALE	17, 18, 19, 20, 25	17, 18, 19, 20, 25	17, 18, 19, 20, 25
	GIGAS CLAW	8, 16, 23	8, 9, 16, 23, 28, 29, 30, 31	8, 9, 16, 23, 28, 29, 30, 31
	HARD SHELL	3, 4, 5, 14	3, 4, 5, 14	3, 4, 5, 14
	MYTHRIL	1, 2, 10	1, 2, 10	1, 2, 10
	THUNDERBALL	6, 7, 11, 12, 13, 15, 21, 22, 24, 26, 27	6, 7, 11, 12, 13, 15, 21, 22, 24, 26, 27	6, 7, 11, 12, 13, 15, 21, 22, 24, 26, 27
ARTIFACTS (TREASURES)	BOOK OF LIGHT	I	–	–
	CAT'S BELL	I	I	–
	CHICKEN KNIFE	–	–	H
	DRILL	H	–	–
	FAERIE RING	–	I	I
	GOLD HAIRPIN	–	–	I
	GREEN BERET	E	–	–
	HEAVY ARMBAND	–	E	E
	MAGE MASHER	I	–	–
	MAIN GAUCHE	H	H	–
	MASQUERADE	–	–	E
	MJOLLNIR	–	E	E
	MOON PENDANT	F	F	–
	ONION SWORD	–	–	E
	POWER WRISTBAND	E	E	–
	RAT'S TAIL	–	H	H
	RING OF THUNDER	F	F	F
	RUNE BELL	–	I	I
	TOME OF ULTIMA	–	–	I
	TWISTED HEADBAND	E	E	–
	WONDER WAND	I	I	–

Kilanda Islands

You will not be able to set foot on Mt. Kilanda until your fourth year. Saving your game is not an option on the mountain, so use your travel money wisely.

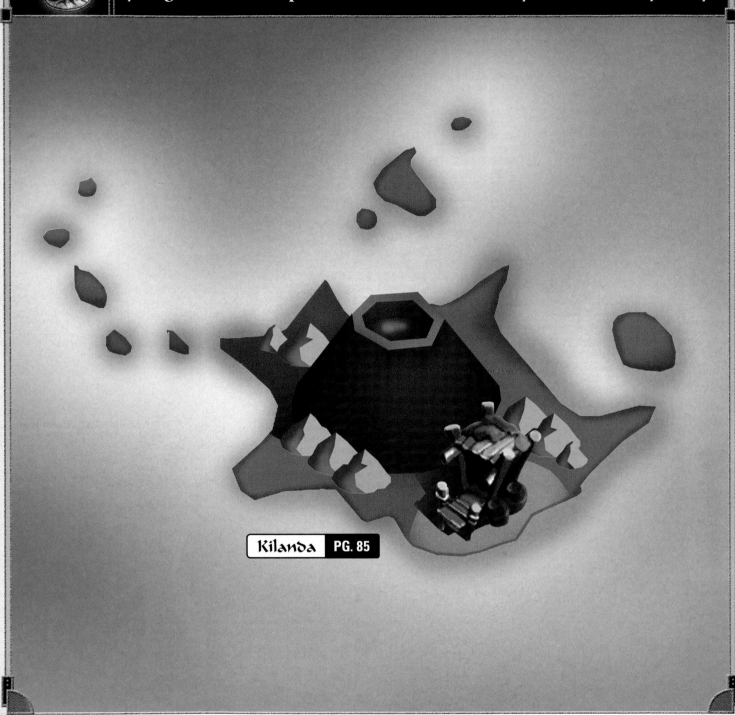

Kilanda   **PG. 85**

Kilanda

Flame-resistant armor and accessories will aid you greatly against the creatures that inhabit this smoldering wasteland.

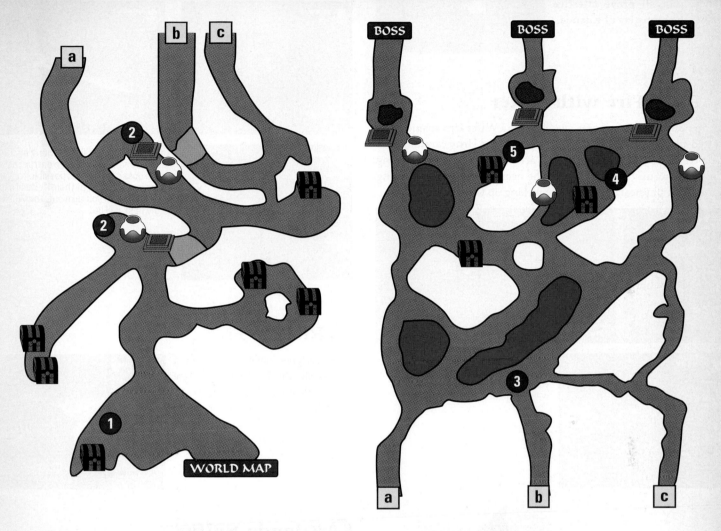

MONSTERS		
Blazer Beetle Cycles: All	PG. 123	
Coeurl Cycles: All	PG. 123	
Lamia Cycles: All	PG. 125	
Lava Ahriman Cycles: All	PG. 125	
Lava Mu Cycles: All	PG. 125	
Ogre (Kilanda) Cycles: All	PG. 127	

MAP KEY	
Treasure Chest	
Switch	
Water Urn	

① Magicite-Seeking

First things first—head southwest from the shore to find a treasure chest that contains a Fire, Thunder, Blizzard or Cure Magicite. Thundara, Blizzaga and Gravity will all prove effective against the monsters of Kilanda.

② Fight Fire with Water

At two points in the first area, you'll notice a Water Urn suspiciously located near a minivolcano. Placing the Water Urns carefully into their respective minivolcanoes will activate rising bridges, giving you access to new areas. Fend off the nearby Lava Ahriman using Gravity and physical attacks before picking up the Water Urns.

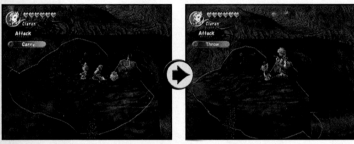

If you drop the Water Urn outside of the minivolcano or an enemy knocks it from your hands, don't worry—the bridges will rise on their own eventually.

③ Goblin Giftgiver

When you enter the second area of Kilanda, you'll see a Goblin carrying a giant sword. Strike the Goblin to make it drop the sword before it delivers the weapon to its lord. Though your valiance has no immediate rewards, it will give you an advantage when fighting the boss of Kilanda.

There are three Goblins couriers, each headed for one of the three entrances to the boss's lair, and it's possible to stop more than one of them if you are quick. The more you take out, the weaker the boss will be.

④ Ring of Fire

Unlike Ogres you've encountered previously, the Kilanda Ogres are vulnerable to Lightning spells. If you take out the Ogre near point 4, it might drop a Fire Ring—you'll have the option to choose it as an artifact after defeating the boss.

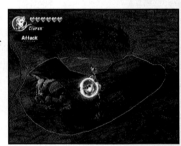

⑤ Kilanda Sulfur

The boat captain, Tristan, yearns for a rare item called Kilanda Sulfur. If you bring it to him, he'll give you a permanent discount on his fare. The item can occasionally be found inside the treasure chest at point 5.

The best time to get Kilanda Sulfur is from the treasure chest at point 5 during cycle three. In cycles one and two it appears very sporadically.

Iron Giant

The Iron Giant's attacks differ depending on whether he is carrying a sword. Stay out of close range when he's armed—his sweeping attack is hard to avoid. In multiplayer mode, one player can draw the Iron Giant's attacks while others lay waste from behind.

RESISTANCE	
FIRE	2
BLIZZARD	2
THUNDER	3
SLOW	3
STOP	3
GRAVITY	3
HOLY	0

When the Iron Giant is wielding his sword, he releases a long-range spinning projectile that will damage and paralyze you. Learn his pattern and move around him quickly to avoid it. Use the in-between time to charge up a spell, or stay near a minivolcano to draw the Iron Giant into a trap.

If the Iron Giant's sword breaks, you'll have a short amount of time to attack him when he is most vulnerable. Run out of close range when he raises his arms to avoid a damaging shockwave. He will eventually grab another sword and repeat the cycle until he runs out of swords.

Dropping a Water Urn into a minivolcano will cause a gust of damaging gas to emerge from the nearby wall. Draw the Iron Giant—with or without his sword—near a minivolcano to activate it and damage him. The gas will hurt you as well, so run away after completing the task.

Iron Giant: Cycles Two and Three

When you fight the Iron Giant in cycles two and three, he will cast a new gravity-based spell when he is without a sword. The attack has a wide range but does minimal damage. Battle the Iron Giant the same way you did in cycle one, keeping in mind his increased strength.

		DROPPED ITEM SETS			
		CYCLE 1	CYCLE 2	CYCLE 3	ARTIFACTS
SET 1	1P	More than 0 pts.	—	—	ENGETSURIN
	2P	More than 0 pts.	—	—	BOOK OF LIGHT
	3P	More than 0 pts.	—	—	DRILL
	4P	More than 0 pts.	—	—	MOON PENDANT
SET 2	1P	More than 102 pts.	—	—	POWER WRISTBAND
	2P	More than 110 pts.	—	—	KRIS
	3P	More than 125 pts.	—	—	DRILL
	4P	More than 137 pts.	—	—	STAR PENDANT
SET 3	1P	More than 127 pts.	More than 0 pts.	—	GREEN BERET
	2P	More than 137 pts.	More than 0 pts.	—	SILVER BRACER
	3P	More than 156 pts.	More than 0 pts.	—	MAIN GAUCHE
	4P	More than 171 pts.	More than 0 pts.	—	RING OF FIRE
SET 4	1P	More than 159 pts.	More than 102 pts.	—	FANG CHARM
	2P	More than 172 pts.	More than 110 pts.	—	CAT'S BELL
	3P	More than 195 pts.	More than 125 pts.	—	DRILL
	4P	More than 214 pts.	More than 137 pts.	—	RING OF FIRE
SET 5	1P	—	More than 127 pts.	More than 0 pts.	MJOLLNIR
	2P	—	More than 137 pts.	More than 0 pts.	RED SLIPPERS
	3P	—	More than 156 pts.	More than 0 pts.	CHICKEN KNIFE
	4P	—	More than 171 pts.	More than 0 pts.	STAR PENDANT
SET 6	1P	—	More than 159 pts.	More than 102 pts.	FLAMETONGUE
	2P	—	More than 172 pts.	More than 110 pts.	MAGE'S STAFF
	3P	—	More than 195 pts.	More than 125 pts.	RING OF FIRE
	4P	—	More than 214 pts.	More than 137 pts.	ORICHALCUM
SET 7	1P	—	—	More than 127 pts.	TWISTED HEADBAND
	2P	—	—	More than 137 pts.	WONDER WAND
	3P	—	—	More than 156 pts.	LEGENDARY WEAPON
	4P	—	—	More than 171 pts.	RED EYE
SET 8	1P	—	—	More than 159 pts.	MASAMUNE
	2P	—	—	More than 172 pts.	RUNE BELL
	3P	—	—	More than 195 pts.	MAIN GAUCHE
	4P	—	—	More than 214 pts.	CELESTIAL WEAPON

Scrolls, Materials, and Artifacts

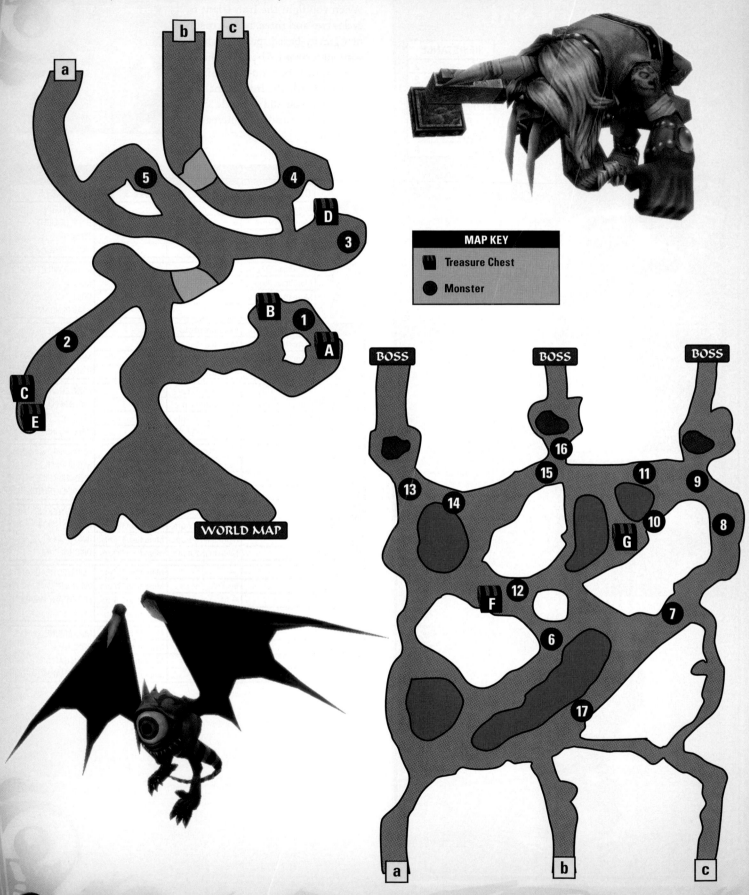

MAP KEY

🗯 Treasure Chest

● Monster

a
b
c

5
4
D
3

B
1
A

2

C
E

WORLD MAP

BOSS
BOSS
BOSS

13
14
16
15
11
9
10
G
8
F
12
7
6
17

a
b
c

		CYCLE 1	CYCLE 2	CYCLE 3
SCROLLS	DIAMOND ARMOR	–	–	6, 8, 15
	FLAME ARMOR	–	A, B	A, B
	FLAME BELT	D	D	D
	FLAME CRAFT	A, B	A, B	–
	FLAME GLOVES	D	D	D
	FLAME SALLET	D	D	D
	FLAME SHIELD	D	D	D
	HEALING KIT	–	–	A, B
	LEGENDARY WEAPON	–	–	F, G
	MASTER'S WEAPON	C	C	C
	MIGHTY WEAPON	–	–	C
	VALIANT WEAPON	–	C	C
	VICTORIOUS WEAPON	–	–	C
	WARRIOR'S WEAPON	C	–	–
	ZEAL KIT	–	A, B	A, B

		CYCLE 1	CYCLE 2	CYCLE 3
MATERIALS	ALLOY	–	E	E
	ANCIENT POTION	–	–	11, 14
	ANGEL'S TEAR	–	–	16, 17*
	COEURL'S WHISKER	11, 14	11, 14	11, 14
	DIAMOND ORE	–	–	E
	FAERIE'S TEAR	1, 2, 5, 13, 16, 17*	1, 2, 5, 13, 16, 17*	1, 2, 5
	HARD SHELL	3,4	3,4	3,4
	IRON	E	E	–
	MAGMA ROCK	1, 2, 5, 13, 16, 17*	1, 2, 5, 13, 16, 17*	1, 2 ,5, 13, 16, 17*
	MYTHRIL	E	E	E
	OGRE FANG	6, 8, 15	6, 8, 15	6, 8, 15

		CYCLE 1	CYCLE 2	CYCLE 3
ARTIFACTS (TREASURES)	BLACK HOOD	7	7	–
	BUCKLER	7	–	–
	CAT'S BELL	12	–	–
	CHICKEN KNIFE	–	7	7
	ENGETSURIN	9	9	–
	FAERIE RING	12	–	–
	FLAMETONGUE	9	–	–
	GIANT'S GLOVE	9	9	–
	GOLD HAIRPIN	–	–	12
	HEAVY ARMBAND	–	9	9
	KRIS	–	12	12
	MASQUERADE	–	–	9
	MOON PENDANT	10	10	10
	NOAH'S LUTE	12	12	–
	ONION SWORD	–	–	9
	POWER WRISTBAND	9	–	–
	RED SLIPPERS	-	12	12
	RING OF FIRE	10	10	10
	SAGE'S STAFF	12	12	–
	STAR PENDANT	–	–	10
	TEDDY BEAR	–	–	7
	TWISTED HEADBAND	–	9	9
	WONDER WAND	–	–	12

*The monster emerges only when three or four characters are playing.

Rebena Plains

Depending on what year you enter Rebena Plains, you may have to change the chalice's element before crossing Jegon River.

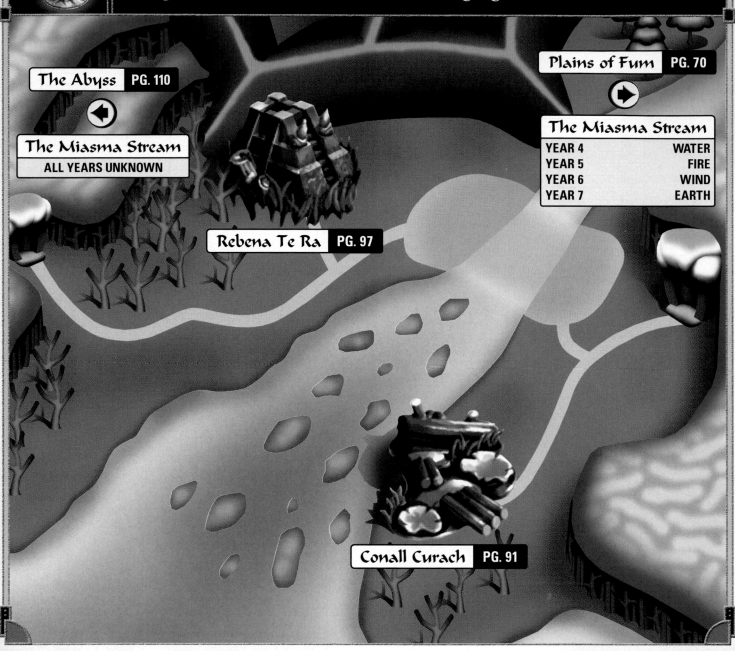

The Abyss PG. 110

The Miasma Stream
ALL YEARS UNKNOWN

Plains of Fum PG. 70

The Miasma Stream

YEAR 4	WATER
YEAR 5	FIRE
YEAR 6	WIND
YEAR 7	EARTH

Rebena Te Ra PG. 97

Conall Curach PG. 91

The Unknown Element "?"

On the east side of Rebena Plains you'll find the fifth Miasma stream, which will lead you to the final area. To pass through it, you'll need to set your chalice to the unknown element ("?") by completing a series of puzzles in Lynari Desert (see page 106). Once you've done so, you will be able to travel freely through all Miasma Streams. Be careful not to change it back to one of the other four elements accidentally, or you'll have to return to Lynari Desert and change it back.

Conall Curach

Monsters and treasure chests exist in great numbers throughout the massive Conall Curach.

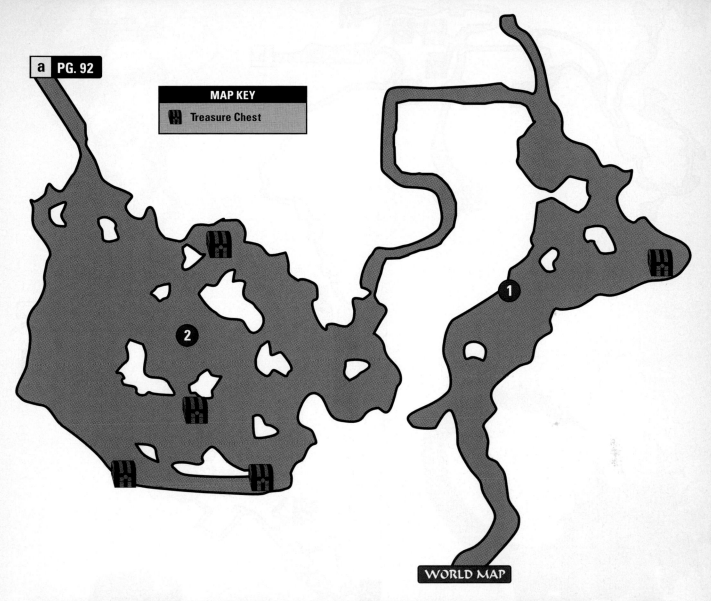

a PG. 92

MAP KEY

Treasure Chest

WORLD MAP

MONSTERS					
Abaddon Cycles: All	PG. 122	Gigan Toad (Conall Curach) Cycles: All	PG. 124	Sahagin Lord Cycles: All	PG. 128
Behemoth Cycles: All	PG. 122	Ice Bomb Cycles: All	PG. 125	Snow Mu Cycles: All	PG. 129
Dark Flan Cycles: All	PG. 123	Magic Plant Cycles: All	PG. 126	Stone Sahagin Cycles: All	PG. 129
Flan (Conall Curach) Cycles: All	PG. 124	Sahagin Cycles: All	PG. 128	Thunder Bomb Cycles: All	PG. 130
Ghost Cycles: All	PG. 124				

a PG. 91

b

BOSS

3

4

5 6

b

① Mysterious Stone

At point 1 you'll find the first of five stones with ancient Selkic script inscribed on them. Your character must be a Selkie to translate them. The messages help explain the history of Selkies in Conall Curach but aren't necessary to finish the level.

② Sneaky Sahagins

The marsh lends itself well to the Sahagins, who will jump from the swampy puddles and surprise you. Lead them away from the stationary Magic Plants to spread out your enemies and avoid getting caught in a trap.

③ Cause and Effect

To continue on, you must have destroyed a bridge in Daemon's Court by detonating a Bomb (pg. 72). After you've destroyed the bridge twice, enough logs will float downriver to allow you to reach a new area with multiple treasure chests.

④ Paint the Moogle Red

Search the area just north of the tree until the Examine icon pops up. Enter the Moogle Nest to get your next stamp and paint your Moogle. In single-player mode, painting it red will allow you to see monster locations if you have a GBA connected to Controller slot 2.

Multiplayer

Sinking Bridge Sections

Sticking close together is usually a good strategy. In Conall Curach, however, you must be wary of the Selkies' shoddy bridge work. Certain sections will sink if too many characters, including monsters, are on them. The Miasma in the water will damage you, so be careful.

⑤ Gravity of the Situation

Most magic has no effect on the Stone Sahagins that litter the later part of Conall Curach. Fear not, magic user! Casting Gravity will ease your troubles.

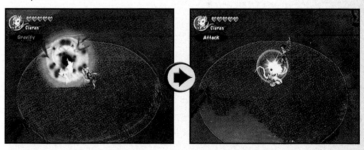

Gravity is used mostly for flying creatures, but in Conall Curach you can cast Gravity to reduce a Stone Sahagin's HP by half. The spell will work only once per creature. Cast Gravity, then move in with physical attacks to finish the job.

⑥ Thunderstruck

Behemoths are nasty creatures, especially when Stone Sahagins are running rampant around them. Use Thunder spells to inflict damage. Cast Thundaga if you can—it will paralyze the Behemoths and give you a second to collect yourself.

Dragon Zombie

The massive Dragon Zombie leaves you little room to maneuver. Move from side to side to dodge its attacks, making sure you don't get trapped by the Stone Sahagins it sends your way. Take out the Stone Sahagins first, then hit the Dragon Zombie with Holy spells—Holy will continue to do damage when the boss is fully visible.

RESISTANCE	
FIRE	1
BLIZZARD	2
THUNDER	2
SLOW	3
STOP	3
GRAVITY	3
HOLY	0

The Dragon Zombie can blow you backward and do significant damage. Avoid his attack by running to the left or right edge of the platform when you see the gust coming. In multiplayer mode, the platform can get very crowded. Assign specific tasks to each player to cut down on the confusion.

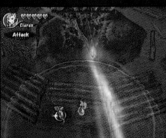

The narrow beam of light the Dragon Zombie emits won't do damage, but it will petrify you. If you get hit, move the Control Stick rapidly from side to side to break free. Be quick—standing in one place is an invitation for the Stone Sahagins to wail on you. If you dodge the attack, you'll have an opportunity to get in close and cast Holy.

The Dragon Zombie will occasionally let out a poison gas that covers almost the entire platform. When it starts spraying the gas, run to the opposite side of the platform and stay as close to the edge as possible.

Dragon Zombie: Cycles Two and Three

The Dragon Zombie in cycles two and three fights with the same routine, but it is much stronger. Fusing Holyra is the most efficient way to damage the boss. You'll face more Stone Sahagins than before—use Gravity and physical attacks to destroy them.

DROPPED ITEM SETS					
		CYCLE 1	CYCLE 2	CYCLE 3	ARTIFACTS
SET 1	1P	More than 0 pts.	—	—	GIANT'S GLOVE
	2P	More than 0 pts.	—	—	GOBLIN POCKET
	3P	More than 0 pts.	—	—	RAT'S TAIL
	4P	More than 0 pts.	—	—	SAGE'S STAFF
SET 2	1P	More than 193 pts.	—	—	FLAMETONGUE
	2P	More than 208 pts.	—	—	GOLD HAIRPIN
	3P	More than 237 pts.	—	—	RING OF CURE
	4P	More than 260 pts.	—	—	TEDDY BEAR
SET 3	1P	More than 240 pts.	More than 0 pts.	—	ICE BRAND
	2P	More than 260 pts.	More than 0 pts.	—	STAR PENDANT
	3P	More than 295 pts.	More than 0 pts.	—	WONDER WAND
	4P	More than 324 pts.	More than 0 pts.	—	WONDER BANGLE
SET 4	1P	More than 301 pts.	More than 193 pts.	—	LOADED DICE
	2P	More than 325 pts.	More than 208 pts.	—	RAT'S TAIL
	3P	More than 370 pts.	More than 237 pts.	—	RING OF CURE
	4P	More than 406 pts.	More than 260 pts.	—	RUNE BELL
SET 5	1P	—	More than 240 pts.	More than 0 pts.	GOLD HAIRPIN
	2P	—	More than 260 pts.	More than 0 pts.	OGREKILLER
	3P	—	More than 295 pts.	More than 0 pts.	STAR PENDANT
	4P	—	More than 324 pts.	More than 0 pts.	TEDDY BEAR
SET 6	1P	—	More than 301 pts.	More than 193 pts.	KRIS
	2P	—	More than 325 pts.	More than 208 pts.	ORICHALCUM
	3P	—	More than 370 pts.	More than 237 pts.	RING OF CURE
	4P	—	More than 406 pts.	More than 260 pts.	SASUKE'S BLADE
SET 7	1P	—	—	More than 240 pts.	DRAGON'S FANG
	2P	—	—	More than 260 pts.	LUNAR WEAPON
	3P	—	—	More than 295 pts.	RED SLIPPERS
	4P	—	—	More than 324 pts.	TWISTED HEADBAND
SET 8	1P	—	—	More than 301 pts.	DIAMOND ARMOR
	2P	—	—	More than 325 pts.	ENGETSURIN
	3P	—	—	More than 370 pts.	RING OF LIFE
	4P	—	—	More than 406 pts.	TOME OF ULTIMA

Scrolls, Materials and Artifacts

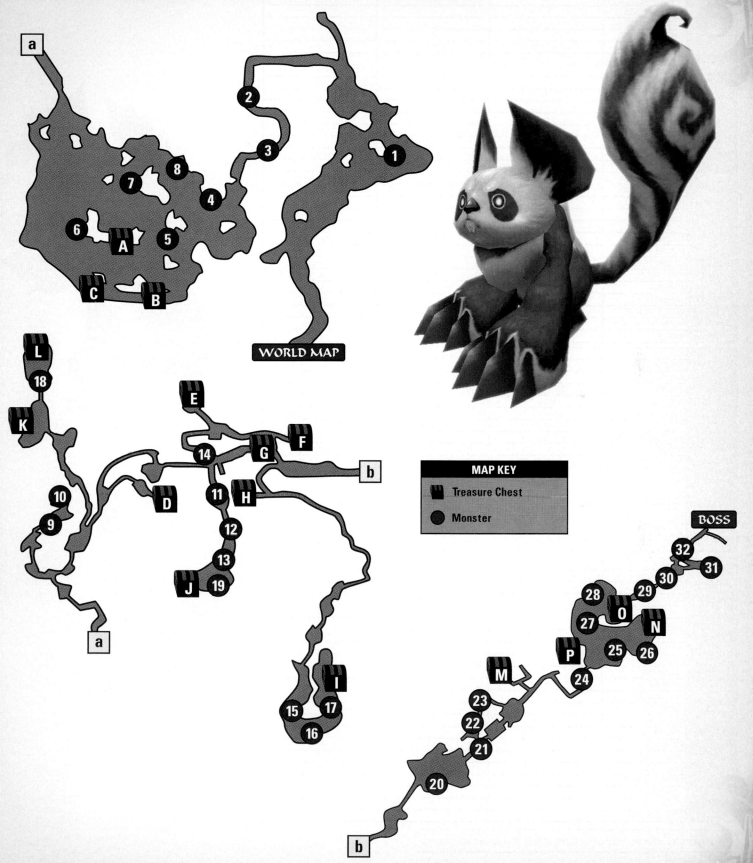

WORLD MAP

MAP KEY

▮ Treasure Chest

● Monster

BOSS

		CYCLE 1	CYCLE 2	CYCLE 3
SCROLLS	DIAMOND ARMOR	–	–	F, K, N
	DIAMOND BELT	–	–	H, O
	DIAMOND GLOVES	–	–	P
	DIAMOND SALLET	–	–	C, O
	DIAMOND SHIELD	–	–	P
	ETERNAL ARMOR	F, K, N	F, K, N	–
	ETERNAL SALLET	–	C	C
	GOLD ARMOR	–	N	N
	GOLD GLOVES	–	G, P	G, P
	HOLY ARMOR	–	F, K	F, K
	HOLY SHIELD	–	B, P	B, P
	LEGENDARY WEAPON	–	–	15, 16, 17, M
	LIGHTNING BELT	H, O	H, O	–
	LIGHTNING GLOVES	G, P	G, P	–
	LIGHTNING SALLET	C, O	C, O	–
	LIGHTNING SHIELD	B	B	–
	MAGIC SHIELD	–	B	B
	MASTER'S WEAPON	A, M	A, M	A
	MIGHTY WEAPON	A, M	A, M	A, M
	MYTHRIL ARMOR	F, K, N	F, K, N	–
	MYTHRIL BELT	H, O	–	–
	MYTHRIL GLOVES	G, P	–	–
	MYTHRIL SALLET	C, O	–	–
	MYTHRIL SHIELD	B, P	–	–
	PURE ARMOR	–	F, K, N	F, K, N
	PURE BELT	–	H, O	H, O
	TIME SALLET	–	C, O	C, O
	VALIANT WEAPON	A, M	A, M	A, M
	VICTORIOUS WEAPON	A, M	A, M	A, M
	WIND BELT	–	H	H
MATERIALS	ALLOY	–	23, 30, 31*	23, 30, 31*
	ANCIENT POTION	–	–	9, 10, 11, 12, 13, 14, 19*
	BLUE SILK	21, 22, 24, 29	21, 22, 24, 29	–
	BRONZE	23, 30, 31*	–	–
	CHILLY GEL	1, 2, 3	1, 2, 3	1, 2, 3
	DIAMOND ORE	–	20, 21, 22, 24, 25, 26, 27, 28, 29, 31*	20, 21, 22, 24, 25, 26, 27, 28, 29, 32
	IRON	23, 30, 31*	23, 30, 31*	–
	JAGGED SCYTHE	15, 16, 17	15, 16, 17	15, 16, 17
	MYTHRIL	–	–	23, 30, 31*
	ORICHALCUM	20, 25, 26, 27, 28	20, 25, 26, 27, 28, 32	20, 25, 26, 27, 28, 32
	PRESSED FLOWER	18	18	18
	REMEDY	18	18	18
	SOUL OF THE DRAGON	–	L	L
	SOUL OF THE LION	L	–	–
	THUNDERBALL	4, 5, 6, 7, 8	4, 5, 6, 7, 8	4, 5, 6, 7, 8
	TOAD OIL	9, 10, 11, 12, 13, 14, 19*	9, 10, 11, 12, 13, 14, 19*	9, 10, 11, 12, 13, 14, 19*
	WHITE SILK	–	–	21, 22, 24, 29
ARTIFACTS (TREASURES)	CANDY RING	E	E	–
	CHICKEN KNIFE	–	–	D
	DARK MATTER	–	–	E
	FAERIE RING	E	–	–
	FLAMETONGUE	–	J	J
	GIANT'S GLOVE	–	–	J
	GREEN BERET	J	J	–
	HEAVY ARMBAND	–	–	J
	KAISER KNUCKLES	J	–	–
	LOADED DICE	J	J	–
	MAGE MASHER	E	–	–
	MAIN GAUCHE	D	D	–
	MANEATER	J	–	–
	MJOLLNIR	–	J	J
	NOAH'S LUTE	–	E	E
	RED SLIPPERS	E	E	–
	RING OF CURE	I	I	I
	SAGE'S STAFF	–	E	E
	SPARKLING BRACER	D	–	–
	STAR PENDANT	I	I	I
	TEDDY BEAR	–	D	D
	TOME OF ULTIMA	–	–	E

*The monster emerges only when three or four characters are playing.

Rebena Te Ra

An ancient relic of days long past, Rebena Te Ra is a confusing labyrinth of puzzles and monsters. It is especially difficult in single-player mode.

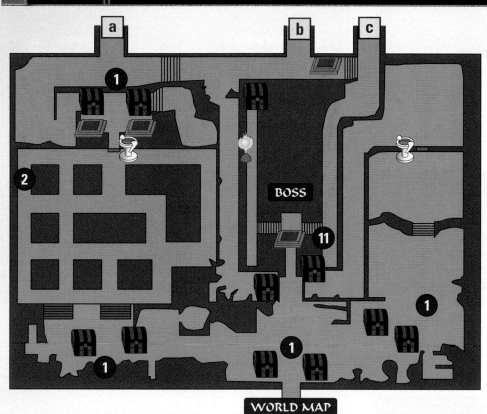

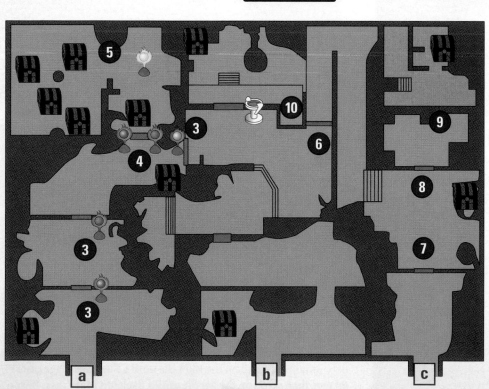

MONSTERS		
Cerberus Cycles: All	PG. 123	
Gargoyle Cycles: All	PG. 124	
Ghost Cycles: All	PG. 124	
Nightmare Cycles: All	PG. 127	
Skeleton Cycles: All	PG. 128	
Skeleton (Mace) Cycles: All	PG. 128	
Skeleton (Spear) Cycles: 2 & 3	PG. 129	
Skeleton Mage (Rebena Te Ra) Cycles: All	PG. 129	
Skeleton Mage (Fire) Cycles: All	PG. 129	
Skeleton Mage (Ice) Cycles: All	PG. 129	
Skeleton Mage (Lightning) Cycles: All	PG. 129	
Vampire Bat Cycles: All	PG. 130	
Wraith Cycles: All	PG. 130	

MAP KEY	
	Treasure Chest
	Switch
	Key Pedestal
	Magic Switch (Blizzard)
	Magic Switch (Fire)
	Magic Switch (Thunder)
	Magic Switch (Any)

❶ The Mimic Gimmick

If you see treasure chests in pairs, one is probably a Mimic in disguise. Cast any spell on the treasure chests—the sharp clanking sound a monster makes when resisting an attack will give away the Mimic. Take it out using physical attacks.

❷ Bat Droppings

Bats are small but feisty. Defeat the bat at point 2 to make it drop a key. Rather than use the key on the nearest door, take it all the way around to the other side of the map. Use it on the easternmost door to unlock a new area and collect an artifact.

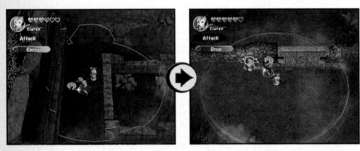

Using the key on the easternmost door is the only way to access the new area. Once inside, you'll find an artifact and another key that you'll need to take back to the westernmost door.

❸ Spells and Switches

The only way to open some doors in Rebena Te Ra is by using magic. Cast Fire, Thunder or Blizzard on the device next to the door. (Which spell you cast depends on the device's color.) Once the device stops glowing, hit it with a physical attack to open the door.

❹ Hang in There, Kupo!

The puzzle at point 4 is easy in multiplayer mode but quite a chore in single-player mode. Both switches must be activated simultaneously to open the door. In single-player mode, you'll need to cast either Fire or Blizzard and hope that your Moogle casts the other. If you position yourself correctly, the Gargoyle on the other side of the door will attack you. Take damage until your Moogle says "Hang in there, Kupo!" Have your Moogle drop the chalice, then charge up a Blizzard spell over the Fire switch. Hold it until your Moogle casts Fire. Quickly move your cursor to the other switch and cast the Blizzard spell. Change to your physical attack and hit both switches before time runs out.

Easy as Pie

You'll have no problem solving the puzzle at point 4 in multiplayer mode. One player must cast Fire while another player casts Blizzard on the corresponding switches. Afterward, change to a physical attack and hit the switches.

❺ More Mimics

The next switch is on the other side of a barrier. Cast a spell (any spell will do) on the switch to open the barrier. You'll find four treasure chests, three of which are Mimics. The real chest holds a very valuable item.

❻ In Harm's Way

Some doors in Rebena Te Ra will open only if you take Fire, Thunder or Blizzard damage while you're standing on a corresponding tile. If you are equipped with items or armor that are resistant to the spell being cast, the door won't open.

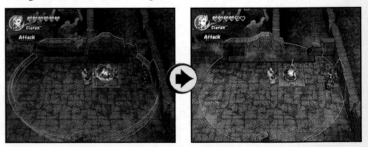

Unequip any items or armor that are resistant to the spell the Skeleton Mage is casting on you. If you destroy the Skeleton Mage before opening the door, don't panic—it will respawn eventually.

❼ Fire and Ice

Taking damage is the name of the game in Rebena Te Ra. To open the door at point 7, stand on the right tile until a Skeleton Mage casts Fire on you, then stand on the left tile until a Skeleton Mage casts Blizzard.

⑧ Four Square

A multitalented Skeleton Mage will show up at point 8. Unequip items or armor resistant to spells, then stand on each tile and take damage until the door opens. Have a Cure spell handy and keep a close eye on your health.

⑨ Trigger Happy

Take out the surrounding monsters before attempting the puzzle at point 9. There are four pairs of switches. One switch in a pair sends a section of the wall up, and the other sends it down. Getting to the other side of the wall is easy, but to reach the key, you'll need to use the Crystal Chalice to trigger a switch.

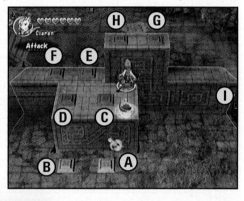

Step on B to move the first section of wall down. Jump on with the chalice and step on C to send the wall back up. Trigger E to bring down the next section of wall. Step on the wall and drop the chalice on G to make the wall rise again. Step off the wall quickly before it rises.

From this point on, you must move fast to complete the puzzle successfully. Step on E then immediately step on D to lower the first section. As soon as you're back on the ground, run to the other section of wall and stand on it before the chalice triggers it to move back up.

You'll need to venture out into the Miasma to collect the key. If you pick up the key, you'll drop it when the Miasma damages you. Instead of picking it up, push it around the wall until you're back within the chalice's safety zone. Pick up the key and jump off the wall at the spot marked "I" on the map. Use the switches to get back on the wall and retrieve the chalice.

Four's a Crowd

Multiplayer mode is a blast, but things can get a little crazy when four people are trying to solve the same puzzle. Assign specific roles—have one player activate the switches while another collects the key. A third player can hold the chalice to make the key-collector's job easier.

⑩ Stamp Collecting

Take your hard-earned key to the final locked door, at point 10 on the map. It will open a small area where you'll find an artifact and a Moogle Nest. Use the opportunity to paint your Moogle and add to your growing stamp collection.

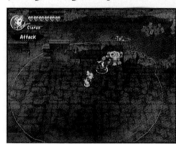

⑪ One Final Task

Head east then down to the passage marked "C" on the map. From there you can access the top of the pyramid. Step on the switch to open the door below that leads to the final boss. On the other side of the pyramid, use magic to trigger one last switch that opens another barrier below. Open the remaining treasure chests, then head back to the beginning of the level and into the pyramid.

Lich

Lich is surrounded by a protective sphere. To remove it, cast magic on the switches on the left and right sides of the room. To make Lich vulnerable, cast Holy on it immediately after triggering the switches. Continue casting Holy to damage Lich, or use physical attacks if your Strength is high.

RESISTANCE	
FIRE	3
BLIZZARD	3
THUNDER	3
SLOW	3
STOP	3
GRAVITY	0
HOLY	0

Lich's meteorite attack is difficult to avoid and deals great damage. The probability that Lich will cast the spell is higher when you are closer to it. Stay out of close range until you are ready to launch an attack.

If you see a black sphere forming, get out of the way. It will take Lich a while to cast, so use the lull as an opportunity to charge up a spell and attack. Gravity will deal a great amount of damage, but it will work only once.

Lich's Thunder spell has a massive range and will paralyze you. When you see it coming, run to the other side of the room. Equipping Thunder-resistant accessories like Badge of the Thunderbolt will prove helpful.

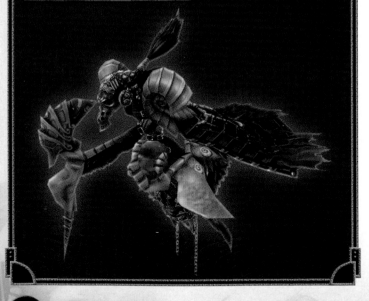

Lich: Cycles Two and Three

In cycles two and three, Lich will launch a ground-shaking attack that won't damage you but will knock you down. Render Lich vulnerable the same way you did in cycle one, then launch an assault using Holy or physical attacks.

		DROPPED ITEM SETS			
		CYCLE 1	**CYCLE 2**	**CYCLE 3**	**ARTIFACTS**
SET 1	1P	More than 0 pts.	—	—	MAIN GAUCHE
	2P	More than 0 pts.	—	—	MJOLLNIR
	3P	More than 0 pts.	—	—	SAGE'S STAFF
	4P	More than 0 pts.	—	—	STAR PENDANT
SET 2	1P	More than 149 pts.	—	—	BLACK HOOD
	2P	More than 160 pts.	—	—	FLAMETONGUE
	3P	More than 182 pts.	—	—	GOBLIN POCKET
	4P	More than 200 pts.	—	—	MAGE'S STAFF
SET 3	1P	More than 186 pts.	More than 0 pts.	—	CHICKEN KNIFE
	2P	More than 200 pts.	More than 0 pts.	—	ICE BRAND
	3P	More than 228 pts.	More than 0 pts.	—	STAR PENDANT
	4P	More than 250 pts.	More than 0 pts.	—	WONDER WAND
SET 4	1P	More than 232 pts.	More than 149 pts.	—	GOBLIN POCKET
	2P	More than 250 pts.	More than 160 pts.	—	HELM OF ARAI
	3P	More than 284 pts.	More than 182 pts.	—	LOADED DICE
	4P	More than 312 pts.	More than 200 pts.	—	RUNE BELL
SET 5	1P	—	More than 186 pts.	More than 0 pts.	ELVEN MANTLE
	2P	—	More than 200 pts.	More than 0 pts.	KRIS
	3P	—	More than 228 pts.	More than 0 pts.	MASQUERADE
	4P	—	More than 250 pts.	More than 0 pts.	STAR PENDANT
SET 6	1P	—	More than 232 pts.	More than 149 pts.	GOBLIN POCKET
	2P	—	More than 250 pts.	More than 160 pts.	NOAH'S LUTE
	3P	—	More than 284 pts.	More than 182 pts.	OGREKILLER
	4P	—	More than 312 pts.	More than 200 pts.	ORICHALCUM
SET 7	1P	—	—	More than 186 pts.	DARK WEAPON
	2P	—	—	More than 200 pts.	ENGETSURIN
	3P	—	—	More than 228 pts.	ETHEREAL ORB
	4P	—	—	More than 250 pts.	RED SLIPPERS
SET 8	1P	—	—	More than 232 pts.	DRILL
	2P	—	—	More than 250 pts.	FORBIDDEN TOME
	3P	—	—	More than 284 pts.	RIBBON
	4P	—	—	More than 312 pts.	TWISTED HEADBAND

Scrolls, Materials, and Artifacts

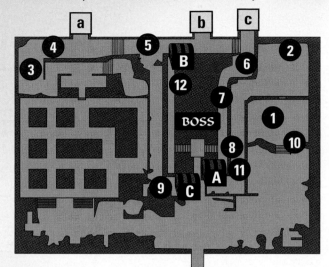

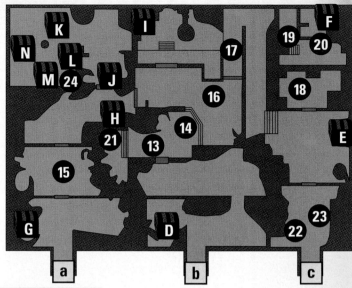

WORLD MAP

MAP KEY

🗄	Treasure Chest
⚫	Monster

		CYCLE 1	CYCLE 2	CYCLE 3
SCROLLS	BLUE YARN	B, D, G	B, D, G	B, D, G
	DIAMOND ARMOR	—	—	F, K, L, M, N
	ETERNAL SALLET	F	F	—
	GOLD GLOVES	F	F	—
	HOLY ARMOR	—	F, K, L, M, N	F, K, L, M, N
	HOLY SHIELD	K, L, M, N	K, L, M, N	—
	PURE ARMOR	—	F, K, L, M, N	F, K, L, M, N
	PURE BELT	K, L, M, N	K, L, M, N	—
	TOME OF MAGIC	C, E	C, E	C, E
	TOME OF SORCERY	—	—	C, E
	WHITE YARN	B, D, G	B, D, G	B, D, G
MATERIALS	ALLOY	—	3, 9	3, 9
	ANCIENT POTION	—	—	B, D, G
	BLUE SILK	7, 8, 10*	7, 8, 10*	—
	CERBERUS'S FANG	2, 13, 16, 21	2, 13, 16, 21	2, 13, 16, 21
	DEVIL'S CLAW	—	—	1, 4, 5, 6
	DIAMOND ORE	—	7, 8, 10*, 14, 15, 17, 19, 20, 24	3, 7, 8, 9, 10*, 14, 15, 17, 19, 20, 24
	FIEND'S CLAW	1, 4, 5, 6	1, 4, 5, 6	—
	GEAR	18, 22, 23	11, 12, 22, 23	11, 12, 22, 23
	HEAVENLY DUST	14, 15, 17, 19, 20, 24	14, 15, 17, 19, 20, 24	14, 15, 17, 19, 20, 24
	HOLY WATER	14, 15, 17, 19, 20, 24	14, 15, 17, 19, 20, 24	14, 15, 17, 19, 20, 24
	MYTHRIL	—	1, 2, 4, 5, 6, 13, 16, 21	1, 2, 4, 5, 6, 13, 16, 21
	TINY CRYSTAL	3, 9	3, 9	—
	WHITE SILK	—	—	7, 8, 10*
ARTIFACTS (TREASURES)	CAT'S BELL	—	J	J
	CHICKEN KNIFE	—	—	I
	ELVEN MANTLE	I	I	—
	ENGETSURIN	-	A	A
	FANG CHARM	A	A	—
	GIANT'S GLOVE	—	—	A
	GOBLIN POCKET	H	H	H
	GOLD HAIRPIN	—	—	J
	HEAVY ARMBAND	—	A	A
	ICE BRAND	A	A	—
	MAGE MASHER	—	J	J
	MAGE STAFF	—	—	J
	ONION SWORD	—	—	A
	POWER WRISTBAND	A	—	—
	RUNE BELL	J	J	—
	RUNE STAFF	J	—	—
	SHURIKEN	A	—	—
	SILVER BRACER	J	—	—
	SILVER SPECTACLES	I	—	—
	STAR PENDANT	H	H	H
	TEDDY BEAR	—	I	I
	WINGED CAP	J	J	—

*The monster emerges only when three or four characters are playing.

Lynari Isle

Lynari Isle consists of Lynari Desert and the Selkie village of Leuda. When the Jegon River dries up, you can visit the isle from Port Tipa.

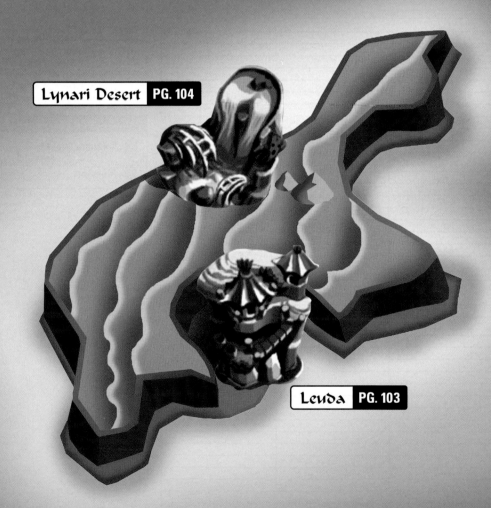

Lynari Desert PG. 104

Leuda PG. 103

Leuda

Leuda is home to the nomadic Selkies. The quaint port town offers two shops and a unique jumping game for fellow Selkies.

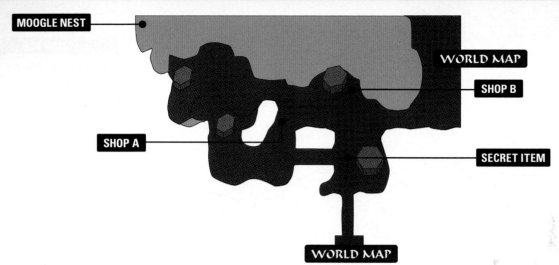

- MOOGLE NEST
- WORLD MAP
- SHOP B
- SHOP A
- SECRET ITEM
- WORLD MAP

Watch Your Wallet

Each time you speak to one of Leuda's residents, the scamp will pick your pockets. Though each person pilfers 10 gil or less, it adds up. Even thieves can be compassionate, however—if you're a fellow Selkie or have less than 100 gil, they won't steal from you.

Selkie Jumping Game

Selkie children take pride in their jumping skills. If your character is a Selkie, you can play a fun jumping minigame in Leuda. Speak to the Selkie boy near the net in the center of town to start playing. Listen to the child's instructions and press the buttons at the right time to score points. Use the Control Pad to roll left and right while you jump to earn double points. You can win the prizes displayed below.

SHOP A	
BRONZE	300
IRON	500
MYTHRIL	5,000
CRYSTAL BALL	100
RUBY	200
JADE	200
ALLOY	250

SHOP B	
VALIANT WEAPON	500
MIGHTY WEAPON	500
VICTORIOUS WEAPON	500
MYTHRIL ARMOR	300
MYTHRIL SHIELD	250
MYTHRIL GLOVES	250
MYTHRIL SALLET	250
MYTHRIL BELT	250

A Nest with a View

A lone Moogle lives by the ocean in a secluded corner of Leuda. Walk to the pink tent in Leuda's upper-left corner, then slip behind the tent to find a door in the rock face. Examine the door to discover the Moogle Nest. Don't forget to get your stamp!

Port Travel

If you visit Lynari Isle via Port Tipa when the Jegon River is dried up, your only other possible destination will be Mount Kilanda. When the Jegon River is flowing normally, you can also visit Jegon River (East) and Jegon River (West) from Leuda.

COMMAND	POINTS
A OR B	1 POINT
A, A OR B, B	2 POINTS
A, B OR B, A	3 POINTS
A, A, B OR B, B, A	4 POINTS
A, B, B, A OR B, A, A, B	5 POINTS
A, B, A, B, A OR B, A, B, A, B	6 POINTS

POINTS	PRIZE
More than 500 points	BRONZE
More than 1,000 points	IRON
More than 2,000 points	MYTHRIL
More than 4,000 points	ORICHALCUM

DESTINATION	FARE
Jegon River (East)	300
Jegon River (West)	300
Mount Kilanda	500
Port Tipa	300

Lynari Desert

Cut Mog's hair, because you're headed for the hottest spot in town.
Status ailments are legion here, especially poison and petrification.

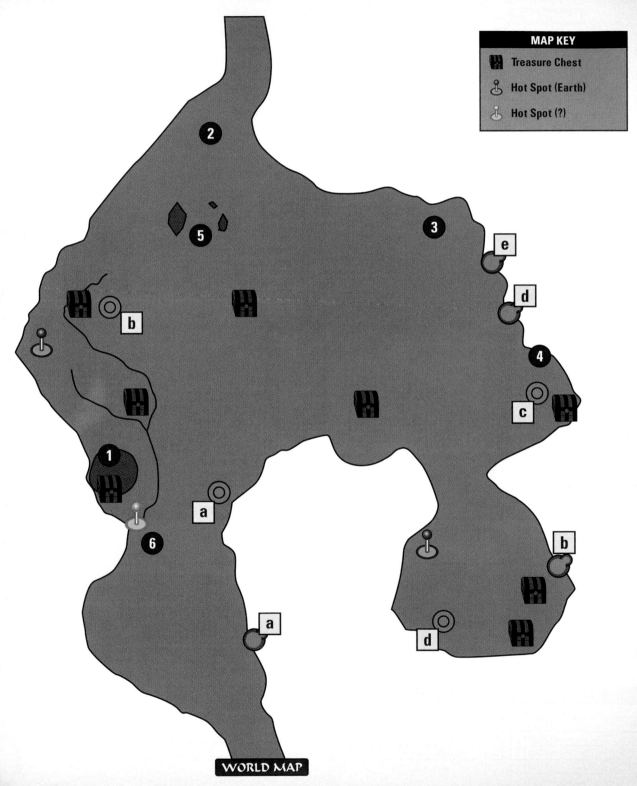

MAP KEY

🗃 Treasure Chest

⚲ Hot Spot (Earth)

⚲ Hot Spot (?)

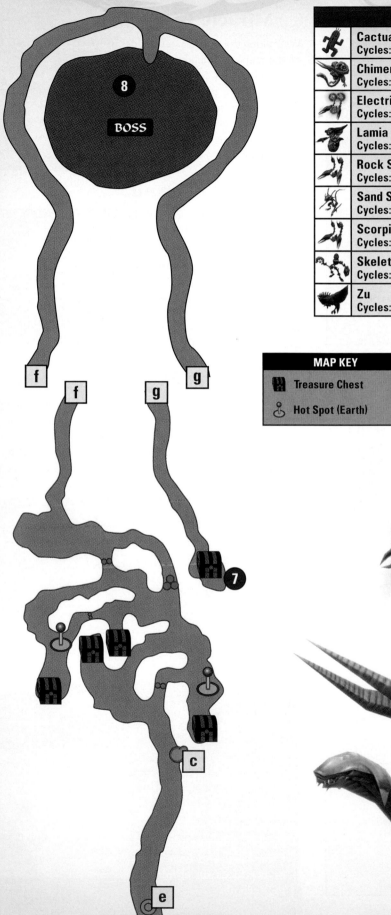

MONSTERS		
Cactuar Cycles: All	PG. 123	
Chimera Cycles: All	PG. 123	
Electric Scorpion Cycles: 2 & 3	PG. 124	
Lamia Cycles: All	PG. 125	
Rock Scorpion Cycles: 2 & 3	PG. 128	
Sand Sahagin Cycles: All	PG. 128	
Scorpion Cycles: All	PG. 128	
Skeleton Mage Cycles: 2 & 3	PG. 129	
Zu Cycles: All	PG. 130	

MAP KEY	
Treasure Chest	
Hot Spot (Earth)	

1 Hidden Treasure

The Moogle Nest is on the far western side of the desert, inside a small cave. You'll have to open a treasure chest to clear the way. If you want the chest's contents, make sure you press the B Button when the Pick Up icon appears, not the Examine icon.

2 The Quest Begins

While in the desert, you can gain access to a mystery element that will allow you to pass through all Miasma Streams. To do so, you must follow tips 2 through 6 in order. For starters, go to the large cactus at the north end of the map and cast Thunder on it.

3 High-Gravity Camping

For the second part of the quest, you need to cast Gravity on an abandoned tent in the northeast portion of the map. Note that for all of the quest-requirement spells, you can use magic from the same family (Gravara on the tent, for example).

4 A Tasty Grilled Mushroom

Walk to the far eastern edge of the desert and look for a mushroom-shaped rock on top of a small dune. When you find the rock, cast Fire on it. The rock is tough to reach—you may have better luck hitting it with Fira or Firaga.

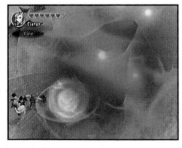

5 A Cast of Three

After you flame one rock, it's time to freeze three. Head back across the desert until you're just south of the large cactus from tip 2, and look for three rocks standing close to each other. Hit them with Blizzard, moving from the smallest rock to the biggest.

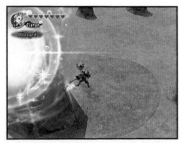

6 Miracle Grow

Walk along the southeastern edge of the map—don't take the path that leads to the Moogle Nest—and look for a pale pink flower. Cast Holy on the plant to turn it into a Hot Spot. When you place the chalice there, it will be infused with the unknown element.

7 Burial Ground

To reach the second section of the desert, jump into the sandpit marked with a "C." Once you do, head up and left until you find a small cactus. Hit the plant to get a Cactus Flower, which you can give to the ferryman. It doesn't always work—you may have to come back to the level a couple of times.

8 Scorpion Minions

The desert boss is a smart cookie—it has a number of small monster lackeys that attack anyone foolish enough to enter its lair. When you go into the boss area, you will face three waves of various scorpions. Each time you beat a wave, the level of the sand will drop, revealing more and more of a cave. When you eliminate all three waves, the boss will emerge and take you on.

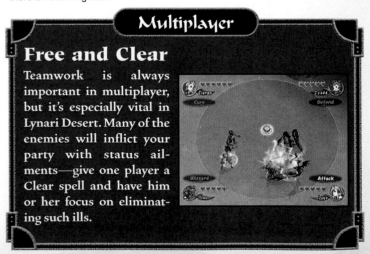

You can leave the boss lair during any of the scorpion fights, so if you're getting whupped, feel free to retreat and regroup. Once you beat the final wave, however, there is no turning back.

Multiplayer

Free and Clear

Teamwork is always important in multiplayer, but it's especially vital in Lynari Desert. Many of the enemies will inflict your party with status ailments—give one player a Clear spell and have him or her focus on eliminating such ills.

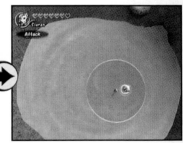

Antlion

The Antlion is a huge bug that's partially buried. Because of its size and the tiny confines of its lair, you'll be forced to engage it from very close range. Hit it once with Gravity and once with Holy, then go to work with Blizzara or Blizzaga.

RESISTANCE	
FIRE	2
BLIZZARD	2
THUNDER	3
SLOW	3
STOP	3
GRAVITY	1
HOLY	0

Do everything you can to avoid the front of the Antlion. If you stand there, it will attack you with its huge mandible. You're also more likely to get hit by breath attacks that can petrify and poison you.

The key to fighting the Antlion is to keep moving in a circle. Run around the beast until it stops to cast a breath attack, then move slightly to the side and attack. A strong magic user can use ice-based spells to wear it down quickly, while melee fighters are in for a bit of a struggle.

If you can get behind the Antlion, that's even better—it's too large to turn around quickly. When the beast is almost done for, it will begin attacking with its legs and fire a huge laser from its mouth. Keep running in circles and attack only when it strikes at you and misses. If you cast Blizzaga, start moving as soon as the ice crystals begin to form—don't stand around watching, or you'll be hit.

Antlion: Cycles Two and Three

The second and third cycles are very similar to the first, except that the Antlion gets a little stronger and faster on each one. If you're having trouble in later cycles, try to find a Blizzard Ring and boost your magic before fighting it.

DROPPED ITEM SETS					
		CYCLE 1	CYCLE 2	CYCLE 3	ARTIFACTS
SET 1	1P	More than 0 pts.	—	—	MAIN GAUCHE
	2P	More than 0 pts.	—	—	MASQUERADE
	3P	More than 0 pts.	—	—	STAR PENDANT
	4P	More than 0 pts.	—	—	SAGE'S STAFF
SET 2	1P	More than 144 pts.	—	—	BLACK HOOD
	2P	More than 156 pts.	—	—	FLAMETONGUE
	3P	More than 177 pts.	—	—	GOBLIN POCKET
	4P	More than 194 pts.	—	—	NOAH'S LUTE
SET 3	1P	More than 180 pts.	More than 0 pts.	—	CHICKEN KNIFE
	2P	More than 195 pts.	More than 0 pts.	—	GOBLIN POCKET
	3P	More than 221 pts.	More than 0 pts.	—	ICE BRAND
	4P	More than 243 pts.	More than 0 pts.	—	WONDER WAND
SET 4	1P	More than 226 pts.	More than 144 pts.	—	HEAVY ARMBAND
	2P	More than 224 pts.	More than 156 pts.	—	HELM OF ARAI
	3P	More than 277 pts.	More than 177 pts.	—	RUNE BELL
	4P	More than 304 pts.	More than 194 pts.	—	STAR PENDANT
SET 5	1P	—	More than 180 pts.	More than 0 pts.	DARK MATTER
	2P	—	More than 195 pts.	More than 0 pts.	ELVEN MANTLE
	3P	—	More than 221 pts.	More than 0 pts.	HERO'S WEAPON
	4P	—	More than 243 pts.	More than 0 pts.	LOADED DICE
SET 6	1P	—	More than 226 pts.	More than 144 pts.	KRIS
	2P	—	More than 244 pts.	More than 156 pts.	OGREKILLER
	3P	—	More than 277 pts.	More than 177 pts.	ORICHALCUM
	4P	—	More than 304 pts.	More than 194 pts.	WONDER BANGLE
SET 7	1P	—	—	More than 180 pts.	DESERT FANG
	2P	—	—	More than 195 pts.	ENGETSURIN
	3P	—	—	More than 221 pts.	GOBLIN POCKET
	4P	—	—	More than 243 pts.	RED SLIPPERS
SET 8	1P	—	—	More than 226 pts.	DIAMOND ARMOR
	2P	—	—	More than 244 pts.	SUN PENDANT
	3P	—	—	More than 277 pts.	TOME OF ULTIMA
	4P	—	—	More than 304 pts.	TWISTED HEADBAND

Scrolls, Materials and Artifacts

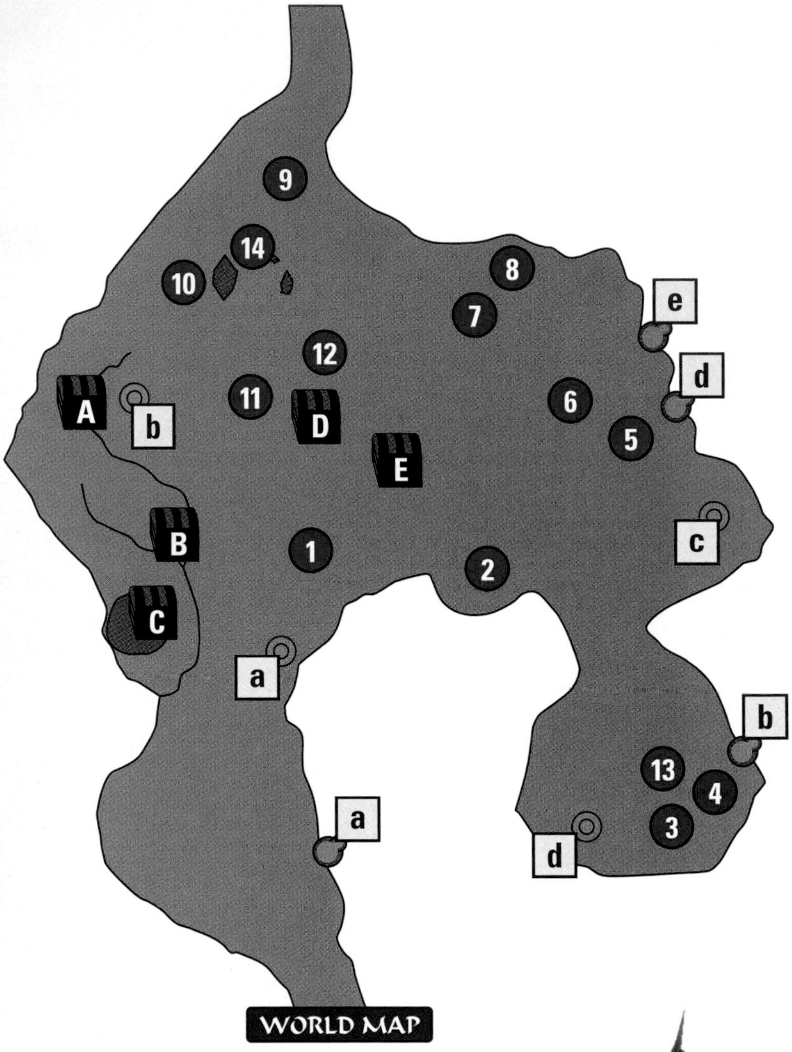

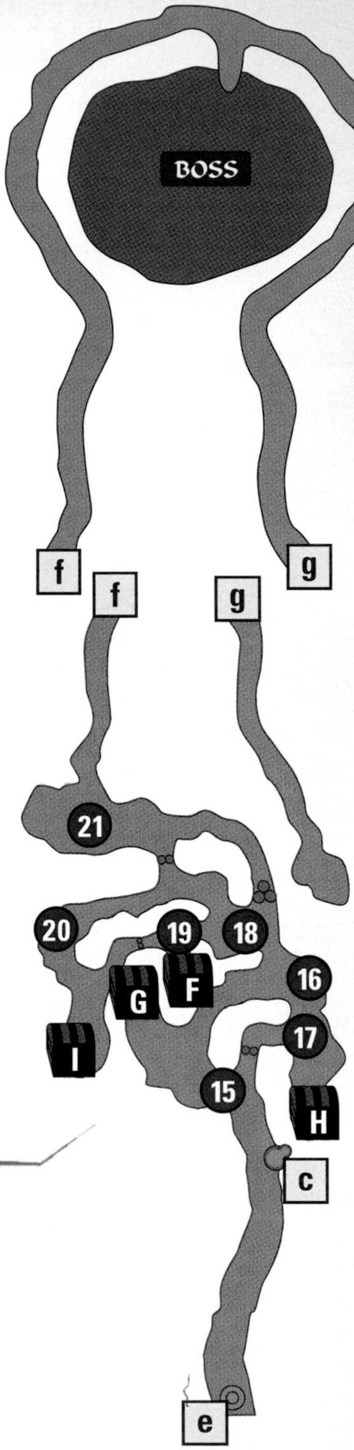

WORLD MAP

BOSS

MAP KEY

▮ Treasure Chest

● Monster

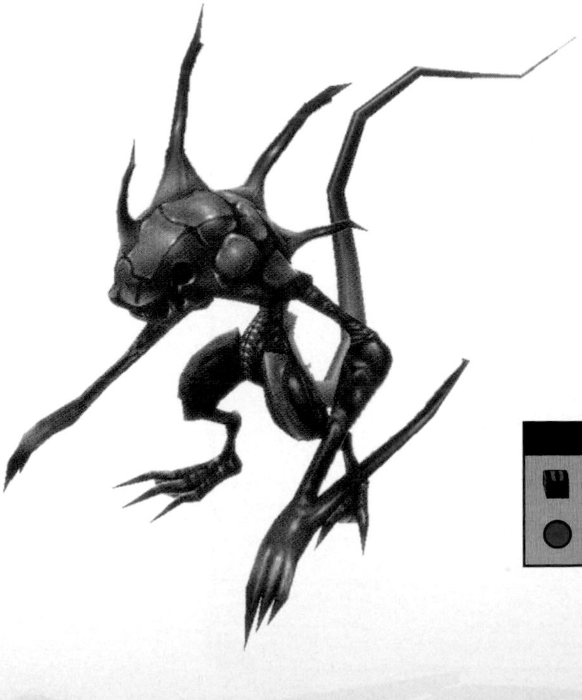

		CYCLE 1	CYCLE 2	CYCLE 3
SCROLLS	CLOCKWORK	E	E	E
	DESIGNER GOGGLES	–	–	G
	DIAMOND ARMOR	–	–	B
	ETERNAL ARMOR	B	B	–
	FLAME CRAFT	D	D	D
	FROST CRAFT	D	D	D
	GOGGLE TECHNIQUES	G	G	G
	GOLD ARMOR	–	B	B
	GOLD CRAFT	E	E	E
	LEGENDARY WEAPON	–	–	15, 18, 20, 21, A
	LIGHTNING CRAFT	D	D	D
	MASTER'S WEAPON	A	A	–
	MIGHTY WEAPON	A	A	A
	MYTHRIL ARMOR	B	B	–
	NEW CLOCKWORK	E	E	E
	PURE ARMOR	–	B	B
	RADIANT ARMOR	–	–	I
	VALIANT WEAPON	A	A	A
	VICTORIOUS WEAPON	A	A	A
MATERIALS	ALLOY	3, 9	3, 9	3, 9
	CHIMERA'S HORN	15, 18, 20, 21	15, 18, 20, 21	15, 18, 20, 21
	DIAMOND ORE	–	–	3, 9
	NEEDLE	7, 12, 16, 17, 19	7, 12, 16, 17, 19	7, 12, 16, 17, 19
	ORICHALCUM	–	–	1, 2, 4, 5, 6, 8, 10, 11
	THUNDERBALL	–	13*	13*, 14
	ZU'S BEAK	1, 2, 4, 5, 6, 8, 10, 11	1, 2, 4, 5, 6, 8, 10, 11	1, 2, 4, 5, 6, 8, 10, 11
ARTIFACTS (TREASURES)	ASHURA	F	–	–
	BOOK OF LIGHT	H	–	–
	DARK MATTER	–	H	H
	DOUBLE AXE	F	F	–
	DRAGON'S WHISKER	H	–	–
	DRILL	I	–	–
	FANG CHARM	F	–	–
	GIANT'S GLOVE	–	–	F
	GOBLIN POCKET	C	C	C
	GOLD HAIRPIN	–	–	H
	HELM OF ARAI	I	I	–
	ICE BRAND	–	F	F
	LOADED DICE	F	F	–
	MAGE'S STAFF	–	H	H
	MASQUERADE	–	–	F
	OGREKILLER	–	F	F
	SILVER BRACER	H	H	–
	STAR PENDANT	C	C	C
	TEDDY BEAR	–	I	I
	TOME OF ULTIMA	–	–	H
	WONDER BANGLE	–	–	I
	WONDER WAND	H	H	–

*The monster emerges only when three or four characters are playing.

The Abyss

Your toughest battle begins at the end of the world. The Abyss is the source of Miasma and the place where you make your final stand.

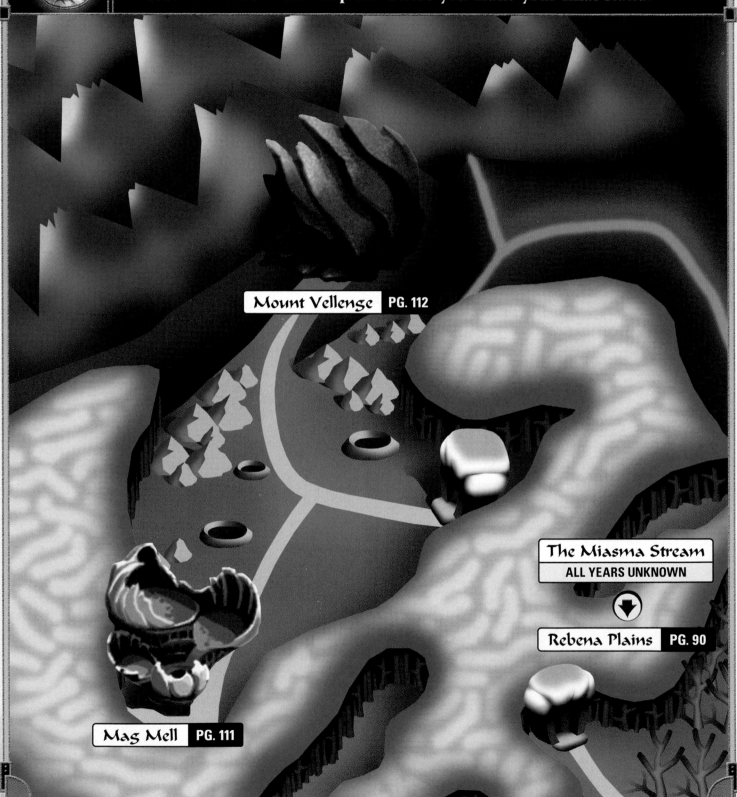

Mount Vellenge PG. 112

The Miasma Stream
ALL YEARS UNKNOWN

Rebena Plains PG. 90

Mag Mell PG. 111

Mag Mell

Rumors of a sleepy town called Mag Mell have been floated for generations. Tread lightly—you're the first visitor in a long, long time.

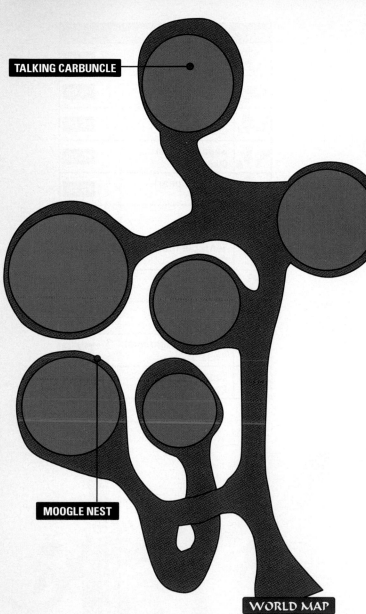

TALKING CARBUNCLE

MOOGLE NEST

WORLD MAP

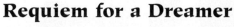

Requiem for a Dreamer

When you go through the mysterious Miasma Stream (you will need to complete the Lynari Desert event to do so—see page 104), you will see a large green creature known as a Carbuncle. In Mag Mell, you can find many of the critters asleep inside cocoons.

Nesting Comfortably

The Moogle Nest is well hidden in the tall grass and dense fog of Mag Mell. When you enter the area, take the first left then the first right. Walk to the back side of the large, round Carbuncle cocoon and examine the wall for an opening.

One Carbuncle is only pretending to sleep. On your first visit he will just make snoring noises, but if you return the next year he'll start to talk. Visit for six years in a row to hear everything he has to say.

Final Fantasy: Crystal Chronicles **111**

Mount Vellenge

The boss of Mount Vellenge is also the game's final boss—so you won't take artifacts or Myrrh away from the battle. Plan carefully!

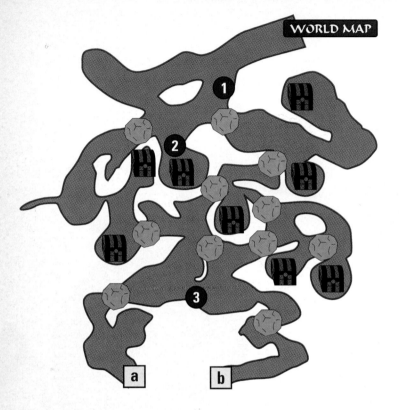

WORLD MAP

1
2
3
a
b

MONSTERS		
	Chimera Cycle: 1	PG. 123
	Death Knight Cycle: 1	PG. 123
	Shade Cycle: 1	PG. 128
	Shade (Mace) Cycle: 1	PG. 128
	Shade (Spear) Cycle: 1	PG. 129
	Sphere Cycle: 1	PG. 129
	Tentacle (Dark) Cycle: 1	PG. 130
	Tentacle (Fire) Cycle: 1	PG. 130
	Tentacle (Ice) Cycle: 1	PG. 130
	Tentacle (Lightning) Cycle: 1	PG. 130
	Tonberry Cycle: 1	PG. 130

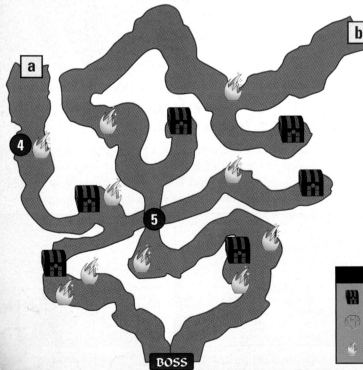

a
b
4
5
BOSS

MAP KEY	
	Treasure Chest
	Rock
	Dark Crystal

1 Batter the Rock

Many of the paths in Mount Vellenge are blocked with large boulders. To clear the way, smash the boulders six times with your weapon. The rocks are immune to magic, so you'll need to strike them with melee attacks.

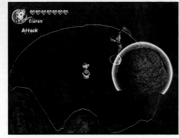

2 The Picky Shopper

Every treasure chest contains an artifact—which means there are more than you can hold. Before you pick up an artifact, check the map and chart on page 115 to see what it could be. You won't keep any of them permanently, but you will reap their benefits for the duration of the dungeon.

3 Two Roads Diverge

Mount Vellenge is divided into two areas, and there are two paths to the second area. When you reach a fork in the road, take the left-hand path—it's the only way to reach the Moogle Nest.

4 In the Age of Wonder

The second area of the dungeon contains a handful of dark crystals that will nullify the effect of the Crystal Chalice if you get too close. The crystals glow with purple light and are usually guarded by powerful monsters.

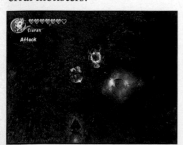

Like the rocks, the dark crystals can be damaged only with melee weapons. If you have a long-distance Focus Attack, use it so the chalice doesn't conk out on you. Otherwise, get in and hit it quickly.

Multiplayer

Breaking the Crystals

The dark crystals won't break any faster if multiple people attack them—it will take six hits from the same player to bring one down. To that end, have one character attack the crystal while the others fend off monsters or heal the damage caused by incoming Miasma.

5 Lowered Property Values

Who knew that a cute Moogle would take up residence in such a dank, evil place? To find the furry homesteader, go to the place where roads converge in the second section of the dungeon, then look for a hole in the wall under a stone overpass.

Meteor Parasite

The Meteor Parasite is the source of Miasma. Once you cause enough damage, it will change its form. Don't get in close or you'll be sliced to ribbons—stay as far away as you can and strike it with Focus Attacks or magic spells. You'll want to have Fire, Blizzard and Thunder spells set in your inventory, as well as Cure and Clear spells (if you have the room). The fight is easier with magic than with weapons, but use whatever gives your character an advantage.

RESISTANCE	
FIRE	2
BLIZZARD	2
THUNDER	2
SLOW	3
STOP	3
GRAVITY	3
HOLY	3

The First Form

Tentacles will spring up on either side of the parasite—take them out, then worry about the main body. Attack the tentacles with their opposite element (Blizzard for Fire Tentacles and so on), or use a strong weapon and a few good hits. Some of the tentacles will poison you, so have the Clear spell ready.

To attack the Meteor Parasite directly, you must strike its vulnerable point—the long, slender part that emerges from its core. Wait for the parasite to strike and miss, then move in and counterattack. It doesn't have any real weaknesses, so you can use your weapon or your most powerful spell.

The Second Form

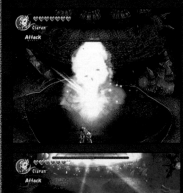

In its second form, the parasite will cast magic spells that cause a lot of damage. Look for a pink circle to appear on the ground—when it does, you'll have about two seconds to get out of the way before the ground explodes. When you're not avoiding attacks, take out the tentacles and strike at the vulnerable spot sticking out of the core.

The parasite's second attack is a laser beam that sweeps across the entire screen. The boss will fire the beam only when the vulnerable point is hidden from view. To avoid the laser, move as close as you can to the parasite or stand at the very edge of the screen.

The Third Form

The parasite will continue to cast the magic spell with the pink targeting circle. The spell can reach you anywhere on-screen, so your only hope is to run away. If you're attacking with magic in a single-player game, don't use three spells linked together—it takes too much time to cast.

The beast's final move is an attack that fires a hail of blue bullets wildly across the screen. One bullet won't do a whole lot, but if three or more hit you at the same time, you'll be in a bad way. Stand near the edge of the screen to avoid the barrage.

Artifacts (No Scrolls or Materials)

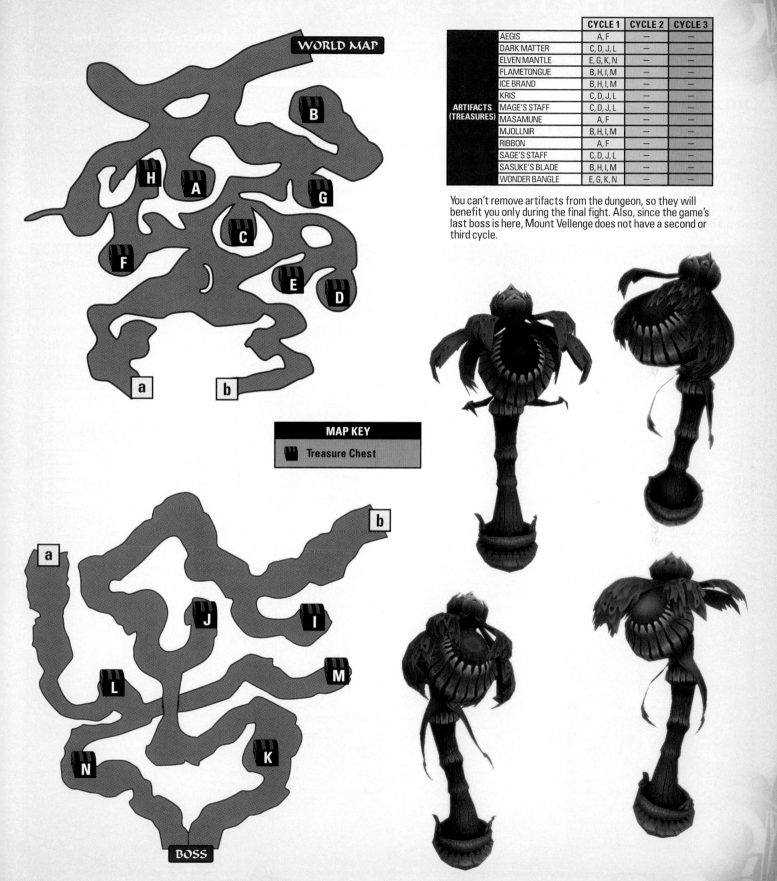

		CYCLE 1	CYCLE 2	CYCLE 3
ARTIFACTS (TREASURES)	AEGIS	A, F	–	–
	DARK MATTER	C, D, J, L	–	–
	ELVEN MANTLE	E, G, K, N	–	–
	FLAMETONGUE	B, H, I, M	–	–
	ICE BRAND	B, H, I, M	–	–
	KRIS	C, D, J, L	–	–
	MAGE'S STAFF	C, D, J, L	–	–
	MASAMUNE	A, F	–	–
	MJOLLNIR	B, H, I, M	–	–
	RIBBON	A, F	–	–
	SAGE'S STAFF	C, D, J, L	–	–
	SASUKE'S BLADE	B, H, I, M	–	–
	WONDER BANGLE	E, G, K, N	–	–

You can't remove artifacts from the dungeon, so they will benefit you only during the final fight. Also, since the game's last boss is here, Mount Vellenge does not have a second or third cycle.

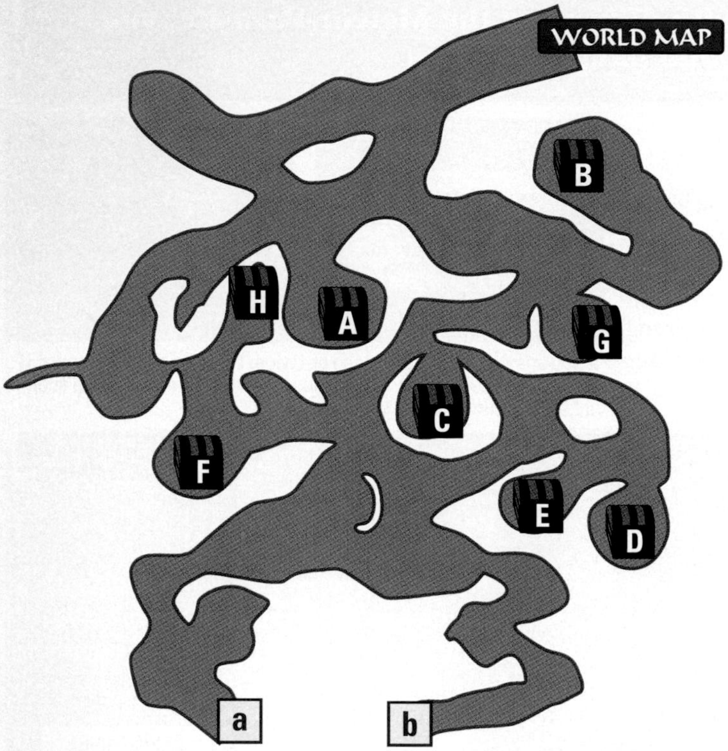

MAP KEY
Treasure Chest

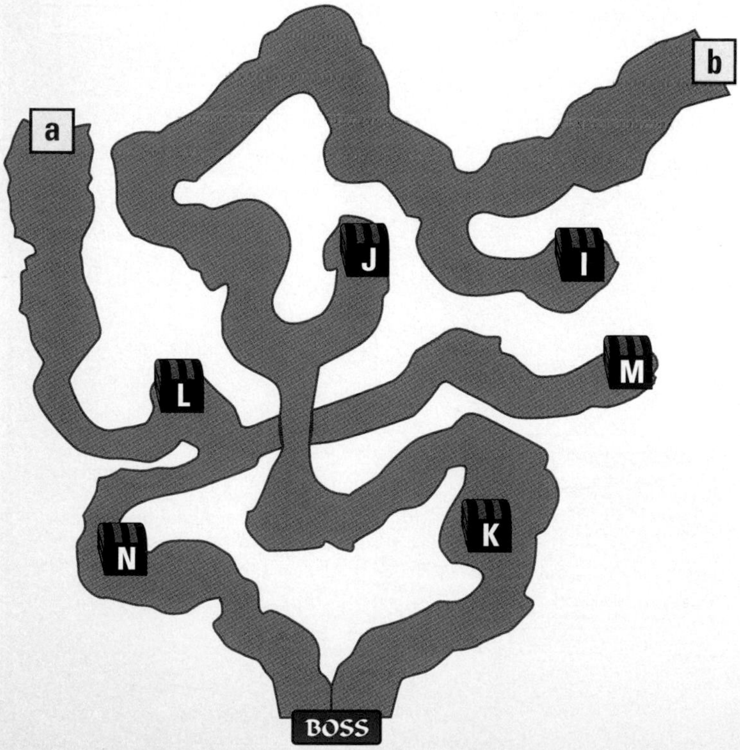

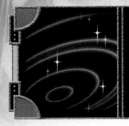

The Nest of Memories

When you're within a hairsbreadth of beating the Meteor Parasite, you will be transported to a strange and dangerous area.

Quiz Show

In the Nest of Memories, you will meet a girl who appears as a shimmering ball of light. She will ask you five questions about your journey—some easy, and some very hard. (The answers are in your diary, but you won't be able to look them up, so do your research before you start the level.) You will move on whether you get the answer right or not, but you will lose memories each time you give a wrong answer. If your memory count falls below 10, the game will end. (Use a GBA to see how many memories you have.)

If you answer incorrectly once or twice, two Minions will appear. If you miss three or more, Monstrous Minions will arrive on the scene. Take them out when they arrive.

Raem

Raem is a tough cookie without any major weaknesses. Attack him with whatever is your character's strong suit, be it hand-to-hand combat or magic, and try to keep your distance when he unleashes big attacks. His Minion friends are quite fast.

They can do a lot of damage and overwhelm you if you aren't prepared, so always keep one eye out for them. Once you eliminate Raem, you'll enter a secret, final battle that will require you to clear your head … and your memories.

RESISTANCE	
FIRE	2
BLIZZARD	2
THUNDER	2
SLOW	3
STOP	3
GRAVITY	3
HOLY	3

Raem will fire pairs of bubbles, much like the Giant Crab's from River Belle Path. They move rather slowly, so avoiding them isn't much of a problem. Try to lure the bubbles together, then duck out of the way so you can dodge them both at once.

When Raem spreads his wings, run between them and right up to the boss's face. It's your best chance to unleash a powerful attack, so make the most of it.

Raem also has a laser beam at his disposal. The laser itself doesn't do a lot of damage, but the ensuing explosion is a killer. As soon as the laser hits the ground, run—it will detonate in about a second.

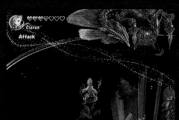

Minions approach two at a time, but don't take them both out. If you do, they will reappear within a very short time. Instead, take out one then avoid the second for as long as is feasible. Use Slow and Stop to make the job easier.

Data Appendices

On the Road

The main story is related through cinema scenes that occur on the road between dungeons. Most caravan events can happen multiple times.

Moogle Teacher

You'll meet Mog the Moogle as soon as you set out from your hometown (as long as you're playing in single-player mode). He will agree to join your quest.

The Black Knight's Story

The Black Knight's storyline is a sad one. The knight is a Lilty who has mysteriously lost his memories. Although you won't see him for a few years, you will hear about his fearsomeness from other caravans. His events are listed below.

The Black Knight's Story: Part 1

After you receive your first drop of Myrrh, you'll meet a caravan from Alfitaria led by Sol Racht. He will tell you about the legend of the Black Knight.

The Black Knight's Story: Part 2

When you get four drops of Myrrh, you will meet a traveler who claims to have been attacked by the Black Knight—a frightening prospect indeed!

The Black Knight's Story: Part 3

After you receive your seventh drop of Myrrh, you'll encounter a caravan that defends the honor of the Black Knight. Do the caravanners believe him, or has he frightened them into silence?

The Black Knight's Story: Part 4

In the fourth year, after you get your tenth drop of Myrrh, Sol Racht will reappear and tell you more about the mysterious fighter.

The Black Knight's Story: Part 5

You meet at last! When you claim your thirteenth drop of Myrrh, you will encounter the Black Knight himself on one of the roads. Listen well to his words.

The Black Knight's Story: Part 6

The Black Knight's story comes to a terrible end after you find your sixteenth drop of Myrrh. Once it's done, you can go back to Alfitaria and talk to some of the main players.

Gurdy's Story

Gurdy is a curly-haired traveler with a shady past. Some think he's a savior, others a swindler. The only thing sure about Gurdy is his knowledge about the world—his poetry and songs will teach you the secret of Lynari Desert.

Gurdy's Story: Part 1

If you get eight drops of Myrrh, you will meet the caravan from Marr's Pass. Gurdy will be with the group, and they won't seem incredibly pleased about the company.

Gurdy's Story: Part 2

After you get 11 drops of Myrrh, you will meet Gurdy and the caravan from the Fields of Fum. He will ask you to lend him 1,000 gil. If you lend him the money, you'll never see it again.

Gurdy's Story: Part 3

When you get 14 drops of Myrrh, you will encounter Gurdy yet again—this time hitching a ride with the Shella caravan. Apparently his hitchhiking skills are as renowned as his silver tongue.

Gurdy's Story: Part 4

Your seventeenth drop of Myrrh is the trigger for another Gurdy event. He will be traveling with the Leuda caravan and tell you a story about his brother.

Gurdy's Story: Part 5

Gurdy's final event will happen randomly any time you have both a Striped Apple and thousands of gil. During the event, a group of bandits will ask you to pay a ransom for Gurdy. You can give them cash or the Striped Apple to set him free. (You can also give them nothing, but don't be a scrooge—go ahead and part with the apple.)

The Bandit Band's Story

A band of clumsy bandits is patrolling the roads. There are three of them: Bal Dat the leader, Artemicion the Moogle and Meh Gaj the aged Selkie. They'll try to intimidate you, but don't be scared—they're not very skilled in the burgling business.

The Bandit Band's Story: Part 1

The first time you meet the bandit band, they will try to steal some of your things—after pretending to be your good friends, of course. Any of the items listed below are fair game for the thieves.

STEALABLE ITEMS	
ALLOY	IRON SHARD
BRONZE	JADE
BRONZE SHARD	MYTHRIL
CHERRY CLUSTER	RAINBOW GRAPES
CRYSTAL BALL	ROUND CORN
GOLD	RUBY
GOURD POTATO	SILVER
IRON	STRIPED APPLE

The Bandit Band's Story: Part 2

When you get your fifth drop of Myrrh, the bandits will appear again. They'll pretend to be an innocent caravan—don't fall for the ruse.

The Bandit Band's Story: Part 3

After the third year, the bandits will block your path and demand a ransom. You can either pay up or break through by knocking over the Moogle. If you don't pay, their story will end—so you'll have to shell out gil if you want to see the remaining portions.

The Bandit Band's Story: Part 4

Sometime after the fourth year, assuming that you paid the bandits in the third part of the story, you'll meet them again. If you have a Striped Apple and 1,000 gil, the bandits will take the apple.

The Bandit Band's Story: Part 5

If you completed the other parts of the bandits' story and also the last part of Gurdy's story, you can wrap up the bandits' tale. Like most of the stories, it ends in tragedy.

The Alfitaria Caravan

The caravan from Alfitaria is a proud and polite bunch of travelers. Pay close attention to their advice—it is both sage and timely.

Event 1

Sometime during the first three years, you will meet the caravan for the first time. It's a chance to bid them a good day and exchange pleasantries.

Event 2

At some point between the second and fifth years, the leader of the caravan, Sol Racht, will give you a gift. The possible presents are a Striped Apple, a Cherry Cluster, Rainbow Grapes, a Star Carrot, a Gourd Potato and a piece of Round Corn.

Event 3

The Alfitaria Caravan is full of useful info about the monsters listed below—their behavior, attack patterns and dislikes. This portion of the story can happen multiple times and yield different information.

MONSTERS			
ABADDON	COEURL	GREMLIN	NIGHTMARE
AHRIMAN	DRAGON ZOMBIE	GRIFFIN	OCHU
ANTLION	ELECTRIC JELLYFISH	HEDGEHOG PIE	OGRE
ARMSTRONG	FLAN	HELL PLANT	ORC
BEHEMOTH	GARGOYLE	IRON GIANT	ORC KING
BLAZER BEETLE	GHOST	KILLER BEE	SAHAGIN
BOMB	GIANT CRAB	LAMIA	SCORPION
CACTAUR	GIGAN TOAD	LICH	SKELETON
CARRION WORM	GIGAS	LIZARD KING	SONIC BAT
CAVE WORM	GIGAS LORD	LIZARDMAN	TONBERRY CHEF
CERBERUS	GOBLIN	MALBORO	WRAITH
CHIMERA	GOBLIN KING	MIMIC	ZU
COCKATRICE	GOLEM	MU	

Event 4

After you complete the fourth year of your journey, the caravans from Alfitaria and Marr's Pass will engage in a shouting match at one of the crossroads.

Event 5

When you complete the sixth year, you can meet the caravan and speak to them about the history of the Lilty people.

Event 6

Once you complete the eighth year of your quest, you can see the final part of the story—which involves the retirement of Sol Racht. The caravan will give you monster info even after year eight, however.

The Marr's Pass Caravan

The caravan from Marr's Pass is made up of aggressive, but ultimately harmless, Lilties. The small ones will offer you gifts. They also run a trading shop out of the back of their wagon.

Event 1

The first time you see the Marr's Pass caravan, it will be chasing a monster down the road—this event will happen again and again throughout your journey. The second time, and each time thereafter, the caravan will give you info about the creature in question.

Event 2

Sometime after the second year, you'll meet up with the caravan. If you have room in your inventory, the party will give you a special weapon that you can't get anywhere else.

Event 3

Sometime after the second year, you'll meet up with the caravan again. If you have room in your inventory, the group will give you an item from the list below.

Event 4

After the fourth year, you can start selling material to the Marr's Pass caravan. You determine the price, but it must be from 0% to 150% of the price listed below. For example, you can give them a piece of bronze for free or charge up to 450 gil.

MATERIALS			
BRONZE	300	FIEND'S CLAW	1,000
IRON	500	FAERIE'S TEAR	1,000
MYTHRIL	5,000	GRIFFIN'S WING	5,000
GOLD	500	CERBERUS'S FANG	5,000
SILVER	500	NEEDLE	5,000
BRONZE SHARD	100	HARD SHELL	5,000
IRON SHARD	100	WORM ANTENNA	5,000
CRYSTAL BALL	100	TOAD OIL	5,000
RUBY	200	JAGGED SCYTHE	5,000
JADE	200	OGRE FANG	5,000
ALLOY	250	CHIMERA'S HORN	5,000
MAGMA ROCK	1,000	COEURL'S WHISKER	5,000
CHILLY GEL	1,000	ZU'S BEAK	5,000
THUNDERBALL	1,000	COCKATRICE SCALE	5,000
HOLY WATER	1,000	SHINY SHARD	1,000
HEAVENLY DUST	1,000	GIGAS CLAW	5,000
BLUE SILK	1,000	GEAR	1,000

The chart above lists all the material you can sell to the caravan, along with the base price. You'll have to wait a while to sell them some of the more expensive items.

The Fum Caravan

The Fum caravan is a peaceful group of farmers who care more for eating and raising crops than for anything else. You'll meet up with them a lot—and get plenty of free food out of the deal—making theirs one of the best stories in the game.

Event 1

The first time you meet the caravan there will be introductions all around. They will tell you a bit about the life of a farmer and talk about the land and how much they love it.

Event 2

The second time you meet up, the farmers will invite you to snack on one of the items listed below—assuming that you have room in your inventory for the leftovers. This event will happen multiple times.

FOOD
STRIPED APPLE
CHERRY CLUSTER
RAINBOW GRAPES
STAR CARROT
GOURD POTATO
ROUND CORN

Event 3

After the third year, you can meet the caravan for a chat about the intricacies of growing fruit. After you talk, they will send a Fruit Seed to your family.

Event 4

Also after the third year, you can start trading with the caravan—if you have space in your inventory. They will offer to sell you a random item and name a price, which you can then raise or lower. If you offer double the price, they will give you two items.

The Shella Caravan

The Yukes in the Shella caravan appear to be a couple of tacos short of a combo plate—but they are actually quite wise in the ways of the world. Play along with the questions and see where they lead.

Event 1

Amidatty is the leader of the caravan, and the first time you meet him he will ask you to trade an item. He always offers a fair bargain, so make the trade.

Event 2

Sometimes the caravan will offer to tell you about monsters for the small fee of 10 gil. The info is somewhat interesting (and 10 gil isn't a lot of money), but you can take or leave the offer as you see fit.

Event 3

To trigger the third event, you must have space in your inventory, be in year six or later and have seen the third part of Gurdy's story. If you satisfy the requirements, you can see Amidatty compare the world to a loaf of bread.

Event 4

If you saw the third event, you can see the fourth when you complete another year. The bread-as-world theory will surely confound scholars for decades to come.

Event 5

After the seventh year, Amidatty will complete his analysis of the Bannock Loaf. Perhaps he's not as wacky as he first appeared—or maybe he's nutty as a fruitcake. You'll have to watch and decide for yourself.

The Leuda Caravan

The Leuda caravan is a pair of out-cast females who spend more time bickering and singing than collecting Myrrh. Hopefully the town has a backup caravan some-where....

Event 1

Meeting the caravan for the first time is a treat. The girls are an opti-mistic and upbeat pair who encourage you in your quest.

Event 2

After the second year—and with a chalice that's two-thirds full—you can see the second event. The caravanners are not quite as happy as they were the first time, and their nonstop arguments will fill your screen with verbal jabs.

Event 3

After the third year, the duo will offer to sell you materials at a slight discount. Pick up something if you're low on supplies, but it's not necessary to advance the story.

Event 4

Sometime after year four, you will encounter the caravan in an open field. The girls will be dancing to a rhythm all their own, and the movements are assured and intoxicating. Stick around and watch the show if you have the time.

If you pay 100 gil, you can see a longer version of the dance. Your caravan members will join in the fun.

Monster Data

Cactuars and Dark Flans and Hell Plants, oh my! If you need to learn the lowdown on a creepy critter, you're in the right place.

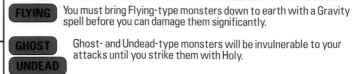

NAME / **STATS**

Abaddon — FLYING

HP	32	FIRE	1	STOP	0
STR	6	BLIZZARD	1	GRAVITY	0
DEF	5	THUNDER	1	HOLY	0
MAG	6	SLOW	0		

RESISTANT TO —
VULNERABLE TO —

FLYING — You must bring Flying-type monsters down to earth with a Gravity spell before you can damage them significantly.

GHOST / **UNDEAD** — Ghost- and Undead-type monsters will be invulnerable to your attacks until you strike them with Holy.

These are the monster's resistance ratings. A small number means that the monster is weak against the element, while large numbers mean that the monster is strong against the element.

If a monster is listed as resistant to an element, it cannot be hurt by it. If it is vulnerable, that means it has an extreme weakness beyond the normal zero rating.

Notes on Monster Stats

Each monster's HP, Strength, Defense and Magic numbers represent the creature's stats in the first cycle of a one-player game. If you play in the second or third cycle—or with multiple players—the monster's stats will increase. Check the chart below to see how the stats are boosted.

	1 player	2 players	3 players	4 players
CYCLE 1	—	x1.25	x1.50	x1.75
CYCLE 2	x1.5	x1.875	x2.25	x2.625
CYCLE 3	x2.5	x3.125	x3.75	x4.375

Abaddon — FLYING

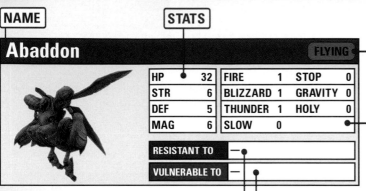

HP	32	FIRE	1	STOP	0
STR	6	BLIZZARD	1	GRAVITY	0
DEF	5	THUNDER	1	HOLY	0
MAG	6	SLOW	0		

RESISTANT TO —
VULNERABLE TO —

Ahriman — FLYING

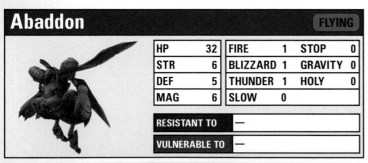

HP	10	FIRE	0	STOP	3
STR	4	BLIZZARD	2	GRAVITY	0
DEF	2	THUNDER	2	HOLY	0
MAG	4	SLOW	3		

RESISTANT TO —
VULNERABLE TO Fire

Bat — FLYING

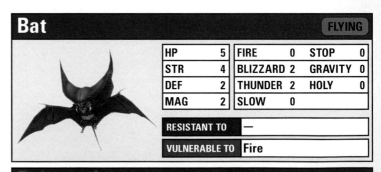

HP	5	FIRE	0	STOP	0
STR	4	BLIZZARD	2	GRAVITY	0
DEF	2	THUNDER	2	HOLY	0
MAG	2	SLOW	0		

RESISTANT TO —
VULNERABLE TO Fire

Behemoth

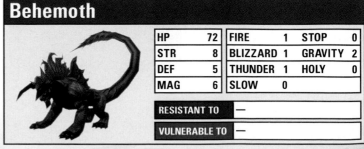

HP	72	FIRE	1	STOP	0
STR	8	BLIZZARD	1	GRAVITY	2
DEF	5	THUNDER	1	HOLY	0
MAG	6	SLOW	0		

RESISTANT TO —
VULNERABLE TO

Blazer Beetle

HP	32	FIRE	0	STOP	0
STR	6	BLIZZARD	0	GRAVITY	1
DEF	5	THUNDER	0	HOLY	0
MAG	2	SLOW	0		

RESISTANT TO —

VULNERABLE TO Fire, Ice, Lightning

Bomb

HP	12	FIRE	3	STOP	0
STR	4	BLIZZARD	0	GRAVITY	0
DEF	2	THUNDER	0	HOLY	0
MAG	4	SLOW	0		

RESISTANT TO —

VULNERABLE TO Ice, Lightning

Cactuar

HP	15	FIRE	0	STOP	3
STR	6	BLIZZARD	1	GRAVITY	0
DEF	5	THUNDER	3	HOLY	0
MAG	6	SLOW	3		

RESISTANT TO Lightning

VULNERABLE TO Fire

Carrion Worm (Mushroom Forest)

HP	24	FIRE	0	STOP	3
STR	4	BLIZZARD	1	GRAVITY	2
DEF	2	THUNDER	3	HOLY	0
MAG	4	SLOW	3		

RESISTANT TO Lightning

VULNERABLE TO Fire

Carrion Worm (Tida)

HP	24	FIRE	0	STOP	0
STR	5	BLIZZARD	1	GRAVITY	2
DEF	3	THUNDER	3	HOLY	0
MAG	5	SLOW	0		

RESISTANT TO Lightning

VULNERABLE TO Fire

Cerberus

HP	32	FIRE	2	STOP	0
STR	6	BLIZZARD	0	GRAVITY	1
DEF	5	THUNDER	1	HOLY	0
MAG	6	SLOW	0		

RESISTANT TO —

VULNERABLE TO Ice

Chimera

HP	48	FIRE	2	STOP	0
STR	6	BLIZZARD	2	GRAVITY	2
DEF	5	THUNDER	2	HOLY	0
MAG	7	SLOW	0		

RESISTANT TO —

VULNERABLE TO —

Cockatrice

HP	18	FIRE	0	STOP	0
STR	5	BLIZZARD	2	GRAVITY	0
DEF	4	THUNDER	1	HOLY	0
MAG	2	SLOW	0		

RESISTANT TO —

VULNERABLE TO Fire

Coeurl

HP	20	FIRE	2	STOP	3
STR	4	BLIZZARD	2	GRAVITY	3
DEF	3	THUNDER	2	HOLY	0
MAG	5	SLOW	3		

RESISTANT TO —

VULNERABLE TO —

Dark Flan   `UNDEAD`

HP	20	FIRE	0	STOP	3
STR	6	BLIZZARD	2	GRAVITY	0
DEF	4	THUNDER	2	HOLY	0
MAG	3	SLOW	3		

RESISTANT TO —

VULNERABLE TO Fire

Dark Hedgehog   `UNDEAD`

HP	15	FIRE	2	STOP	0
STR	4	BLIZZARD	2	GRAVITY	0
DEF	2	THUNDER	2	HOLY	0
MAG	4	SLOW	0		

RESISTANT TO —

VULNERABLE TO —

Death Knight

HP	48	FIRE	1	STOP	0
STR	12	BLIZZARD	1	GRAVITY	2
DEF	10	THUNDER	1	HOLY	0
MAG	12	SLOW	0		

RESISTANT TO —

VULNERABLE TO —

Electric Jellyfish

HP	12	FIRE	1	STOP	0
STR	4	BLIZZARD	0	GRAVITY	0
DEF	2	THUNDER	3	HOLY	0
MAG	4	SLOW	0		

RESISTANT TO	Lightning
VULNERABLE TO	Ice

Electric Scorpion

HP	15	FIRE	2	STOP	0
STR	6	BLIZZARD	0	GRAVITY	0
DEF	5	THUNDER	3	HOLY	0
MAG	6	SLOW	0		

RESISTANT TO	Lightning
VULNERABLE TO	Ice

Flan

HP	10	FIRE	0	STOP	3
STR	4	BLIZZARD	1	GRAVITY	0
DEF	2	THUNDER	2	HOLY	0
MAG	3	SLOW	3		

RESISTANT TO	—
VULNERABLE TO	Fire

Flan (Conall Curach)

HP	20	FIRE	0	STOP	3
STR	6	BLIZZARD	1	GRAVITY	0
DEF	5	THUNDER	1	HOLY	0
MAG	6	SLOW	3		

RESISTANT TO	—
VULNERABLE TO	Fire

Gargoyle `FLYING`

HP	5	FIRE	3	STOP	3
STR	4	BLIZZARD	3	GRAVITY	0
DEF	16	THUNDER	3	HOLY	3
MAG	4	SLOW	3		

RESISTANT TO	Fire, Ice, Lightning
VULNERABLE TO	—

Ghost `GHOST`

HP	20	FIRE	1	STOP	0
STR	5	BLIZZARD	3	GRAVITY	0
DEF	4	THUNDER	0	HOLY	0
MAG	6	SLOW	0		

RESISTANT TO	Ice
VULNERABLE TO	Lightning

Gigan Toad

HP	24	FIRE	0	STOP	3
STR	5	BLIZZARD	3	GRAVITY	0
DEF	3	THUNDER	1	HOLY	0
MAG	5	SLOW	3		

RESISTANT TO	Ice
VULNERABLE TO	Fire

Gigan Toad (Conall Curach)

HP	32	FIRE	0	STOP	0
STR	6	BLIZZARD	3	GRAVITY	0
DEF	6	THUNDER	1	HOLY	0
MAG	6	SLOW	0		

RESISTANT TO	Ice
VULNERABLE TO	Fire

Gigas

HP	60	FIRE	0	STOP	0
STR	5	BLIZZARD	3	GRAVITY	2
DEF	4	THUNDER	1	HOLY	0
MAG	5	SLOW	0		

RESISTANT TO	Ice
VULNERABLE TO	Fire

Goblin

HP	12	FIRE	0	STOP	0
STR	4	BLIZZARD	1	GRAVITY	0
DEF	2	THUNDER	0	HOLY	0
MAG	2	SLOW	0		

RESISTANT TO	—
VULNERABLE TO	Fire, Lightning

Goblin (Mace)

HP	18	FIRE	0	STOP	0
STR	4	BLIZZARD	1	GRAVITY	0
DEF	2	THUNDER	0	HOLY	0
MAG	2	SLOW	0		

RESISTANT TO	—
VULNERABLE TO	Fire, Lightning

Goblin (Spear)

HP	15	FIRE	0	STOP	0
STR	4	BLIZZARD	1	GRAVITY	0
DEF	2	THUNDER	0	HOLY	0
MAG	2	SLOW	0		

RESISTANT TO	—
VULNERABLE TO	Fire, Lightning

Goblin Chieftain

HP	24	FIRE	0	STOP	1
STR	4	BLIZZARD	1	GRAVITY	1
DEF	3	THUNDER	1	HOLY	0
MAG	2	SLOW	1		

RESISTANT TO	—
VULNERABLE TO	Fire

Ice Ahriman · FLYING

HP	20	FIRE	0	STOP	3
STR	6	BLIZZARD	3	GRAVITY	0
DEF	2	THUNDER	2	HOLY	0
MAG	5	SLOW	3		

RESISTANT TO	Ice
VULNERABLE TO	Fire

Goblin Mage

HP	12	FIRE	0	STOP	0
STR	2	BLIZZARD	1	GRAVITY	0
DEF	2	THUNDER	0	HOLY	0
MAG	4	SLOW	0		

RESISTANT TO	—
VULNERABLE TO	Fire

Ice Bomb

HP	15	FIRE	0	STOP	0
STR	5	BLIZZARD	3	GRAVITY	0
DEF	3	THUNDER	0	HOLY	0
MAG	5	SLOW	0		

RESISTANT TO	Ice
VULNERABLE TO	Fire, Lightning

Gremlin

HP	12	FIRE	2	STOP	0
STR	4	BLIZZARD	0	GRAVITY	0
DEF	2	THUNDER	1	HOLY	0
MAG	2	SLOW	0		

RESISTANT TO	—
VULNERABLE TO	Ice

Killer Bee · FLYING

HP	6	FIRE	0	STOP	0
STR	5	BLIZZARD	2	GRAVITY	0
DEF	2	THUNDER	2	HOLY	0
MAG	5	SLOW	0		

RESISTANT TO	—
VULNERABLE TO	Fire

Griffin

HP	32	FIRE	0	STOP	3
STR	5	BLIZZARD	1	GRAVITY	2
DEF	4	THUNDER	2	HOLY	0
MAG	2	SLOW	1		

RESISTANT TO	—
VULNERABLE TO	Fire

Lamia

HP	15	FIRE	2	STOP	3
STR	6	BLIZZARD	0	GRAVITY	0
DEF	6	THUNDER	1	HOLY	0
MAG	6	SLOW	3		

RESISTANT TO	—
VULNERABLE TO	Ice

Hedgehog Pie · FLYING · GHOST

HP	12	FIRE	2	STOP	0
STR	4	BLIZZARD	0	GRAVITY	0
DEF	2	THUNDER	0	HOLY	0
MAG	4	SLOW	0		

RESISTANT TO	
VULNERABLE TO	Ice, Lightning

Lava Ahriman · FLYING

HP	20	FIRE	3	STOP	3
STR	6	BLIZZARD	2	GRAVITY	0
DEF	2	THUNDER	2	HOLY	0
MAG	5	SLOW	3		

RESISTANT TO	Fire
VULNERABLE TO	—

Hell Plant

HP	12	FIRE	0	STOP	0
STR	4	BLIZZARD	1	GRAVITY	0
DEF	2	THUNDER	1	HOLY	0
MAG	2	SLOW	0		

RESISTANT TO	—
VULNERABLE TO	Fire

Lava Mu

HP	18	FIRE	3	STOP	0
STR	6	BLIZZARD	0	GRAVITY	0
DEF	4	THUNDER	1	HOLY	0
MAG	2	SLOW	0		

RESISTANT TO	Fire
VULNERABLE TO	Ice

Lizard Captain

HP	15	FIRE	2	STOP	0
STR	5	BLIZZARD	1	GRAVITY	1
DEF	4	THUNDER	1	HOLY	0
MAG	5	SLOW	0		

RESISTANT TO	—
VULNERABLE TO	—

Lizard Mage

HP	15	FIRE	2	STOP	0
STR	2	BLIZZARD	0	GRAVITY	0
DEF	3	THUNDER	1	HOLY	0
MAG	5	SLOW	0		

RESISTANT TO	—
VULNERABLE TO	Ice

Lizard Skirmisher

HP	18	FIRE	2	STOP	0
STR	5	BLIZZARD	0	GRAVITY	0
DEF	4	THUNDER	1	HOLY	0
MAG	2	SLOW	0		

RESISTANT TO	—
VULNERABLE TO	Ice

Lizard Skirmisher (Gold)

HP	18	FIRE	2	STOP	0
STR	5	BLIZZARD	0	GRAVITY	0
DEF	4	THUNDER	1	HOLY	0
MAG	2	SLOW	0		

RESISTANT TO	—
VULNERABLE TO	Ice

Lizard Soldier

HP	18	FIRE	2	STOP	0
STR	5	BLIZZARD	0	GRAVITY	0
DEF	4	THUNDER	1	HOLY	0
MAG	2	SLOW	0		

RESISTANT TO	—
VULNERABLE TO	Ice

Lizard Warrior

HP	30	FIRE	2	STOP	0
STR	5	BLIZZARD	0	GRAVITY	0
DEF	4	THUNDER	1	HOLY	0
MAG	2	SLOW	0		

RESISTANT TO	—
VULNERABLE TO	Ice

Lizard Wizard

HP	18	FIRE	2	STOP	0
STR	2	BLIZZARD	0	GRAVITY	0
DEF	4	THUNDER	1	HOLY	0
MAG	5	SLOW	0		

RESISTANT TO	—
VULNERABLE TO	Ice

Lizardman

HP	15	FIRE	2	STOP	0
STR	5	BLIZZARD	0	GRAVITY	0
DEF	3	THUNDER	1	HOLY	0
MAG	2	SLOW	0		

RESISTANT TO	—
VULNERABLE TO	Ice

Lizardman (Mace)

HP	15	FIRE	2	STOP	0
STR	5	BLIZZARD	0	GRAVITY	0
DEF	3	THUNDER	1	HOLY	0
MAG	2	SLOW	0		

RESISTANT TO	—
VULNERABLE TO	Ice

Lizardman (Spear)

HP	15	FIRE	2	STOP	0
STR	5	BLIZZARD	0	GRAVITY	0
DEF	3	THUNDER	1	HOLY	0
MAG	2	SLOW	0		

RESISTANT TO	—
VULNERABLE TO	Ice

Magic Plant

HP	18	FIRE	2	STOP	3
STR	5	BLIZZARD	2	GRAVITY	2
DEF	4	THUNDER	2	HOLY	0
MAG	6	SLOW	3		

RESISTANT TO	—
VULNERABLE TO	—

Mimic

HP	20	FIRE	3	STOP	3
STR	6	BLIZZARD	3	GRAVITY	3
DEF	5	THUNDER	3	HOLY	3
MAG	6	SLOW	3		

RESISTANT TO	Fire, Ice, Lightning
VULNERABLE TO	—

Minion (Blue)

HP	15	FIRE	1	STOP	0
STR	11	BLIZZARD	1	GRAVITY	0
DEF	9	THUNDER	1	HOLY	0
MAG	2	SLOW	0		

RESISTANT TO	—
VULNERABLE TO	

Minion (Blue Magic)

HP	24	FIRE	1	STOP	0
STR	2	BLIZZARD	1	GRAVITY	0
DEF	9	THUNDER	1	HOLY	0
MAG	11	SLOW	0		

RESISTANT TO	—
VULNERABLE TO	

Minion (Red)

HP	24	FIRE	1	STOP	0
STR	12	BLIZZARD	1	GRAVITY	0
DEF	9	THUNDER	1	HOLY	0
MAG	2	SLOW	0		

RESISTANT TO	—
VULNERABLE TO	

Monstrous Minion

HP	120	FIRE	1	STOP	0
STR	12	BLIZZARD	1	GRAVITY	0
DEF	9	THUNDER	1	HOLY	0
MAG	12	SLOW	0		

RESISTANT TO	
VULNERABLE TO	

Mu

HP	10	FIRE	0	STOP	0
STR	4	BLIZZARD	0	GRAVITY	0
DEF	2	THUNDER	1	HOLY	0
MAG	4	SLOW	0		

RESISTANT TO	—
VULNERABLE TO	Fire, Ice

Nightmare GHOST

HP	30	FIRE	1	STOP	3
STR	6	BLIZZARD	1	GRAVITY	1
DEF	4	THUNDER	1	HOLY	0
MAG	6	SLOW	3		

RESISTANT TO	
VULNERABLE TO	

Ochu

HP	40	FIRE	0	STOP	0
STR	5	BLIZZARD	2	GRAVITY	2
DEF	3	THUNDER	2	HOLY	0
MAG	5	SLOW	0		

RESISTANT TO	—
VULNERABLE TO	Fire

Ogre

HP	48	FIRE	1	STOP	3
STR	5	BLIZZARD	1	GRAVITY	2
DEF	2	THUNDER	0	HOLY	0
MAG	2	SLOW	1		

RESISTANT TO	Lightning
VULNERABLE TO	—

Ogre (Kilanda)

HP	48	FIRE	1	STOP	3
STR	6	BLIZZARD	1	GRAVITY	2
DEF	5	THUNDER	0	HOLY	0
MAG	2	SLOW	1		

RESISTANT TO	—
VULNERABLE TO	Lightning

Orc

HP	16	FIRE	0	STOP	0
STR	4	BLIZZARD	1	GRAVITY	0
DEF	2	THUNDER	1	HOLY	0
MAG	2	SLOW	0		

RESISTANT TO	—
VULNERABLE TO	Fire

Orc (Mace)

HP	16	FIRE	0	STOP	0
STR	4	BLIZZARD	1	GRAVITY	0
DEF	2	THUNDER	1	HOLY	0
MAG	2	SLOW	0		

RESISTANT TO	—
VULNERABLE TO	Fire

Orc (Spear)

HP	20	FIRE	0	STOP	0
STR	4	BLIZZARD	1	GRAVITY	0
DEF	2	THUNDER	1	HOLY	0
MAG	2	SLOW	0		

RESISTANT TO	
VULNERABLE TO	Fire

Orc Mage

HP	16	FIRE	0	STOP	0
STR	2	BLIZZARD	1	GRAVITY	0
DEF	2	THUNDER	1	HOLY	0
MAG	4	SLOW	0		

RESISTANT TO	—
VULNERABLE TO	Fire

Practice Goblin

HP	12	FIRE	0	STOP	0
STR	4	BLIZZARD	1	GRAVITY	0
DEF	2	THUNDER	0	HOLY	0
MAG	2	SLOW	0		

RESISTANT TO	—
VULNERABLE TO	Fire, Lightning

Rock Scorpion

HP	6	FIRE	3	STOP	3
STR	6	BLIZZARD	3	GRAVITY	0
DEF	16	THUNDER	3	HOLY	3
MAG	6	SLOW	3		

RESISTANT TO	Fire, Ice, Lightning
VULNERABLE TO	—

Sahagin

HP	18	FIRE	0	STOP	0
STR	5	BLIZZARD	2	GRAVITY	0
DEF	4	THUNDER	1	HOLY	0
MAG	5	SLOW	0		

RESISTANT TO	—
VULNERABLE TO	Fire

Sahagin Lord

HP	30	FIRE	1	STOP	0
STR	7	BLIZZARD	1	GRAVITY	2
DEF	6	THUNDER	1	HOLY	0
MAG	7	SLOW	0		

RESISTANT TO	—
VULNERABLE TO	—

Sand Sahagin

HP	18	FIRE	2	STOP	0
STR	6	BLIZZARD	0	GRAVITY	0
DEF	6	THUNDER	1	HOLY	0
MAG	6	SLOW	0		

RESISTANT TO	—
VULNERABLE TO	Ice

Scorpion

HP	15	FIRE	2	STOP	0
STR	6	BLIZZARD	0	GRAVITY	0
DEF	5	THUNDER	1	HOLY	0
MAG	6	SLOW	0		

RESISTANT TO	—
VULNERABLE TO	Ice

Shade GHOST

HP	25	FIRE	1	STOP	0
STR	11	BLIZZARD	1	GRAVITY	3
DEF	7	THUNDER	1	HOLY	0
MAG	11	SLOW	0		

RESISTANT TO	—
VULNERABLE TO	

Shade (Mace) GHOST

HP	25	FIRE	1	STOP	0
STR	11	BLIZZARD	1	GRAVITY	3
DEF	7	THUNDER	1	HOLY	0
MAG	11	SLOW	0		

RESISTANT TO	—
VULNERABLE TO	

Shade (Spear) GHOST

HP	25	FIRE	1	STOP	0
STR	11	BLIZZARD	1	GRAVITY	3
DEF	7	THUNDER	1	HOLY	0
MAG	11	SLOW	0		

RESISTANT TO	—
VULNERABLE TO	

Skeleton

HP	15	FIRE	0	STOP	0
STR	5	BLIZZARD	1	GRAVITY	0
DEF	3	THUNDER	1	HOLY	0
MAG	2	SLOW	0		

RESISTANT TO	—
VULNERABLE TO	Fire

Skeleton (Mace)

HP	15	FIRE	0	STOP	0
STR	5	BLIZZARD	1	GRAVITY	0
DEF	3	THUNDER	1	HOLY	0
MAG	2	SLOW	0		

RESISTANT TO	—
VULNERABLE TO	Fire

Skeleton (Spear)

HP	18	FIRE	0	STOP	0
STR	5	BLIZZARD	1	GRAVITY	0
DEF	3	THUNDER	1	HOLY	0
MAG	2	SLOW	0		

RESISTANT TO —
VULNERABLE TO Fire

Skeleton Mage

HP	15	FIRE	0	STOP	0
STR	2	BLIZZARD	1	GRAVITY	0
DEF	3	THUNDER	1	HOLY	0
MAG	5	SLOW	0		

RESISTANT TO —
VULNERABLE TO Fire

Skeleton Mage (Fire)

HP	9	FIRE	0	STOP	3
STR	2	BLIZZARD	3	GRAVITY	3
DEF	4	THUNDER	3	HOLY	3
MAG	4	SLOW	3		

RESISTANT TO Ice, Lightning
VULNERABLE TO Fire

Skeleton Mage (Ice)

HP	9	FIRE	3	STOP	3
STR	2	BLIZZARD	0	GRAVITY	3
DEF	4	THUNDER	3	HOLY	3
MAG	4	SLOW	3		

RESISTANT TO Fire, Lightning
VULNERABLE TO Ice

Skeleton Mage (Lightning)

HP	9	FIRE	3	STOP	3
STR	2	BLIZZARD	3	GRAVITY	3
DEF	4	THUNDER	0	HOLY	3
MAG	4	SLOW	3		

RESISTANT TO Fire, Ice
VULNERABLE TO Lightning

Skeleton Mage (Rebena Te Ra)

HP	18	FIRE	0	STOP	0
STR	2	BLIZZARD	1	GRAVITY	0
DEF	4	THUNDER	1	HOLY	0
MAG	6	SLOW	0		

RESISTANT TO —
VULNERABLE TO Fire

Snow Mu

HP	18	FIRE	0	STOP	0
STR	6	BLIZZARD	3	GRAVITY	0
DEF	4	THUNDER	1	HOLY	0
MAG	2	SLOW	0		

RESISTANT TO Ice
VULNERABLE TO Fire

Sonic Bat `FLYING`

HP	6	FIRE	0	STOP	0
STR	4	BLIZZARD	2	GRAVITY	0
DEF	2	THUNDER	2	HOLY	0
MAG	2	SLOW	0		

RESISTANT TO —
VULNERABLE TO Fire

Sphere `FLYING`

HP	18	FIRE	2	STOP	3
STR	12	BLIZZARD	2	GRAVITY	0
DEF	7	THUNDER	2	HOLY	0
MAG	12	SLOW	3		

RESISTANT TO —
VULNERABLE TO —

Stone Hedgehog

HP	8	FIRE	3	STOP	3
STR	4	BLIZZARD	3	GRAVITY	0
DEF	16	THUNDER	3	HOLY	0
MAG	4	SLOW	3		

RESISTANT TO Fire, Ice, Lightning
VULNERABLE TO —

Stone Plant

HP	8	FIRE	3	STOP	3
STR	4	BLIZZARD	3	GRAVITY	0
DEF	16	THUNDER	3	HOLY	3
MAG	2	SLOW	3		

RESISTANT TO Fire, Ice, Lightning
VULNERABLE TO —

Stone Sahagin

HP	8	FIRE	3	STOP	3
STR	6	BLIZZARD	3	GRAVITY	0
DEF	16	THUNDER	3	HOLY	3
MAG	6	SLOW	3		

RESISTANT TO Fire, Ice, Lightning
VULNERABLE TO —

Tentacle (Dark)

HP	48	FIRE	1	STOP	3
STR	12	BLIZZARD	1	GRAVITY	3
DEF	9	THUNDER	1	HOLY	0
MAG	12	SLOW	3		

RESISTANT TO	—
VULNERABLE TO	—

Tonberry

HP	24	FIRE	1	STOP	3
STR	12	BLIZZARD	1	GRAVITY	3
DEF	10	THUNDER	1	HOLY	0
MAG	12	SLOW	3		

RESISTANT TO	—
VULNERABLE TO	—

Tentacle (Fire)

HP	48	FIRE	3	STOP	0
STR	12	BLIZZARD	0	GRAVITY	2
DEF	9	THUNDER	1	HOLY	0
MAG	12	SLOW	0		

RESISTANT TO	Fire
VULNERABLE TO	Ice

Tonberry Chef

HP	15	FIRE	1	STOP	3
STR	4	BLIZZARD	1	GRAVITY	1
DEF	3	THUNDER	1	HOLY	0
MAG	4	SLOW	3		

RESISTANT TO	—
VULNERABLE TO	—

Tentacle (Ice)

HP	48	FIRE	0	STOP	0
STR	12	BLIZZARD	3	GRAVITY	2
DEF	9	THUNDER	1	HOLY	0
MAG	12	SLOW	0		

RESISTANT TO	Ice
VULNERABLE TO	Fire

Vampire Bat — FLYING GHOST

HP	20	FIRE	0	STOP	0
STR	6	BLIZZARD	2	GRAVITY	0
DEF	2	THUNDER	2	HOLY	0
MAG	2	SLOW	0		

RESISTANT TO	—
VULNERABLE TO	Fire

Tentacle (Lightning)

HP	48	FIRE	1	STOP	0
STR	12	BLIZZARD	1	GRAVITY	2
DEF	9	THUNDER	3	HOLY	0
MAG	12	SLOW	0		

RESISTANT TO	Lightning
VULNERABLE TO	—

Water Flan

HP	14	FIRE	0	STOP	3
STR	5	BLIZZARD	3	GRAVITY	0
DEF	3	THUNDER	2	HOLY	0
MAG	3	SLOW	3		

RESISTANT TO	Ice
VULNERABLE TO	Fire

Thunder Bomb

HP	15	FIRE	0	STOP	0
STR	5	BLIZZARD	0	GRAVITY	0
DEF	3	THUNDER	3	HOLY	0
MAG	5	SLOW	0		

RESISTANT TO	Lightning
VULNERABLE TO	Fire, Ice

Wraith — GHOST

HP	20	FIRE	0	STOP	0
STR	6	BLIZZARD	0	GRAVITY	0
DEF	4	THUNDER	0	HOLY	0
MAG	4	SLOW	0		

RESISTANT TO	—
VULNERABLE TO	Fire, Ice, Lightning

Tiny Worm

HP	12	FIRE	0	STOP	3
STR	4	BLIZZARD	1	GRAVITY	0
DEF	2	THUNDER	3	HOLY	0
MAG	2	SLOW	3		

RESISTANT TO	Lightning
VULNERABLE TO	Fire

Zu — FLYING

HP	48	FIRE	0	STOP	3
STR	7	BLIZZARD	2	GRAVITY	0
DEF	3	THUNDER	2	HOLY	0
MAG	7	SLOW	3		

RESISTANT TO	—
VULNERABLE TO	Fire

Item Data

All you need to make your trip a success can be found on the following pages. Items are listed with the race or sex that can use them, when applicable.

Swords   CLAVATS

	NAME	STRENGTH	FOCUS ATTACK	SCROLL REQUIRED	MATERIALS	PRICE
	BASTARD SWORD	32	Piercing Sweep	Mighty Weapon	Iron x2, Jagged Scythe	500
	COPPER SWORD	15	Power Slash	—	—	—
	DEFENDER	31	Bash	Victorious Weapon	Iron x2, Ogre Fang	500
	EXCALIBUR	33	Soulshot	Legendary Weapon	Alloy, Orichalcum, Ancient Potion	2,500
	FATHER'S SWORD	32	Piercing Sweep	—	—	—
	FEATHER SABER	31	Power Slash	Valiant Weapon	Bronze x3, Cerberus's Fang	500
	IRON SWORD	20	Piercing Sweep	Novice's Weapon	Iron	100
	MARR SWORD	22	Piercing Sweep	—	—	—
	RAGNAROK	35	Shadowblade	Dark Weapon	Cursed Crook, Orichalcum, Ancient Sword	5,000
	RUNE BLADE	30	Soulshot	Master's Weapon	Mythril, Alloy	700
	STEEL BLADE	25	Bash	Warrior's Weapon	Iron, Alloy	300
	TREASURED SWORD	18	Power Slash	—	—	—
	ULTIMA SWORD	35	Piercing Sweep	Greatest Weapon	Orichalcum, Ultimite	50,000

Spears   LILTIES

	NAME	STRENGTH	FOCUS ATTACK	SCROLL REQUIRED	MATERIALS	PRICE
	DRAGON LANCE	30	Pulse Thrust	Master's Weapon	Mythril, Alloy	700
	DRAGOON'S SPEAR	33	Pulse Thrust	Hero's Weapon	Chimera's Horn, Orichalcum, Dragon's Fang	5,000
	FATHER'S SPEAR	32	Psi Blast	—	—	—
	GUNGNIR	35	Cross Slash	Legendary Weapon	Alloy, Orichalcum, Ancient Potion	2,500
	HALBERD	32	Psi Blast	Mighty Weapon	Iron x2, Jagged Scythe	500
	HIGHWIND	31	Avalanche	Victorious Weapon	Iron x2, Ogre Fang	500
	IRON LANCE	15	Cyclone Slash	—	—	—
	LONGINUS	40	Bladestorm	Celestial Weapon	Dragon's Fang, Orichalcum x2, Red Eye	8,000
	MARR SPEAR	22	Psi Blast	—	—	—

Spears (continued)

	NAME	STRENGTH	FOCUS ATTACK	SCROLL REQUIRED	MATERIALS	PRICE
	PARTISAN	20	Psi Blast	Novice's Weapon	Iron	100
	SONIC LANCE	25	Avalanche	Warrior's Weapon	Iron, Alloy	300
	TITAN LANCE	31	Cyclone Slash	Valiant Weapon	Bronze x3, Cerberus's Fang	500
	TREASURED SPEAR	18	Cyclone Slash	—	—	—
	ULTIMA LANCE	35	Psi Blast	Greatest Weapon	Orichalcum, Ultimite	50,000

Hammers

YUKES

	NAME	STRENGTH	FOCUS ATTACK	SCROLL REQUIRED	MATERIALS	PRICE
	FATHER'S HAMMER	32	Wave Bomb	—	—	—
	GOBLIN HAMMER	31	Power Bomb	Valiant Weapon	Bronze x3, Cerberus's Fang	500
	MARR HAMMER	22	Wave Bomb	—	—	—
	MYSTIC HAMMER	35	Magic Bomb	Legendary Weapon	Alloy, Orichalcum, Ancient Potion	2,500
	MYTHRIL HAMMER	30	Shock Bomb	Master's Weapon	Mythril, Alloy	700
	ORC HAMMER	15	Power Bomb	—	—	—
	PRISM HAMMER	31	Shock Bomb	Victorious Weapon	Iron x2, Ogre Fang	500
	RUNE HAMMER	25	Shock Bomb	Warrior's Weapon	Iron, Alloy	300
	SONIC HAMMER	32	Wave Bomb	Mighty Weapon	Iron x2, Jagged Scythe	500
	TREASURED HAMMER	18	Power Bomb	—	—	—
	ULTIMA HAMMER	35	Wave Bomb	Greatest Weapon	Orichalcum, Ultimite	50,000
	WAVE HAMMER	20	Wave Bomb	Novice's Weapon	Iron	100

Rackets

SELKIES

	NAME	STRENGTH	FOCUS ATTACK	SCROLL REQUIRED	MATERIALS	PRICE
	AURA RACKET	15	Aura Blast	—	—	—
	BUTTERFLY HEAD	30	Power Kick	Master's Weapon	Mythril, Alloy	700
	DREAMCATCHER	35	Meteor Blast	Lunar Weapon	Wind Crystal, Orichalcum, Desert Fang	5,000
	DUAL SHOOTER	25	Dual Blast	Warrior's Weapon	Iron, Alloy	300
	ELEMENTAL CUDGEL	31	Aura Blast	Valiant Weapon	Bronze x3, Cerberus's Fang	500
	FATHER'S MAUL	32	Stampede	—	—	—
	MARR MAUL	22	Stampede	—	—	—
	PRISM BLUDGEON	31	Dual Blast	Victorious Weapon	Iron x2, Ogre Fang	500

Rackets (continued)

	NAME	STRENGTH	FOCUS ATTACK	SCROLL REQUIRED	MATERIALS	PRICE
	QUEEN'S HEEL	33	Power Kick	Legendary Weapon	Alloy, Orichalcum, Ancient Potion	2,500
	SOLID RACKET	20	Stampede	Novice's Weapon	Iron	100
	STEEL CUDGEL	32	Stampede	Mighty Weapon	Iron x2, Jagged Scythe	500
	TREASURED MAUL	18	Aura Blast	—	—	—
	ULTIMA MAUL	35	Stampede	Greatest Weapon	Orichalcum, Ultimite	50,000

IMPORTANT NOTE: Some pieces of armor and accessories will protect you from Fire, Ice or Lightning. Using such an item won't reduce the amount of damage you take from the spell—it will only eliminate the Burning, Freezing or Paralysis status effects.

Armor
CLAVATS, LILTIES, YUKES, SELKIES

NAME	DEFENSE	SPECIAL EFFECT	SCROLL REQUIRED	MATERIALS	PRICE
BLESSED MAIL	23	Resist Poison +1	Pure Armor	Mythril, Holy Water	500
BRONZE PLATE	13	—	Bronze Armor	Bronze	100
CRYSTAL MAIL	24	Resist Miasma	Radiant Armor	Mythril, Tiny Crystal	500
DIAMOND PLATE	27	—	Diamond Armor	Diamond Ore, Orichalcum, Hard Shell	2,500
ETERNAL MAIL	23	Resist Stasis +1	Eternal Armor	Mythril, Toad Oil	500
FLAME MAIL	24	Resist Fire +1	Flame Armor	Iron x3, Magma Rock x2	500
FROST MAIL	24	Resist Ice +1	Frost Armor	Iron x3, Chilly Gel x2	500
GAIA PLATE *	30	—	Earth Armor	Lord's Robe, Orichalcum x2, King's Scale	5,000
GOLD MAIL	24	Resist Stone +1	Gold Armor	Mythril, Gold, Shiny Shard	500
IRON PLATE	17	—	Iron Armor	Iron	200
MYTHRIL PLATE	22	—	Mythril Armor	Mythril	500
SAINTLY MAIL	23	Resist Curse +1	Holy Armor	Mythril, Heavenly Dust	500
STORM MAIL	24	Resist Lightning +1	Lightning Armor	Iron x3, Thunderball x2	500
TIME MAIL	23	Resist Slow +1	Time Armor	Mythril, Worm Antenna	500
TRAVEL CLOTHES	10	—	—	—	—

* Usable only by Clavats

Shields
CLAVATS

	NAME	DEFENSE	SPECIAL EFFECT	SCROLL REQUIRED	MATERIALS	PRICE
	CHOCOBO SHIELD	25	—	Legendary Shield	Orichalcum x2, Yellow Feather	3,000
	DIAMOND SHIELD	22	—	Diamond Shield	Orichalcum, Diamond Ore	2,000
	FLAME SHIELD	17	Resist Fire +1	Flame Shield	Iron x2, Magma Rock	400
	FROST SHIELD	17	Resist Ice +1	Frost Shield	Iron x2, Chilly Gel	400
	IRON SHIELD	10	—	Iron Shield	Iron	150
	MAKESHIFT SHIELD	7	—	—	—	—
	MYTHRIL SHIELD	15	—	Mythril Shield	Mythril	400
	RUNE SHIELD	18	Spell range +20	Magic Shield	Bronze, Coeurl's Whisker x2	400
	SAINTLY SHIELD	18	Resist Curse +1	Holy Shield	Mythril, Heavenly Dust	400
	STORM SHIELD	17	Resist Lightning +1	Lightning Shield	Iron x2, Thunderball	400

Gloves

NAME	DEFENSE	SPECIAL EFFECT	SCROLL REQUIRED	MATERIALS	PRICE
BRONZE GAUNTLETS	8	—	Bronze Gloves	Bronze	80
DIAMOND ARMLETS	22	—	Diamond Gloves	Orichalcum, Diamond Ore	2,000
FLAME ARMLETS	17	Resist Fire +1	Flame Gloves	Iron x2, Magma Rock	400
FROST ARMLETS	17	Resist Ice +1	Frost Gloves	Iron x2, Chilly Gel	400
GAUNTLETS	5	—	—	—	—
GOLD ARMLETS	18	Resist Stone +1	Gold Gloves	Gold, Mythril, Cockatrice Scale	400
IRON GAUNTLETS	12	—	Iron Gloves	Iron	150
MYTHRIL GAUNTLETS	15	—	Mythril Gloves	Mythril	400
STORM ARMLETS	17	Resist Lightning +1	Lightning Gloves	Iron x2, Thunderball	400

Helms

NAME	DEFENSE	SPECIAL EFFECT	SCROLL REQUIRED	MATERIALS	PRICE
BRONZE HELM	8	—	Bronze Sallet	Bronze	80
DIAMOND HELM	22	—	Diamond Sallet	Orichalcum, Diamond Ore	2,000
ETERNAL HELM	18	Resist Stasis +1	Eternal Sallet	Mythril, Toad Oil	400
FLAME HELM	17	Resist Fire +1	Flame Sallet	Iron x2, Magma Rock	400
FROST HELM	17	Resist Ice +1	Frost Sallet	Iron x2, Chilly Gel	400
HELM	5	—	—	—	—
IRON HELM	12	—	Iron Sallet	Iron	150
MYTHRIL HELM	15	—	Mythril Sallet	Mythril	400
STORM HELM	17	Resist Lightning +1	Lightning Sallet	Iron x2, Thunderball	400
TIME HELM	18	Resist Slow +1	Time Sallet	Mythril, Worm Antenna	400

Belts

NAME	DEFENSE	SPECIAL EFFECT	SCROLL REQUIRED	MATERIALS	PRICE
BLESSED SASH	18	Resist Poison +1	Pure Belt	Mythril, Holy Water	400
BRONZE BELT	8	—	Bronze Belt	Bronze	80
DIAMOND BELT	22	—	Diamond Belt	Orichalcum, Diamond Ore	2,000
FLAME SASH	17	Resist Fire +1	Flame Belt	Iron x2, Magma Rock	400
FROST SASH	17	Resist Ice +1	Frost Belt	Iron x2, Chilly Gel	400
IRON BELT	12	—	Iron Belt	Iron	150
MYTHRIL BELT	15	—	Mythril Belt	Mythril	400
OLD BELT	5	—	—	—	—
STORM SASH	17	Resist Lightning +1	Lightning Belt	Iron x2, Thunderball	400
WINGED BELT	18	Focus Attack range +20	Wind Belt	Mythril, Griffin's Wing x2	400

Accessories

NAME	SPECIAL EFFECT	SCROLL REQUIRED	MATERIALS	RACE	PRICE
ACCURATE WATCH	Resist Slow +1	Clockwork	Worm Antenna, Bronze Shard x3, Gear	All	300
ANGEL'S EARRING	Resist status changes +60	Angel Kit	Silver, Angel's Tear	Selkie	1,200
BADGE OF THE FLAME	Resist Fire +1	Flame Craft	Iron Shard x2, Magma Rock	All	300
BADGE OF THE FROST	Resist Ice +1	Frost Craft	Iron Shard x2, Chilly Gel	All	300
BADGE OF THE THUNDERBOLT	Resist Lightning +1	Lightning Craft	Iron Shard x2, Thunderball	All	300
BISHOP'S SOUL	Magic Power +3	Tome of Sorcery	Jade x2, Cursed Crook	Yuke	2,000
BLUE MISANGA	Resist Poison +1	Blue Yarn	Needle, Blue Silk	All	300
CHARM OF SPEED	Focus Attack charge time -5	Tome of Speed	Needle, Gigas Claw	Selkie	400
CHARM OF WISDOM	Casting time -10	Tome of Wisdom	Needle, Coeurl's Whisker	Yuke	400
CRYSTAL RING	Resist Miasma +30	Ring of Light	Tiny Crystal, Silver	All	1,000
DAEMON'S EARRING	Status change effects +30	Fiend Kit	Silver, Fiend's Claw	Yuke	400
DEVIL'S EARRING	Status change effects +60	Daemon Kit	Silver, Devil's Claw	Clavat	1,200
DRAGON'S HEART	Focus Attack +3	Soul of the Dragon	Dragon's Fang, Ruby x2, Orc Belt	Lilty	2,000
EAGLE GOGGLES	Focus Attack range +20	Designer Goggles	Iron, Crystal Ball x2, Griffin's Wing	Selkie	1,200
ELEMENTAL'S SOUL	Spell damage +5	Forbidden Tome	Dweomer Spore, Ethereal Orb, Malboro Seed	Yuke	5,000
FLOWER BRACER	Casting time -5	Lady's Accessories	Ruby, Silver x2, Pressed Flower	Female	400
FORCE RING	Resist attack +1	Ring of Invincibility	Orichalcum, Dark Sphere	All	50,000
GOLD NECKLACE	Resist Stone +1	Gold Craft	Gold x2, Cockatrice Scale	All	300
HEADBAND OF HEALING	Increased regeneration	Healing Kit	White Silk, Tiny Crystal, Remedy	Male	2,500
HEADBAND OF ZEAL	Focus Attack charge time -5	Zeal Kit	Blue Silk, Tiny Crystal, Remedy	Male	400
JADE BRACER	Increased regeneration	Fashion Kit	Jade, Silver x2, Pressed Flower	Female	2,500
LION'S HEART	Focus Attack +1	Soul of the Lion	Ruby, Cerberus's Fang	Lilty	800
PIXIE'S EARRING	Resist status changes +30	Faerie Kit	Silver, Faerie's Tear	Lilty	400
POWER GOGGLES	Focus Attack range +20	Goggle Techniques	Crystal Ball, Bronze	Lilty	400
TALISMAN OF SPEED	Focus Attack charge time -10	Secrets of Speed	Needle, Zu's Beak	Selkie	1,200
TALISMAN OF WISDOM	Casting time -15	Secrets of Wisdom	Needle, Chimera's Horn	Clavat	1,200
THIEF'S EMBLEM	Focus Attack charge time -15	Brigandology	Wind Crystal, Orc Belt, Green Sphere	Selkie	5,000
TWISTED SCOPE	Spell range +20	Designer Glasses	Gold, Crystal Ball x2, Chimera's Horn	Clavat	1,200
TWISTED SPECTACLES	Spell range +20	Eyewear Techniques	Crystal Ball x2, Silver	Yuke	400
UNFALTERING WATCH	Resist Stasis +1	New Clockwork	Toad Oil, Bronze Shard x3, Gear	All	300
WHITE MISANGA	Resist Curse +1	White Yarn	Needle, White Silk	All	300
WIZARD'S SOUL	Spell damage +1	Tome of Magic	Jade, Coeurl's Whisker	Yuke	800

Materials

NAME	COMMON LOCATION	USE	BUY	SELL
ALLOY	Most merchants	Varies	250	62
ANCIENT POTION	Kilanda	Legendary Weapon	—	5,000
ANCIENT SWORD	River Belle Path (Boss)	Ragnarok	—	7,500
ANGEL'S TEAR	Kilanda (Cycle 3)	Angel's Earring	—	250
BLUE SILK	Tida (Cycle 2)	Blue Misanga, Headband of Zeal	1,000	250
BRONZE	Most merchants	Varies	300	75
BRONZE SHARD	Most merchants	Accurate Watch, Unfaltering Watch	100	25
CERBERUS'S FANG	Rebena Te Ra	Valiant Weapon, Lion's Heart	—	750
CHILLY GEL	Tipa (Merchant Lv. 2 or 3)	Frost Protector, Badge of the Frost	1,000	250
CHIMERA'S HORN	Lynari Desert	Dragoon's Spear, Talisman of Wisdom, Twisted Scope	—	625

Materials (continued)

NAME	COMMON LOCATION	USE	BUY	SELL
COCKATRICE SCALE	Selepation Cave	Gold Armlets, Gold Necklace	—	500
COEURL'S WHISKER	Daemon's Court	Rune Shield, Charm of Wisdom, Wizard's Soul	—	500
CRYSTAL BALL	Mushroom Forest	Twisted Spectacles, Twisted Scope, Power Goggles, Eagle Goggles	100	25
CURSED CROOK	Goblin Wall (Boss)	Ragnarok, Bishop's Soul	—	7,500
DARK SPHERE	Tipa (Merchant Lv. 3)	Force Ring	50,000	12,500
DESERT FANG	Lynari Desert (Boss)	Dreamcatcher	—	7,500
DEVIL'S CLAW	Rebena Te Ra (Cycle 3)	Devil's Earring	—	750
DIAMOND ORE	Mushroom Forest (Cycle 2)	Diamond Protector	—	750
DRAGON'S FANG	Conall Curach (Boss)	Dragoon's Spear, Longinus, Dragon's Heart	—	7,500
DWEOMER SPORE	Tida (Boss)	Elemental's Soul	—	7,500
ETHEREAL ORB	Mushroom Forest (Boss)	Elemental's Soul	—	7,500
FAERIE'S TEAR	Mushroom Forest	Pixie's Earring	1,000	250
FIEND'S CLAW	Leuda	Daemon's Earring	1,000	250
GEAR	Rebena Te Ra	Accurate Watch, Unfaltering Watch	—	250
GIGAS CLAW	Selepation Cave	Charm of Speed	—	625
GOLD	Mushroom Forest (Cycle 2)	Gold Armlets, Twisted Scope, Gold Necklace	500	125
GREEN SPHERE	Tida (Boss)	Thief's Emblem	—	7,500
GRIFFIN'S WING	Veo Lu Sluice	Winged Belt, Eagle Goggles	—	500
HARD SHELL	Selepation Cave	Diamond Plate	—	500
HEAVENLY DUST	Daemon's Court	Saintly Mail, Saintly Shield	1,000	250
HOLY WATER	Moschet Manor	Blessed Mail, Blessed Sash	1,000	250
IRON	Most merchants	Various	500	125
IRON SHARD	Most merchants	Flame Craft, Ice Craft, Lightning Craft	100	25
JADE	Leuda	Fashion Kit, Wizard's Soul, Bishop's Soul	200	50
JAGGED SCYTHE	Conall Curach	Mighty Weapon	—	1,000
KING'S SCALE	Daemon's Court (Boss)	Gaia Plate	—	7,500
LORD'S ROBE	Moschet Manor (Boss)	Gaia Plate	—	7,500
MAGMA ROCK	Kilanda	Flame Protector, Badge of the Flame	1,000	250
MALBORO SEED	Mushroom Forest (Boss)	Elemental's Soul	—	7,500
MYTHRIL	Most merchants	Various	5,000	1,250
NEEDLE	Lynari Desert	Blue Misanga, White Misanga, Charm of Wisdom, Talisman of Wisdom, Charm of Speed, Talisman of Speed	—	625
OGRE FANG	Kilanda	Victorious Weapon	—	625
ORC BELT	Cathuriges Mine (Boss)	Thief's Emblem, Dragon's Heart	—	7,500
ORICHALCUM	Conall Curach (Cycle 3)	Various	—	5,000
PRESSED FLOWER	Conall Curach	Flower Bracer, Jade Bracer	—	250
RED EYE	Kilanda (Boss)	Longinus	—	7,500
REMEDY	Conall Curach	Headband of Zeal, Headband of Healing	—	250
RUBY	Leuda	Flower Bracer, Lion's Heart, Dragon's Heart	200	50
SHINY SHARD	Tida (Cycle 1 or 2)	Gold Mail	—	250
SILVER	Mushroom Forest (Cycle 2)	Various	500	125
THUNDERBALL	Tipa (Merchant Lv. 2 or 3)	Thunderbolt Protector, Badge of the Thunderbolt	1,000	250
TINY CRYSTAL	Mushroom Forest	Crystal Ring, Headband of Zeal, Headband of Healing	—	250
TOAD OIL	Conall Curach	Eternal Mail, Eternal Helm, Unfaltering Watch	—	500
ULTIMITE	Tipa (Merchant Lv. 3)	Greatest Weapon	50,000	12,500
WHITE SILK	Rebena Te Ra (Cycle 3)	White Misanga, Headband of Healing	—	750
WIND CRYSTAL	Selepation Cave (Boss)	Dreamcatcher, Thief's Emblem	—	7,500
WORM ANTENNA	Tida	Time Mail, Time Helm, Accurate Watch	—	500
YELLOW FEATHER	Moschet Monor (Cycle 3)	Chocobo Shield	—	1,000
ZU'S BEAK	Lynari Desert	Talisman of Speed	—	750

Scrolls

	NAME	COMMON LOCATION	MATERIALS	ITEM CREATED	PRICE
WEAPONS	CELESTIAL WEAPON	Kilanda (Boss)	Orichalcum x 2, Dragon's Fang, Red Eye	Longinus	8,000
	DARK WEAPON	Rebena Te Ra (Boss)	Orichalcum, Cursed Crook, Ancient Sword	Ragnarok	5,000
	GREATEST WEAPON	Tipa (Alchemist Lv. 12)	Orichalcum, Ultimite	Ultima Sword, Ultima Lance, Ultima Hammer, Ultima Maul	50,000
	HERO'S WEAPON	Lynari Desert (Boss)	Orichalcum, Chimera's Horn, Dragon's Fang	Dragoon's Spear	5,000
	LEGENDARY WEAPON	River Belle Path (Boss)	Orichalcum, Alloy, Ancient Potion	Excalibur, Gungnir, Mystic Hammer, Queen's Heel	2,500
	LUNAR WEAPON	Conall Curach (Boss)	Orichalcum, Wind Crystal, Desert Fang	Dreamcatcher	5,000
	MASTER'S WEAPON	Leuda	Mythril, Alloy	Rune Blade, Dragon Lance, Mythril Hammer, Butterfly Head	700
	MIGHTY WEAPON	Leuda	Iron x2, Jagged Scythe	Bastard Sword, Halberd, Sonic Hammer, Steel Cudgel	500
	NOVICE'S WEAPON	River Belle Path (Cycles 1 and 2)	Iron	Iron Sword, Wave Hammer, Partisan, Solid Racket	100
	VALIANT WEAPON	Leuda	Bronze x3, Cerberus's Fang	Feather Saber, Titan Lance, Goblin Hammer, Elemental Cudgel	500
	VICTORIOUS WEAPON	Leuda	Iron x2, Ogre Fang	Defender, Highwind, Prism Hammer, Prism Bludgeon	500
	WARRIOR'S WEAPON	Tipa (Merchant Lv. 2 or 3)	Iron, Alloy	Steel Blade, Rune Hammer, Sonic Lance, Dual Shooter	300
ARMOR	BRONZE ARMOR	Mushroom Forest (Cycles 1 and 2)	Bronze	Bronze Plate	100
	DIAMOND ARMOR	Kilanda (Cycle 3)	Orichalcum, Hard Shell, Diamond Ore	Diamond Plate	2,500
	EARTH ARMOR	Selepation Cave (Boss)	Orichalcum x2, Lord's Robe, King's Scale	Gaia Plate	5,000
	ETERNAL ARMOR	Conall Curach	Mythril, Toad Oil	Eternal Mail	500
	FLAME ARMOR	Kilanda (Cycle 2)	Iron x3, Magma Rock x2	Flame Mail	500
	FROST ARMOR	Veo Lu Sluice (Cycle 2)	Iron x3, Chilly Gel x2	Frost Mail	500
	GOLD ARMOR	Lynari Desert (Cycles 2 and 3)	Mythril, Gold, Shiny Shard	Gold Mail	500
	HOLY ARMOR	Conall Curach	Mythril, Heavenly Dust	Saintly Mail	500
	IRON ARMOR	Tipa (Alchemist Lv. 1)	Iron	Iron Plate	200
	LIGHTNING ARMOR	Leuda	Iron x3, Thunderball x2	Storm Mail	500
	MYTHRIL ARMOR	Most merchants	Mythril	Mythril Plate	500
	PURE ARMOR	Conall Curach	Mythril, Holy Water	Blessed Mail	500
	RADIANT ARMOR	Lynari Desert (Cycle 3)	Mythril, Tiny Crystal	Crystal Mail	500
	TIME ARMOR	Tida (Cycle 2)	Mythril, Worm Antenna	Time Mail	500
SHIELDS	DIAMOND SHIELD	Conall Curach (Cycle 3)	Orichalcum, Diamond Ore	Diamond Shield	2,000
	FLAME SHIELD	Kilanda	Iron x2, Magma Rock	Flame Shield	400
	FROST SHIELD	Tida (Cycle 2)	Iron x2, Chilly Gel	Frost Shield	400
	HOLY SHIELD	Rebena Te Ra	Mythril, Heavenly Dust	Saintly Shield	400
	IRON SHIELD	River Belle Path (Cycle 1)	Iron	Iron Shield	150
	LEGENDARY SHIELD	Moschet Manor (Boss)	Orichalcum x2, Yellow Feather	Chocobo Shield	3,000
	LIGHTNING SHIELD	Selepation Cave	Iron x2, Thunderball	Storm Shield	400
	MAGIC SHIELD	Conall Curach (Cycle 2)	Bronze, Coeurl's Whisker	Rune Shield	400
	MYTHRIL SHIELD	Most merchants	Mythril	Mythril Shield	400
GLOVES	BRONZE GLOVES	River Belle Path (Cycles 1 and 2)	Bronze	Bronze Gauntlets	80
	DIAMOND GLOVES	Conall Curach (Cycle 3)	Orichalcum, Diamond Ore	Diamond Armlets	2,000
	FLAME GLOVES	Kilanda	Iron x2, Magma Rock	Flame Armlets	400
	FROST GLOVES	Tida (Cycle 2)	Iron x2, Chilly Gel	Frost Armlets	400
	GOLD GLOVES	Rebena Te Ra	Mythril, Gold, Cockatrice Scale	Gold Armlets	400
	IRON GLOVES	Goblin Wall (Cycles 1 and 2)	Iron	Iron Gauntlets	150
	LIGHTNING GLOVES	Selepation Cave	Iron x2, Thunderball	Storm Armlets	400
	MYTHRIL GLOVES	Most merchants	Mythril	Mythril Gauntlets	400
HELMS	BRONZE SALLET	River Belle Path (Cycles 1 and 2)	Bronze	Bronze Helm	80
	DIAMOND SALLET	Conall Curach (Cycle 3)	Orichalcum, Diamond Ore	Diamond Helm	2,000
	ETERNAL SALLET	Rebena Te Ra (Cycles 1 and 2)	Mythril, Toad Oil	Eternal Helm	400
	FLAME SALLET	Kilanda	Iron x2, Magma Rock	Flame Helm	400
	FROST SALLET	Veo Lu Sluice	Iron x2, Chilly Gel	Frost Helm	400
	IRON SALLET	Most merchants	Iron	Iron Helm	150

Scrolls (continued)

	NAME	COMMON LOCATION	MATERIALS	ITEM CREATED	PRICE
HELMS	LIGHTNING SALLET	Conall Curach	Iron x2, Thunderball	Storm Helm	400
	MYTHRIL SALLET	Most merchants	Mythril	Mythril Helm	400
	TIME SALLET	Conall Curach	Mythril, Worm Antenna	Time Helm	400
BELTS	BRONZE BELT	River Belle Path (Cycles 1 and 2)	Bronze	Bronze Belt	80
	DIAMOND BELT	Conall Curach (Cycle 3)	Orichalcum, Diamond Ore	Diamond Belt	2,000
	FLAME BELT	Kilanda	Iron x2, Magma Rock	Flame Sash	400
	FROST BELT	Tida (Cycle 2)	Iron x2, Chilly Gel	Frost Sash	400
	IRON BELT	Goblin Wall (Cycles 1 and 2)	Iron	Iron Belt	150
	LIGHTNING BELT	Conall Curach	Iron x2, Thunderball	Storm Sash	400
	MYTHRIL BELT	Most merchants	Mythril	Mythril Belt	400
	PURE BELT	Rebena Te Ra	Mythril, Holy Water	Blessed Sash	400
	WIND BELT	Conall Curach (Cycle 2)	Mythril, Griffin's Wing x3	Winged Belt	400
ACCESSORIES	ANGEL KIT	Tida (Cycle 3)	Silver, Angel's Tear	Angel's Earring	1,200
	BLUE YARN	Shella	Needle, Blue Silk	Blue Misanga	300
	BRIGANDOLOGY	Tida (Boss)	Orc Belt, Green Sphere, Wind Crystal	Thief's Emblem	5,000
	CLOCKWORK	Shella	Bronze Shard x3, Gear, Worm Antenna	Accurate Watch	300
	DAEMON KIT	Mushroom Forest (Cycle 3)	Silver, Devil's Claw	Devil's Earring	1,200
	DESIGNER GLASSES	Daemon's Court (Cycle 3)	Crystal Ball x2, Chimera's Horn, Gold	Twisted Scope	1,200
	DESIGNER GOGGLES	Lynari Desert (Cycle 3)	Crystal Ball x2, Griffin's Wing, Iron	Eagle Goggles	1,200
	EYEWEAR TECHNIQUES	Daemon's Court (Cycles 2 and 3)	Crystal Ball x2, Silver	Twisted Spectacles	400
	FAERIE KIT	Tida (Cycles 2 and 3)	Silver, Faerie's Tear	Pixie's Earring	400
	FASHION KIT	Moschet Manor	Silver x2, Pressed Flower, Jade	Jade Bracer	2,500
	FIEND KIT	Mushroom Forest (Cycles 2 and 3)	Silver, Fiend's Claw	Daemon's Earring	400
	FLAME CRAFT	Shella	Iron Shard x2, Magma Rock	Badge of the Flame	300
	FORBIDDEN TOME	Rebena Te Ra (Boss)	Ethereal Orb, Malboro Seed, Dweomer Spore	Elemental's Soul	5,000
	FROST CRAFT	Shella	Iron Shard x2, Chilly Gel	Badge of the Frost	300
	GOGGLE TECHNIQUES	Lynari Desert (Cycles 2 and 3)	Crystal Ball x2, Bronze	Power Goggles	400
	GOLD CRAFT	Shella	Gold x2, Cockatrice Scale	Gold Necklace	300
	HEALING KIT	Kilanda (Cycle 3)	Tiny Crystal, Remedy, White Silk	Headband of Healing	2,500
	LADY'S ACCESSORIES	Moschet Manor	Silver x2, Pressed Flower, Ruby	Flower Bracer	400
	LIGHTNING CRAFT	Shella	Iron Shard x2, Thunderball	Badge of the Thunderbolt	300
	NEW CLOCKWORK	Shella	Bronze Shard x3, Gear, Toad Oil	Unfaltering Watch	300
	RING OF INVINCIBILITY	Tipa (Alchemist Lv. 11)	Orichalcum, Dark Sphere	Force Ring	50,000
	RING OF LIGHT	Selepation Cave	Tiny Crystal, Silver	Crystal Ring	1,000
	SECRETS OF SPEED	Cathuriges Mine (Cycle 3)	Needle, Zu's Beak	Talisman of Speed	1,200
	SECRETS OF WISDOM	Goblin Wall (Cycle 3)	Needle, Chimera's Fang	Talisman of Wisdom	1,200
	SOUL OF THE DRAGON	Conall Curach (Cycles 2 and 3)	Ruby x2, Orc Belt, Dragon's Fang	Dragon's Heart	2,000
	SOUL OF THE LION	Conall Curach	Ruby, Cerberus's Fang	Lion's Heart	800
	TOME OF MAGIC	Rebena Te Ra (Cycles 2 and 3)	Jade, Coeurl's Whisker	Wizard's Soul	800
	TOME OF SORCERY	Rebena Te Ra (Cycle 3)	Jade x2, Cursed Crook	Bishop's Soul	2,000
	TOME OF SPEED	Cathuriges Mine (Cycles 2 and 3)	Needle, Gigas Claw	Charm of Speed	400
	TOME OF WISDOM	Goblin Wall	Needle, Coeurl's Whisker	Charm of Wisdom	400
	WHITE YARN	Shella	Needle, White Silk	White Misanga	300
	ZEAL KIT	Kilanda	Tiny Crystal, Remedy, Blue Silk	Headband of Zeal	400

Seeds

NAME	ITEM CREATED	PRICE
FLOWER SEED	—	250
FRUIT SEED	Striped Apple, Rainbow Grapes or Cherry Cluster	25
STRANGE SEED	A random fruit or vegetable (not wheat-based)	250

NAME	ITEM CREATED	PRICE
VEGETABLE SEED	Star Carrot, Round Corn or Gourd Potato	25
WHEAT SEED	Bannock, Flour, Wheat	25

Magicite

	NAME	EFFECT		NAME	EFFECT
	BLIZZARD	Enables you to cast Blizzard		FIRE	Enables you to cast Fire
	CLEAR	Enables you to cast Clear		LIFE	Enables you to cast Life
	CURE	Enables you to cast Cure		THUNDER	Enables you to cast Thunder

Food

	NAME	EFFECT	COMMON LOCATION	BUY	SELL
	CHERRY CLUSTER	Restores HP, Magic+2	The Fields of Fum	40	10
	FISH	Restores HP, Strength +2	Alfitaria	40	10
	GOURD POTATO	Restores HP, Defense +2	The Fields of Fum	40	10
	MEAT	Restores HP, Strength +2	Alfitaria	40	10
	RAINBOW GRAPES	Restores HP, Magic +2	The Fields of Fum	40	10
	ROUND CORN	Restores HP, Defense +2	The Fields of Fum	40	10
	STAR CARROT	Restores HP, Defense +2	The Fields of Fum	40	10
	STRIPED APPLE	Restores HP, Magic +2	The Fields of Fum	40	10

Other Items

	NAME	EFFECT	COMMON LOCATION	BUY	SELL
	PHOENIX DOWN	Revives a fallen character	Everywhere	—	25
	BANNOCK	Restores HP	In your hometown, from your family—after sending them Wheat Seeds	—	10
	CACTUS FLOWER	20% discount on ferry rides	Lynari Desert	—	5
	FLOUR	—	In your hometown (if your father is a Miller)	—	50
	KILANDA SULFUR	20% discount on ferry rides	Kilanda	—	5
	MARK OF SHELLA	Allows you to enter Shella	From the Shella merchant, your father (as a Yuke) or Veo Lu Sluice	40	12
	MILK	Restores HP (1 heart)	Most merchants	20	5
	SPRING WATER	Restores HP (1 heart)	Most merchants	20	5
	STRANGE LIQUID	Restores HP (1 or 2 hearts)	Shella	20	5
	WHEAT	—	In your hometown (if your father is a Farmer)	—	50
	WORN BANDANNA	—	Conall Curach	—	5

ARTIFACTS THAT RAISE STRENGTH

NAME	EFFECT	COMMON LOCATION	NAME	EFFECT	COMMON LOCATION
ASHURA	Strength +1	Tida (Cycle 1)	MANEATER	Strength +1	River Belle Path (Cycle 1)
DOUBLE AXE	Strength +1	River Belle Path (Cycle 1)	MASAMUNE	Strength +5	Kilanda (Boss)
ENGETSURIN	Strength +2	Daemon's Court (Cycle 1)	MASQUERADE	Strength +3	Daemon's Court (Cycle 2)
FANG CHARM	Strength +1	Daemon's Court (Cycle 1)	MJOLLNIR	Strength +3	Selepation Cave (Cycle 2)
FLAMETONGUE	Strength +2	Kilanda (Cycle 1)	MURASAME	Strength +4	Cathuriges Mine (Boss)
GEKKABIJIN	Strength +5	Moschet Manor (Boss)	OGREKILLER	Strength +2	Tida (Cycle 1)
GIANT'S GLOVE	Strength +3	Kilanda (Cycle 1)	ONION SWORD	Strength +1	Veo Lu Sluice (Cycle 3)
GREEN BERET	Strength +1	Mushroom Forest (Cycle 1)	POWER WRISTBAND	Strength +1	Veo Lu Sluice (Cycle 1)
HEAVY ARMBAND	Strength +3	Daemon's Court (Cycle 2)	SASUKE'S BLADE	Strength +3	River Belle Path (Cycle 3)
ICE BRAND	Strength +2	Tida (Cycle 1)	SHURIKEN	Strength +1	River Belle Path (Cycle 1)
KAISER KNUCKLES	Strength +1	Tida (Cycle 1)	TWISTED HEADBAND	Strength +2	Veo Lu Sluice (Cycle 1)
LOADED DICE	Strength +2	Conall Curach (Cycle 1)			

ARTIFACTS THAT RAISE MAGIC

NAME	EFFECT	COMMON LOCATION	NAME	EFFECT	COMMON LOCATION
BOOK OF LIGHT	Magic +1	Veo Lu Sluice (Cycle 1)	NOAH'S LUTE	Magic +5	Kilanda (Cycle 1)
CANDY RING	Magic +1	Tida (Cycle 1)	RED SLIPPERS	Magic +3	Conall Curach (Cycle 1)
CAT'S BELL	Magic +1	Selepation Cave (Cycle 1)	RIBBON	Magic +9	Rebena Te Ra (Boss)
DARK MATTER	Magic +5	Tida (Cycle 3)	RUNE BELL	Magic +3	Rebena Te Ra (Cycle 2)
DRAGON'S WHISKER	Magic +1	River Belle Path (Cycle 1)	RUNE STAFF	Magic +1	Moschet Manor (Cycle 1)
FAERIE RING	Magic +1	Tida (Cycle 1)	SAGE'S STAFF	Magic +3	Kilanda (Cycle 1)
GALATYN	Magic +7	Goblin Wall (Boss)	SILVER BRACER	Magic +1	River Belle Path (Cycle 1)
GOLD HAIRPIN	Magic +5	Daemon's Court (Cycle 2)	TAOTIE MOTIF	Magic +7	Veo Lu Sluice (Boss)
KRIS	Magic +3	Veo Lu Sluice (Cycle 1)	TOME OF ULTIMA	Magic +10	Conall Curach (Boss)
MAGE MASHER	Magic +1	River Belle Path (Cycle 1)	WINGED CAP	Magic +1	Tida (Cycle 1)
MAGE'S STAFF	Magic +5	Daemon's Court (Cycles 2 and 3)	WONDER WAND	Magic +3	Tida (Cycle 1)

ARTIFACTS THAT RAISE DEFENSE

NAME	EFFECT	COMMON LOCATION	NAME	EFFECT	COMMON LOCATION
AEGIS	Defense +5	Daemon's Court (Boss)	RAT'S TAIL	Defense +2	Veo Lu Sluice (Cycle 2)
BLACK HOOD	Defense +2	Lynari Desert (Cycle 2)	RING OF PROTECTION	Defense +4	Selepation Cave (Boss)
BUCKLER	Defense +1	River Belle Path (Cycle 1)	SAVE THE QUEEN	Defense +4	River Belle Path (Boss)
CHICKEN KNIFE	Defense +3	Kilanda (Cycle 2)	SILVER SPECTACLES	Defense +1	River Belle Path (Cycle 1)
DRILL	Defense +1	Veo Lu Sluice (Cycle 1)	SPARKLING BRACER	Defense +1	Tida (Cycle 1)
ELVEN MANTLE	Defense +2	Rebena Te Ra (Cycle 1)	TEDDY BEAR	Defense +2	Lynari Desert (Cycle 2)
HELM OF ARAI	Defense +2	Tida (Cycle 1)	WONDER BANGLE	Defense +3	River Belle Path (Cycle 3)
MAIN GAUCHE	Defense +2	Veo Lu Sluice (Cycle 1)			

ARTIFACTS THAT ADD COMMAND LIST SLOTS

NAME	EFFECT	COMMON LOCATION
CHOCOBO POCKET	Gain one command slot	Tida (Cycle 1)
GOBBIE POCKET	Gain one command slot	Lynari Desert (Cycle 1)
MOOGLE POCKET	Gain one command slot	River Belle Path (Cycle 1)
ULTIMATE POCKET	Gain one command slot	Cathuriges Mine (Boss)

ARTIFACTS THAT ADD HEARTS

NAME	EFFECT	COMMON LOCATION
EARTH PENDANT	Gain one heart	River Belle Path (Cycle 1)
MOON PENDANT	Gain one heart	Veo Lu Sluice (Cycle 1)
STAR PENDANT	Gain one heart	Lynari Desert (Cycle 1)
SUN PENDANT	Gain one heart	Lynari Desert (Boss)

ARTIFACTS THAT FUNCTION AS MAGICITE

NAME	EFFECT	COMMON LOCATION
RING OF BLIZZARD	Magic +1, Blizzard	Veo Lu Sluice
RING OF CURE	Magic +1, Cure	Conall Curach
RING OF FIRE	Magic +1, Fire	Kilanda
RING OF LIFE	Magic +1, Life	Selepation Cave (Boss)
RING OF THUNDER	Magic +1, Thunder	Selepation Cave

Magic Data

Need to know how to cast a spell? Wondering how to combine your magic? All of your questions will be answered, traveler.

Fire

NAME	POWER	EFFECT AREA	SINGLE	TIMING	REQUIRED MAGICITE
FIRE	30	Small	OK	—	Fire
FIRA	15 x 3	Medium	OK	Type A	Fire
FIRA +1	15 x 4	Medium	—	Type A	Fire
FIRA +2	15 x 5	Medium	—	Type A	Fire
FIRAGA	60	Large	OK	Type D	Fire
FIRAGA +1	90	Large	—	Type D	Fire
FIRAGA +2	120	Large	—	Type D	Fire

In Single-Player mode, you need two Fire magicites to use Fira and three to use Firaga. An enemy on fire will lose defensive power, but have its speed raised by 1.5. The Power stat refers to the spell's attack power. It is only one of many factors that are taken into account when you cast a spell—you're safe in assuming that the higher the number, the better the spell. Numbers such as 15 x 3 refer to spells that swirl around. The spell has an attack rating of 15, but it also has the possibility to strike an enemy three times, if cast correctly.

Blizzard

NAME	POWER	EFFECT AREA	SINGLE	TIMING	REQUIRED MAGICITE
BLIZZARD	30	Small	OK	—	Blizzard
BLIZZARA	15 x 3	Medium	OK	Type A	Blizzard
BLIZZARA +1	15 x 4	Medium	—	Type A	Blizzard
BLIZZARA +2	15 x 5	Medium	—	Type A	Blizzard
BLIZZAGA	60	Large	OK	Type D	Blizzard
BLIZZAGA +1	90	Large	—	Type D	Blizzard
BLIZZAGA +2	120	Large	—	Type D	Blizzard

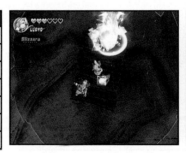

In Single-Player mode, you need two Blizzard Magicites to use Blizzara and three to use Blizzaga. The Blizzard family of spells will often freeze foes in place. If you strike a frozen enemy with a physical attack, you will do twice the normal damage.

Thunder

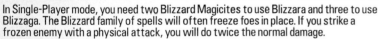

NAME	POWER	EFFECT AREA	SINGLE	TIMING	REQUIRED MAGICITE
THUNDER	30	Small	OK	—	Thunder
THUNDARA	15 x 3	Medium	OK	Type A	Thunder
THUNDARA +1	15 x 4	Medium	—	Type A	Thunder
THUNDARA +2	15 x 5	Medium	—	Type A	Thunder
THUNDAGA	60	Large	OK	Type D	Thunder
THUNDAGA +1	90	Large	—	Type D	Thunder
THUNDAGA +2	120	Large	—	Type D	Thunder

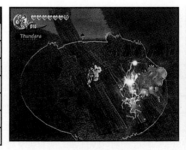

In Single-Player mode, you need two Thunder Magicites to use Thundara and three to use Thundaga. If you hit an enemy with the spell, it will become paralyzed for a short time.

Cure

NAME	POWER	EFFECT AREA	SINGLE	TIMING	REQUIRED MAGICITE
CURE	—	Small	OK	—	Cure
CURAGA	—	Large	—	Type A	Cure

Cure recovers HP for a single character, although other players can share the benefit if they stand next to the targeted character. Curaga restores HP for everyone. To cast Curaga, you need two Cure spells.

Clear

NAME	POWER	EFFECT AREA	SINGLE	TIMING	REQUIRED MAGICITE
CLEAR	—	Small	OK	—	Clear
CLEARAGA	—	Large	—	Type A	Clear

Clear removes any status changes from a character, while Clearaga does the same for the entire party. The spells will also remove helpful status changes, such as Haste. To cast Clearaga, you need two Clear spells.

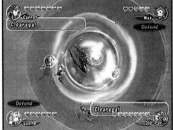

Life

NAME	POWER	EFFECT AREA	SINGLE	TIMING	REQUIRED MAGICITE
LIFE	—	Small	OK	—	Life
FULL-LIFE	—	Small	—	Type E	Life

Life brings a fallen character back to the world of the living, and also restores four hearts to his or her health meter. Full-Life brings a player back and restores all hearts. To cast Full-Life, you need two Life spells.

Gravity

NAME	POWER	EFFECT AREA	SINGLE	TIMING	REQUIRED MAGICITE
GRAVITY	Varies	Small	OK	Type A	Fire, Blizzard, Thunder
GRAVIRA	Varies	Medium	—	Type C	Fire, Blizzard, Thunder
GRAVIGA	Varies	Large	—	Type A	Fire, Blizzard, Thunder

Gravity will bring a flying monster crashing to the ground, and can also damage certain creatures. (If the monster's resistance is 0, you can drain half its HP. If its resistance is 1, you can drain one-fourth of its HP. If its resistance is 2, you can drain one-tenth of its HP.) You need a combination of Fire, Blizzard and Thunder (two of the three) to use Gravity. You must fuse one Fire, Blizzard and Thunder spell to use Gravira or Graviga.

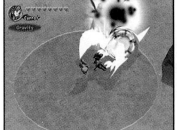

Holy

NAME	POWER	EFFECT AREA	SINGLE	TIMING	REQUIRED MAGICITE
HOLY	30	Small	OK	Type A	Life, Fire, Blizzard, Thunder
HOLYRA	25 x3	Middle	—	Type C	Life, Fire, Blizzard, Thunder
HOLYRA +1	25 x4	Middle	—	Type C	Life, Fire, Blizzard, Thunder

Holy turns Ghost- and Undead-type monsters solid, which gives you the ability to damage them. You need one Life spell and one Fire, Blizzard or Thunder spell to use Holy. You need one additional Life spell to use Holyra, and two additional Life spells to use Holyra +1. Place Life below the other magic in the command list to get Holy.

Haste

NAME	POWER	EFFECT AREA	SINGLE	TIMING	REQUIRED MAGICITE
HASTE	—	Small	OK	Type B	Life, Cure
HASTEGA	—	Large	—	Type B	Life, Cure

Haste increases your movement by 1.5 times and cuts in half the time required for Focus Attacks and charging spells. You need one Life spell and two Cure spells to use Haste. You need one additional Cure spell to use Hastega.

Slow

NAME	POWER	EFFECT AREA	SINGLE	TIMING	REQUIRED MAGICITE
SLOW	—	Small	OK	Type B	Life, Fire, Blizzard, Thunder
SLOWGA	—	Large	—	Type B	Life, Fire, Blizzard, Thunder

Slow drops the speed and movement of a character. You need one Fire, Blizzard or Thunder spell and one Life spell to create Slow. You need one Life spell and two Fire, Blizzard or Thunder spells (they must be different) to use Slowga. Place Life above the other magic in the command list to get Slow.

Stop

NAME	POWER	EFFECT AREA	SINGLE	TIMING	REQUIRED MAGICITE
STOP	—	Small	OK	Type E	Life, Fire, Blizzard, Thunder

Stop freezes a monster in its tracks. You need one Life spell and two Fire, Blizzard or Thunder spells (they must be different) to use Stop.

Spell Fusion Timing

There are five different spell fusion timings in multiplayer mode. To read the following charts, assume that all players have their targeting rings placed and ready to go. As soon as player one releases his or her A Button, the timer begins ticking. The other players must then release their A Buttons within the time period shown on the chart. So for a Type A spell, players 2, 3 and 4 must release the A Button within .33 seconds of player 1's release. Use the charts to give you an idea of the timing—don't try to break out the stopwatch.

TYPE A	0s	0.33s	0.66s	1.00s	1.33s	1.66s	2.00s	2.33s	2.66s
PLAYER 1									
PLAYER 2	Magic 2								
PLAYER 3	Magic 3								
PLAYER 4	Magic 4								

TYPE B	0s	0.33s	0.66s	1.00s	1.33s	1.66s	2.00s	2.33s	2.66s
PLAYER 1									
PLAYER 2		Magic 2							
PLAYER 3		Magic 3							
PLAYER 4		Magic 4							

TYPE C	0s	0.33s	0.66s	1.00s	1.33s	1.66s	2.00s	2.33s	2.66s
PLAYER 1									
PLAYER 2	Magic 2								
PLAYER 3		Magic 3							
PLAYER 4			Magic 4						

TYPE D	0s	0.33s	0.66s	1.00s	1.33s	1.66s	2.00s	2.33s	2.66s
PLAYER 1									
PLAYER 2				Magic 2					
PLAYER 3						Magic 3			
PLAYER 4									Magic 4

TYPE E	0s	0.33s	0.66s	1.00s	1.33s	1.66s	2.00s	2.33s	2.66s
PLAYER 1									
PLAYER 2		Magic 2							
PLAYER 3			Magic 3						

Focus Attacks and Magic Strikes

Every Focus Attack is listed below, along with the three magic strikes that you can create.

Clavats

NAME	TYPE	POWER	RANGE	WEAPONS
BASH	Move	15 x 2	50	Steel Blade, Defender
PIERCING SWEEP	Charge	15	50	Iron Sword, Marr Sword, Bastard Sword, Father's Sword, Ultima Sword
POWER SLASH	Move	20	50	Copper Sword, Treasured Sword, Feather Saber
SHADOWBLADE	Move	25 x 3	35	Ragnarok
SOULSHOT	Leaping	35	60	Rune Blade, Excalibur

Lilties

NAME	TYPE	POWER	RANGE	WEAPONS
AVALANCHE	Move	15 x 2	50	Sonic Lance, Highwind
BLADESTORM	Move	15 x 5	55	Longinus
CROSS SLASH	Charge	25 x 2	55	Gungnir
CYCLONE SLASH	Charge	15 x 2	55	Iron Lance, Treasured Spear, Titan Lance
PULSE THRUST	Unstoppable	25	60	Dragon Lance, Dragoon's Spear
PSI BLAST	Leaping	25	70	Halberd, Marr Spear, Father's Spear, Ultima Lance, Partisan

Yukes

NAME	TYPE	POWER	RANGE	WEAPONS
MAGIC BOMB	Move	20,40,80	30	Mystic Hammer
POWER BOMB	Move	20	30	Orc Hammer, Treasured Spear, Goblin Hammer
SHOCK BOMB	Move	20	30	Rune Hammer, Prism Hammer, Mythril Hammer
WAVE BOMB	Move	20	30	Wave Hammer, Marr Hammer, Sonic Hammer, Father's Hammer, Ultima Hammer

Selkies

NAME	TYPE	POWER	RANGE	WEAPONS
AURA BLAST	Leaping	20	65	Aura Racket, Elemental Cudgel, Treasured Maul
DUAL BLAST	Leaping	20 x 2	65	Dual Shooter, Prism Bludgeon
METEOR BLAST	Unstoppable	35	45	Dreamcatcher
POWER KICK	Move	25 x 2	55	Butterfly Head, Queen's Heel
STAMPEDE	Move	25	55	Solid Racket, Steel Cudgel, Father's Maul, Marr Maul, Ultima Maul

Magic Strikes

NAME	COMBINATION	POWER	STATUS EFFECT
FLAMESTRIKE	Fire and weapon	Varies	Burning
ICESTRIKE	Blizzard and weapon	Varies	Freezing
THUNDERSTRIKE	Thunder and weapon	Varies	Paralysis